# LINUS PAULING
# A Man and his Science

## ANTHONY SERAFINI

Foreword by
ISAAC ASIMOV

PARAGON HOUSE
*New York*

First paperback edition, 1991

Published in the United States by

Paragon House
90 Fifth Avenue
New York, NY 10011

Library of Congress Cataloging-in-Publication Data

Serafini, Anthony.
   Linus Pauling : a man and his science / Anthony Serafini ; foreword by Isaac Asimov.
      p.  cm.
   Bibliography: p.
   Includes index.
   ISBN 1-55778-440-X
    1. Pauling, Linus, 1901–  .  2. Chemists—United States—
Biography.  I. Title.
QD22.P35S47   1989
540'.92'4—dc19
[B]                                            88-28348
                                                CIP

Manufactured in the United States of America

10  9  8  7  6  5  4  3  2  1

# Contents

# Acknowledgments

I would like to thank the following persons for their generous offers of time and their willingness to talk to me about Linus Pauling and his work.

First, special thanks to Roy Benedek of Argonne National Laboratory, and Robert Olby, author of *The Path to the Double Helix* and Professor in the Division at the History and Philosophy of Science, Department of Philosophy of the University of Leeds. Both devoted many hours scrutinizing the manuscript for errors and patiently discussed assorted important scientific concepts with me. Since I have followed their advice almost, but not quite 100 percent of the time, all scientific errors are my own responsibility.

I am, of course, deeply grateful to my subject, Dr. Linus Pauling, for making himself available to me.

Also, I am especially grateful to both my wife, Tina Serafini, and my editor, Laura Greeney, for superb and tactful editing, as well as for displaying more patience than a person could reasonably be expected to endure.

Others who offered to talk with me and who gave generously of their time are: The staff of the library at Centenary College, for repeatedly offering their extensive resources and knowledge, and Isaac Asimov, for generously writing the foreword. I am also indebted to the scientists and engineers of the John D. Walsh

Company, Inc. of Glen Rock, New Jersey, for their kindness and hospitality.

I, too, wish to thank:
Horace Freeland Judson of Johns Hopkins University
Barry Commoner
John Archibald Wheeler
P.W. Anderson of Princeton University
William F. Buckley, Jr.
Otto Bastiansen of the University of Oslo
Francis Crick
Erwin Chargaff
Sten Samson
Edward Teller
Jonathan Singer
The Sterling Library and staff at Yale University and the faculty club of Yale for its kindness and hospitality
The Bulletin of the Atomic Scientists
The Royal Society
The staff of the Sophia Smith Collection at Smith College
Anne Sayre, author of *Rosalind Franklin and DNA*
The American Medical Association
The American Psychiatric Association
Florence Meiman White
The Cambridge Scientific Periodicals Library
The editors and staff of *The New England Journal of Medicine*
Dr. Lee DuBridge of the California Institute of Technology
The staff of the Stanford University Archives
Dr. Thomas Jukes
Professor Zoran Petrovich
The library staff of the University of Illinois
The library staff of the University of Indiana
Layne Woolschlager of The Oregon Historical Society
Nathan Reingold, Editor of the Joseph Henry Papers of the Smithsonian Institute
The Library of Congress
Laurie Micklos, Archivist of the Cold Spring Harbor Laboratory
Suzanne Roethel of The American Chemical Society

The Multnomah County Library of Portland, Oregon
The Staff of *Physcial Review Letters* and the American Institute of Physics
Dr. Charles Moertel of the Mayo Clinic
The staff of The Center for the Study of Democratic Institutions
The Brotherton Library of the University of Leeds
Verner Schomaker of the University of Washington
The Institute Archives of the Massachusetts Institute of Technology
The staff of the Robert A. Millikan Library at the California Institute of Technology
Jerry Donahue
Margaret Rossiter
Cushing Strout
Edward Jay Epstein
Robert Kargon, the Willis K. Shepard Professor of the History of Science at Johns Hopkins University
Elizabeth Einstein
Alice Richards
Katherine Higby
Al Bauer
Tony Schille
Louis Parrish
William Hedges
Harry Strickhausen
George Waldo of the class of 1922
Alma Scharpf Wiggins of the class of 1922
Harold Granrud of the class of 1922
Dr. Barclay Kamb
Dr. Arthur Robinson and the Oregon Institute of Science and Medicine
Karen Milstein
C. Dickerman Williams of *National Review*
Michele Aldrich, archivist of the American Association for the Advancement of Science
Alice W. Kahler of Princeton, for the hospitality of her home and for many pleasant and informative conversations about

her husband Eric Kahler, and their friendship with Albert Einstein
P.C. Joss of the Massachusetts Institute of Technology
George Fleck of Smith College
Samuel Silverman
Frances Herring
Eric Swenson
W. H. Ferry and his wife, for the kind hospitality at their home in Portland, Oregon
Joseph Koeplfli of the California Institute of Technology
Edward Hughes of the California Institute of Technology
Ernest Swift of the California Institute of Technology
Oliver Wulf of the California Institute of Technology
Jack Roberts of the California Institute of Technology
Richard Marsh of the California Institute of Technology
The staff at the Athenaeum of the California Institute of Technology, for making my stay a most enjoyable one
The Department of Philosophy at Princeton University, for its cordiality in offering me a Visiting Fellowship, where I first began my investigations
The faculty of the Department of Journalistic Studies at the University of Massachusetts, for its kindness and hospitality to me when I was at the university several years ago
Special thanks to Dario Politella of that department
John Edsall
Ruth Hubbard
Helene Schwarz
Ralph Jessem of the class of 1922 at Oregon State University, George Payne of the class of 1922
The sisters-in-law of Linus Pauling, Gorgo and Lillian Miller
William Friedlander of Washington University
The Woodrow Wilson Foundation, for appointing me as a summer Fellow in 1988
Marjorie Senechal of Smith College
Robert Richter, producer of the NOVA program on Linus Pauling and the staff of WGBH-TV in Boston
Dr. David Harker of the Medical Foundation of Buffalo, Inc.
James Ibers of Northwestern University

Libby Frank of the Women's International League for Peace and Freedom

Mildred Scott Olmsted of the Women's International League for Peace and Freedom

John and Laree Caughey

Ralph Coleman of the class of 1922 at Oregon State University

George Rutledge of the class of 1922 at Oregon State University

Oregon State University

The FBI

The Niels Bohr Library

The staff of *The Oregonian*

Finally, I should like to thank the Magnavox Company for creating the *Videowriter*—that marvelous machine which shortened the editing time of this manuscript by at least 50 percent, if not more.

# Foreword

My first interaction with Linus Pauling—in my opinion, the greatest chemist of the twentieth century—was an entirely indirect and entirely uncomfortable one. It came about thus:

My college career at Columbia University spanned the years from 1935 to 1939, and I majored in chemistry. I then went on (still at Columbia) to graduate work in the field of chemistry and got my Master's degree in 1941. Then World War II intervened and there was a five-year hiatus.

Pauling had, in 1932, published his seminal book *The Nature of the Chemical Bond*, in which quantum theory was, for the first time, applied to chemistry, and to organic chemistry in particular. It took a while, however, for the new concept to establish itself within the thought processes of the professors teaching the subject.

All through my pre-war education, then, I was taught organic chemistry in the old-fashioned way (except for a small whiff of electronic matters in Louis Hammett's textbook *Physical Organic Chemistry*). I, of course, was not bright enough, and did not do sufficient outside reading to know that a revolution had taken place, and I was perfectly content to memorize the details of reactions by rote, without any concern for intermediates and electronic shifts.

In 1946 the war was finally over and I returned to Columbia

University in order to continue work toward my doctorate. During the war years, while I was gone, Pauling's views had finally permeated the department and I discovered that organic chemistry was a brand-new subject and that I was a beginner and not only had much to learn, but much to unlearn.

I managed to get my Ph.D. in 1948, but I never felt comfortable in organic chemistry again; just because Pauling was the genius he was, and the chemistry professors were the lesser men they were, and with the hiatus coming when it did, it became inevitable that I would eventually make the decision to leave chemistry and become a full-time writer. On the whole, Pauling did me a huge favor, though I did not think so at the time.

Soon after I got my Ph.D., Pauling exerted a far more direct influence on me. I was spending a year in a post-doctorate program—*still* at Columbia University—and on March 21, 1949, I attended a lecture given at Columbia by Linus Pauling. (Why do I remember the date? No arcane explanations are necessary; I have been keeping a diary for fifty years.)

That talk was the best talk by anyone on any subject that I had ever heard up to that time. I have heard good talks since, notably by George Wald, another Nobel laureate, but nothing yet has ever been clearly superior to Pauling's talk that night.

The amazing thing is this: My first wife attended the talk with me. While an intelligent woman, she knew nothing about chemistry and Pauling's talk was on the structure of molecules. Nevertheless, despite the fact that she understood nothing about the content of the talk, she was fascinated. Pauling had a way of communicating enthusiasm and exerting charisma.

The talk was more than a talk to me. It filled me with a desire of my own to become a speaker. I had up to that time never given a talk before an audience of anything more than my schoolmates, but I now had a wild desire to try my hand at exerting the same charisma as Pauling.

In 1950, I gave my first public talk at a science-fiction convention and was delighted to find that, indeed, the audience laughed when I wanted them to laugh, and reacted, generally, as I wanted them to react. I have since then given somewhere between 1000 and 2000 talks, most of them for inordinate fees, and that, too, I owe to Pauling.

But there's more. At the time I listened to Pauling's talk I had already been a professional writer of science fiction magazine stories for eleven years, and I signed a contract for my first science fiction novel just one week after the talk. However, the talk filled me with the desire to write not only science fiction, but "straight" science. I wanted to explain things as clearly and as attractively as Pauling had.

Almost immediately, I began to try writing essays on science; while I had little luck getting them published at first, I managed eventually. As a result, in the forty years since I heard Pauling's talk, I have published some two hundred books on scientific subjects of one kind or another. And that, too, I owe to Pauling.

My first really *successful* science book was "The Intelligent Man's Guide to Science" (Basic Books, 1960). It was a general overview of every branch of science and I had undertaken it with considerable anxiety and uncertainty. However, as soon as it appeared, my writing income doubled. The reviews were terrific and I was taken seriously as a science writer from then on. (I had had the sneaking fear that my science would be dismissed because I was "just a science fiction writer.")

On June 3, 1961, I heard Pauling speak in Cambridge. I spoke with him afterward, and he told me he had been consulted by Basic Books as to who might do the book and he had strongly recommended me. So one more debt to him may be listed.

I suppose that he recommended me because he reads what I write—some of it anyway. In particular I know that he reads my monthly column in *The Magazine of Fantasy and Science Fiction* (something I have now been writing for thirty years, without missing an issue). I know he reads that because he occasionally writes me to correct an error.

Once, in listing whom I considered to be the greatest scientists of all time, I confused a still-living scientist with his brother, who had died a few years before. So I gave the living scientist a death-date and Pauling wrote to assure me the scientist in question was still alive.

What's more, Pauling told me that he went through the list carefully to make sure that he himself was listed, and was gratified to find that he was. (Of course, he was included. I was astonished to think that he could possibly imagine he wouldn't be.)

On September 14, 1964, he wrote me a letter that went something like this—and I am forced to quote from memory: "Dear Asimov: I have been frequently told that I make errors in my calculations, but *never* have I made an error of 23 orders of magnitude as you have in your article 'First and Rearmost'."

That was all. I broke into a cold perspiration at once, for the article in question, along with a group of others from *F & SF* was soon to appear in book form, and I had to find out what the error was and correct it.

All I had to go by was that "23 orders of magnitude." That had to involve Avogadro's Number ($6.026 \times 10^{23}$), which I had made use of in the article. I went over it tensely and, sure enough, it turned out that I should have taken the *square* of Avogadro's number and had failed to do so (or perhaps I *had* taken the square and shouldn't have, I forget which). In any case, I corrected it for the book appearance with vast relief.

Afterward, I was uncertain whether to be irritated with Pauling for not having bothered to point out where the error was, or to be flattered by the fact that he was clearly of the opinion that I did not *need* to have it pointed out. After considerable thought, I decided I would feel happier if I decided I had been flattered.

But more than the fact that Pauling is a first-class genius, more than the fact that he was a brave man who struggled for peace and against nuclear weapons even during the McCarthy era, when so many worthy men were frightened and browbeaten into silence, is the fact that he is a gentleman in the highest sense of the word. He has *character*. Here's how I know:

In the early 1950s, I had written a series of articles for the

*Journal of Chemical Education.* The last of these was written on August 13, 1954, and it appeared in the February 1955 issue of the *J. C. E.* In it, I discussed the radioactive atoms that occurred naturally in the human body and pointed out that by far the most important of these, and the one that was absolutely bound to have crucial effects upon the body, was carbon-14.

As far as I knew at the time, this was the first occasion on which anyone had pointed out the importance of carbon-14 in this respect. It was an original idea of mine, although I believe Willard Libby, the Nobel laureate who had specialized in work on carbon-14, may have had the idea at the same time.

Nearly four years later, Pauling published a paper in the November 14, 1958, issue of *Science* that discussed the dangers of carbon-14 in a careful and systematic way.

I'm sure that Pauling's article played its part in the eventual agreement on the part of the three chief nuclear powers to suspend atmospheric testing, for Pauling was one of the most prominent and influential critics of such tests, and he pointed to the production of carbon-14 in these tests as one of their chief long-term dangers.

I do not mean to, in any way, dispute priorities with Pauling. I had merely had an idea—which is what I am supposed to have, as a professional science fiction writer—an idea which I did not develop. Pauling developed it thoroughly, on the basis of the work done by Libby.

Still, I did work up the courage to send Pauling a reprint of my *J. C. E.* article by way of a mutual friend, carefully stating that I was not disputing priorities.

Pauling was kind enough to send me the following letter, dated February 11, 1959:

Dear Professor Asimov:

I am pleased that Mr. William Kaufmann should have sent on to me the copy of your carbon-14 paper that appeared in the *Journal of Chemical Education* four years ago. I now remember that I had read the paper when it appeared (I always read the *Journal of Chemical Education*) but I had forgotten about it, except that without doubt the principal argument remained in my mind. I am sorry that I did not mention it in the carbon-14 paper that I published recently, a copy of which is enclosed.

Sincerely yours,

s/ Linus Pauling

It was a sweet and gentle letter. He need not have written it. There was no question but that the credit was all his. However, he was not the person to snatch at everything in sight. He was perfectly content to let me have my idea and was even so incredibly courteous as to imply that it might have influenced him.

I have never forgotten that letter, and whenever I have had the impulse to snatch at "glory" or to make myself out to be bigger than I am, I think of the letter and of the truly great man who wrote it and who took such care to preserve my *amour propre*.

Pauling is not an easy man to live up to, but it does me good to try, even when I give up hope of succeeding.

ISAAC ASIMOV

# Introduction

What is the story of Linus Pauling? A man of conspicuous talents, hard-driving and boundlessly energetic, he could well be considered the American Cowboy of science. Never one to shy away from controversies or challenges, Pauling has always approached them with his own brand of zest and confidence. His works and activities are the epitome of the same pioneering spirit that drove the early settlers to explore and conquer ever-widening frontiers. His ground-breaking work on sickle-cell anemia, the theory of anesthesia, his work on chemical bonding, his near-victory in the DNA race—these and many other projects show the tremendous range of his professional talents and curiosity.

Pauling does have his weaknesses. But in them he also found his greatest strength. His impatience, impulsiveness, and desire to "get there first" were merely the flip side of that other, crucial element of scientific genius: the courage to follow one's intuitions when the scientific data is lacking and the roadmap to knowledge is not clearly marked. One could argue that the quest for data for its own sake can lead to a peculiar brand of scientific paralysis, akin to the dogmatism of a scientist like John Slater. Though Slater is competent, hard-working, ruthlessly accurate and technically correct in his criticisms of Pauling, he will not be judged one of the world's great scientific minds. While those only marginally familiar with science will recognize names like Pauling, Fermi, Oppenheimer, Teller, Bethe, and others, few will remember Slater.

Pauling's crusade for vitamin C, it is true, may well prove to be his Waterloo, like the "key to all mythologies" that Mr. Casaubon pursued in vain in *Middlemarch*. But even in failure, he will have done no worse than the great Einstein himself, who so single-mindedly albeit fruitlessly pursued the dream of the "Unified Field Theory." In any case, this particular odyssey of Pauling's has not yet ended. Only the future will tell if he is right or wrong about vitamin C.

In the interim, the past is, ironically, coming back to haunt him. Just as Pauling once patronized and ignored organic chemistry and criticized Dorothy Wrinch and Art Robinson for being "inappropriately out of their fields," so he now faces an intolerant and hostile medical community. The world's medical establishment steadfastly refuses to take seriously his claims about vitamin C on the grounds that he, too, is "inappropriately out of his field."

Yet because of Pauling's obsession with vitamin C, there is considerable risk that his name may become synonymous with that crusade—as if Pauling had done no "real" scientific work for decades. It is true that his work in the health field is that which the public knows best. And Pauling himself contributes to this myopic public perception, writing and personally promoting a book entitled *How To Live Longer and Feel Better*, which was published in 1986. His TV talk show appearances do foster the public impression of Pauling as a vitamin C crusader and tend to obscure his lesser-known, more serious work. The book itself is informed, thoughtful and, as usual, controversial. In it, Pauling discusses the "new nutrition," "orthomolecular medicine," and the relationships between vitamins and drugs, among other things. In the "Regimen" section, Pauling gives his own rules for better health, discusses the problems generated by the overabundance of food in Western society, and other such issues. Doubtless the medical community will deny that the book contains any new and interesting information about vitamins or nutrients generally. Pauling's credentials as a medical researcher are, they feel, far too weak to be taken seriously (an odd claim about a man who many felt deserved the Nobel prize for his work on sickle-cell anemia.)

Nevertheless, despite appearances to the contrary, nutrition is not the only thing Linus Pauling has investigated over the years. While it may come as a surprise to many, Pauling is still working on the chemical bond and, very recently, has come full circle to the project that launched his career in 1922—the work on structural chemistry with Roscoe Dickinson at the California Institute of Technology. His most recent contribution to that branch of science began in November of 1984, when D. Shechtman and his colleagues discovered a structure with symmetry previously thought impossible, formed when a molten mixture of manganese and aluminum was cooled rapidly. Using his knowledge of the principles governing the structure of intermetallic compounds acquired from Roscoe Dickinson so long ago, Pauling suggested a structure for the manganese-aluminum alloy. What was most interesting about the Pauling structure, perhaps, was that it yielded a theoretical model in seemingly good agreement with the data obtained from X-ray crystallography. Also Pauling's model was a controversial scientific procedure in that, unlike Shechtman and his co-workers, Pauling did not find it necessary to introduce a new, "quasi-crystalline" (as Shechtman dubbed it) state of matter to explain the X-ray observations. Pauling here follows a basic principle of science: no more theoretical assumptions should ever be introduced into a theory than are required to explain the given facts.

Whether this theoretical model will be accepted by physicists working in these areas is conjectural at this point, since current opinion on Pauling's new structure is, so far, divided— a common enough phenomenon in the day-to-day workings of science. But since controversy, be it professional or personal, is Pauling's favorite milieu, he is not worried about generating it.

For the present, the point is that Pauling does not restrict his activities to proselytizing for vitamin C. And if there was any doubt that the scientific community still regards him as a world-class scientist, that was dispelled when on Feb. 29, 1986 the California Institute of Technology threw a party to celebrate

Pauling's eighty-fifth birthday. Among the guests were Nobelist Francis Crick, Pauling's DNA nemesis; Alex Rich of M.I.T.; William N. Lipscomb Jr. of Harvard University's Chemistry Department; and many other greats from the world of science.

All in all, Linus Pauling is a happily unconventional genius who, despite his shortcomings, ranks among the great scientists of history, along with Einstein, Niels Bohr, Francis Crick, Dorothy Wrinch, James Watson, Rosalind Franklin, Enrico Fermi. Marie Curie, and, in contemporary times, Paul Joss and Stephen Hawking, among others. His work on sickle-cell anemia, the application of quantum mechanics to the theory of the chemical bond, crystal structure, molecular biology, the discovery of the alpha-helix and many other accomplishments easily take their place alongside such monumental developments as relativity theory by Einstein, quantum mechanics by Schrödinger and Heisenberg et al. and quantum electrodynamics by Feynman.

As has been said of a few other giants, heroes, rogues, and charmers down through the centuries, if Linus Pauling did not exist, the world would have had to invent him.

# 1

# The Early Days

LINUS CARL PAULING IS A QUINTESSENTIALLY AMERICAN
figure. Born into conflict and combat with the rawest elements
of nature, poverty, and disease, he toughened himself for a lifetime of struggle. Brilliant, undisciplined, and rebellious, Pauling
burst quickly onto the scientific scene. Unflappable in
the face of criticism, unshakably confident in his own genius,
Pauling challenged scientific orthodoxy armed with a minimum
of hard scientific data and a tidal surge of intellectual power.
Before reaching the age of thirty, he ranked among the great
scientists of the world.

Perhaps it was the very remoteness of Oregon in the early
days of the century, coupled with its lack of entertainment, that
drove some to a lifetime love affair with learning. Condon was
indistinguishable from the myriad small towns scattered
through the American West. "God-fearing" folk, hard work, and
the Protestant ethic reigned. And just as California, in 1901, was
only beginning to rise from the confusion and chaos of the Old
West and vigilante justice, Condon had not changed very much.
During the early years of the century there were still the occasional gunfight and barroom brawl. No railroads existed in Condon in 1901 and it was a good forty-five miles to the nearest
"iron-horse" depot. True, Condon had a few qualities uniquely
its own. Over the years, Scotsmen had sought out its fertile

1

landscape—a landscape reminiscent, in many ways, of their native Highlands with streams to ford and timber to clear. And the beautiful and austere land of Oregon had drawn others from many quarters, people who sought opportunities to work on the cattle drives, build bridges and roads, and farm the rich soil. Calvin Neal was one of these. Born in 1824 in Tennessee, he came to Oregon in the famed Wagon Train expedition of 1844. His youngest daughter became the wife of Linus Wilson Darling (born 1855)—Linus Pauling's grandfather.

The conflict and struggle that followed Linus Pauling throughout his life was foreshadowed by a telling event in the Darling family history. When Linus Wilson Darling was seven years old, his father, William Allen Darling, abandoned his family to fight for the North in the early days of the Civil War.

On May 27, 1900, one of Linus Darling's daughters, Lucy Isabelle, married an obscure druggist named Herman W. Pauling. Three children followed quickly. Linus Pauling, born on February 28, 1901, was the first, soon followed by his sister Pauline the next year, and by Frances Lucille in 1904.

If one wishes to speculate about the often brilliant, always quixotic, and occasionally stormy career of Linus Pauling, his maternal relatives provide some fascinating clues. They were an odd bunch, as bizarre as the paternal side was humdrum. There was old Will Darling, Linus Darling's brother, who was a painter and a confirmed spiritualist. Always "in touch" with a dead Indian named Red Cloud, he hoped to find the location of a lost gold mine in the Lone Rock country. Not to be outdone, Linus Pauling's aunt, Stella "Fingers" Darling was known throughout the West for her ability to break open safes. If Linus Pauling's later actions in politics and science were fabulous and unorthodox, he was not, at least, breaking with family tradition.

Like so many who had preceeded them, Herman and Belle Pauling struggled to earn a living. Herman Pauling did his best as a salesman and a druggist and the growing family made do in a one-room tenement apartment near the Chinese part of Oswego. Just as Linus Darling could scarcely extract payment for his legal services, so too Herman Pauling could barely wrench a penny from the poor of Oswego.

It was at about this time that the Paulings moved to Condon. Slightly more well-to-do, Belle Pauling's family there might be counted on as a source of money, at least in absolute emergencies. Herman set up a drugstore—some claim this was where his son developed an early interest in science, by watching his father work. That theory is plausible. In an eerily prophetic advertisement in the March 30, 1906 edition of the Condon *Globe*, Herman Pauling offered twenty-five cent bottles of "Dr. Pfunder's Oregon Blood Purifier." The text of the ad is an uncanny telescope into the future. It claims that the blood purifier is "a . . . cure for all diseases arising from derangements of the liver and kidneys, or an impure condition of the blood, such as scrofulous infections, erysipeias, pimples, blotches, boils, salt rheum, ulcers, cold sores, dropsy and dyspepsia."

The cure for all ills? Was it not just such a miracle cure that Pauling promoted some seventy years later? Who is there to say for certain that the mystical blood purifier did not work, or that it did not contain perhaps a touch of vitamin C, though the vitamin was not discovered until the 1930s?

Pauling, however, denies any very early interest in chemistry. In an interview given many years later, he said that he was about twelve years old when he became interested in chemistry. His father died when he was nine. On the other hand, he does admit to an early interest in science generally. In the interview, he says: "My interest in mathematics was already evident and of course I found that scientific questions interested me as a boy. I was always puzzling about various phenomena such as shadows, optical phenomena that I had observed of one sort or another."[1] Perhaps some sort of "imprinting" took place very early in Pauling's life as he watched his father mix medicines, though he had no active interest in chemistry until later.

Interestingly, there is evidence that Pauling felt some attraction to religion in his early years. In the same interview he says:

I can remember lying in bed in my grandmother's house looking at a . . . drawing of a head of Christ . . . here I was looking at this head of Christ when I saw that a halo appeared above it, a band

of light . . . after . . . investigation I discovered the after-image
effects . . . of the retina and satisfied myself that this was a general
natural phenomenon. . . .[2]

Evidently, whatever environmental pressure there was to practice religion soon resolved itself, and his humanistic and anti-
metaphysical tendencies appeared soon after, when he was still
a boy.

By age nine, Pauling's interest in science was sufficiently
strong that his father wrote the *Oregonian* to ask for help in
cultivating Linus' fascination with learning. Pauling says, "He
. . . had taken an interest in my apparent intellectual ability to
the extent of writing a letter to the . . . *Oregonian* at a time when
we had already moved to Portland, asking for advice about what
books he might provide . . . or what other actions he might take."[3]

Unlike the stereotypical scientist who inhabits a solipsistic
world of his own creation, Linus Pauling was active, sports-
oriented, and enjoyed the outdoors. On the rare sunny Oregon
afternoon, he and first cousin Mervyn Stephenson would wander
aimlessly through the frontier streets of Condon, swiping at the
occasional butterfly and skipping rocks over the waters of nearby
ponds. In the summers, the pair spent a great deal of time on
the wheat ranch of Mervyn's father, Philip Herbert Stephenson.
Life at the ranch was carefree, punctuated by occasional hunting
expeditions and swims in the nearby streams.

But this bucolic existence was coming to an end. Pauling's
father died soon after the letter to the *Oregonian* was published.
Battling serious financial problems while dedicating himself to
his son's intellectual development had taken its toll. Moreover,
a deepening melancholy over his wife's increasingly bizarre and
unreasonable attitudes toward money and her obsession with
finding ways for Linus to bring in extra income added to his
burden.

A final blow came when the family's move to Portland did
not bolster his financial fortunes as he had hoped. His obituary
notice in the June 12, 1910 issue of the *Oregon Journal* read
simply, "Pauling—In this city, June 11, at his late residence,
Forty-Fifth and Belmont Sts., Herman W. Pauling, aged thirty-

two years, six months, and thirteen days. Funeral services will be held at the Congregational Church at Oswego at 3 P.M. today (Sunday). Friends Invited. Interment Oswego Cemetery."

Then too, Pauling's friend and cousin Mervyn Stephenson had been left behind when the Paulings left Condon for Portland. For four years, he remained without any close friends, withdrawing more and more into science as a consequence.

Pauling and his mother continued to move in different directions as well, despite the mediations of his sisters. His sister-in-law Gorgo Miller commented: "Liney and his mother didn't get along, you see; she was a cranky, sort of snooty type. I don't think she spent much time with Linus and didn't want him to go to college." The practical laboratory of his father's workshop was gone, and Pauling realized he could develop his abilities in science only through books. While Pauling's universe was the universe of thought, reason, and order, his mother's was the world of rowdyism and blue-collar banter. In his quest for privacy, the young Pauling found himself driven to putting a lock on his door in the family boardinghouse to guard his privacy and cherished study periods.

His curiosity about the physical universe in this period took on a kind of insatiability. His sisters could not match either his scientific prowess or his curiosity, but they did try and share his love of nature as best they could and included him in their activities without exception.

Pauling himself has spoken of his very earliest curiosity: "When I was around eleven or twelve, on my own initiative I made a collection of insects. I'd gotten a book from the library and had started collecting insects and classifying them, and I had become interested in minerals."[4] The interest in minerals presages his later and classic work in the study of mineral structures at the California Institute of Technology. For the present, it was only a hobby. Moreover, the Willamette Valley was hardly a good place in which to collect minerals. Still, it was a beginning. As Pauling's interest grew, his sisters continued to find new ways to broaden and nurture it. Feeling that the confines of his narrow and dank study were less than healthy, they began including him on trips to visit Charles and Adelheit Pauling, their paternal grandparents, who lived at the time in a sturdy, Western-style home surrounded by wheat grass and briar. The grandparents' grief at the death of Linus' father was profoundly and deeply felt and the visits of Linus, Pauline, and Lucille filled a void for them as well.

Pauling's intellectual curiosity became increasingly evident. His sister Lucille remembers:

> Linus was always thinking . . . I recall so vividly one time when we were waiting for the train at the Jefferson Street Depot to come out to visit grandma and grandpa at Oswego—it was a very cold morning and mother and I were standing close together and Linus was walking around a little bit in the cold air. He said, "Mama, I know why you don't get so cold if you are moving around. Your feet aren't on the ground but half the time." And to me that was a real clever deduction.

Even if his renowned ability to theorize was still immature, his thirst for knowledge was there. At times, his information came from odd sources. Back in Portland there lived a mountain man by the name of Yokum. Pauling was fascinated. When he felt brave enough to risk his mother's ire, he stopped by the man's den on the way home from school. The mountain man, equally drawn to Pauling, urged him to learn Greek. Apparently having some knowledge of this language himself, he began teaching Pauling.

As the years continued to pass, Pauling gradually began to seriously consider the future. At Washington High School he met his first real source of inspiration, a schoolteacher named Pauline Geballe.

The secondary school system of the day was worth nearly nothing, at least so far as science was concerned. Most of the high schools provided only a general education. Even mathematics was rudimentary and often only a college would provide courses beyond basic algebra. Teachers skilled in basic physics were also in short supply.

However, Washington High was better than average. Pauling was able to take a fair sampling of courses in English, Latin, history, and science. And he was exposed to a fine teacher like Pauline Geballe. Even today, Pauling mentions her influence:

> When I was twelve I had a course in high school . . . in what was called 'physiography,' which was general science. This interested me very much. I can remember the teacher, an old woman, about twenty-four I supposed; she's still alive in Oregon and her name is Geballe. . . . I can remember her carrying out an experiment to show the pressure of the atmosphere. She had a Log Cabin Syrup can with a little water in it. She boiled the water for a while, screwed the top on, and then let it cool and it collapsed. . . .[6]

In December, 1963, Pauline Geballe was a small, white-haired lady of seventy-four. She spoke admiringly of her Nobel Prize-winning former student: "I can remember him as a small, shy, twelve-year-old freshman. He was one of my brightest pupils, but I honestly haven't any idea how I influenced him to become so interested in science."[7]

How could she have known? At best she was a catalyst who helped bring out an interest that was already there. She was well-prepared for the role. She had been finely educated at Smith College in an age where many teachers had no formal credentials at all. One of six women majoring in chemistry at Smith, she had joined Washington High's teaching staff in 1913. No doubt Pauling, whose intellect and intuitive powers were impressive even at that age, saw something special in Pauline Geballe. He paid attention to her—a compliment he would not pay very often later in life.

None of this is to say that she would have approved of all his early "research" into chemistry. One of his efforts consisted of sprinkling the trolley tracks in Portland with some kind of explosive powder. Some reports hold that this was his first "scientific experiment." According to another childhood friend, Paul Emmett (later Pauling's friend and co-worker and eventually his brother-in-law) this happened fairly often: "On some occasions we'd make these explosive chemicals, then go out and put them right on the car tracks so that when the street car came by [the chemicals] just blew up." It seems that such "experimentation" began even earlier than high school.

Hints of Pauling's later traits emerge in accounts of his high school years. In all things, he was always the intellectual frontiersman, very sure of himself and quite unwilling to consider the idea that anyone could tell him much about anything. His high school and college friend George Payne remembers: "He never took to what you'd call 'social studies' though he knew more about politics and all that than anyone."

This fundamental arrogance and undisguised intellectual superiority could and would surface later on with any topic under discussion. Others noticed his hubris. The austere Portland *Oregonian* reported: "Dr. Pauling did not receive his diploma from Washington High School because he refused to take a course in civics. He told the school administration he could absorb all the civics he needed simply through his own reading."

Although Washington High thought this was the last word regarding Linus Pauling's diploma, their own fussiness and protocol came back years later to haunt them. In 1962, they had to relent—Pauling had won his second Nobel Prize and how could Washington High School hold out? They gave him his diploma (a Nobel Peace Prize arguably being the equivalent of a high school course in civics).

Later in high school, few dared oppose him and Pauling had begun to show his contempt for traditional ways of doing things. In this period, he became good friends with a fellow student named Lloyd Jeffress. Pauling's respect for Jeffress, like his respect for Pauline Geballe, was considerable. In many ways, they mirrored one another; both were enormously intelligent, both loved conversation about science, and both appeared headed for academic careers.

Even so, Jeffress was several years younger than Pauling, which gave Pauling something of an edge in conversation and general knowledge. Yet this slight advantage was balanced by the fact that Jeffress had started tinkering with chemistry a bit earlier than he had. He deferred to Jeffress. Pauling recalls:

... I was walking home from high school with a fellow named Lloyd Alexander Jeffress who asked if I would like to see an ... experiment. I said yes. ... I stopped at his home ... where he carried out certain experiments; he mixed potassium chlorate and sugar, putting a drop of sulfuric acid on it which started the reaction liberating water and producing carbon. Very exciting![8]

Events like this fueled his interest in chemistry. But science is an expensive hobby and he needed to find chemicals and equipment, since Jeffress' supply of such things was limited. His old mentor, Mr. Yokum, did give him some equipment, since he worked part time in a chemistry laboratory. But it was not enough to satisfy Pauling's needs. He drew upon his elastic imagination to solve the problem:

I had built a little laboratory in my basement. I found that there were bottles of chemicals in the small chemical laboratory of the Oregon Iron and Steel Company smelter which hadn't been operated for fifteen years perhaps, or even more. The roof had fallen in on the building where these bottles of chemicals were. I, from time to time, 'borrowed' them and took them to Portland; this was in Oswego which involved going seven miles. My grandparents lived there and my grandfather worked for this company as night watchman, so I had access. He was the night watchman at the foundry which was an eighth of a mile away and the smelter was just abandoned. ... So I had a supply of chemicals and I became a chemist.[9]

What Geballe and Jeffress provided was an environment which accelerated Pauling's drive and conquest of chemistry by a year or two at most. Perhaps that is all a mentor can ever provide. Indeed, Pauling spent many happy afternoons at the house Jeffress shared with his aunt and uncle. Almost invariably, the discussions focused on books, ideas, science, and politics, and were always at a high level. He preferred this heady atmosphere to the smoky rooms of his mother's boardinghouse, with its working-class discussions about beer, taxes, and the federal government.

Nonetheless, Pauling had to pay attention to other things besides science and intellectual discussion. There was, and would be for some time to come, the threat of financial trouble—serious financial trouble. To keep this specter from his laboratory door, Pauling delivered milk, operated motion picture projectors and, later, even labored in the shipyards on the Willamette River.

But the extra income he produced was apparently insufficient. As a result, his relations with his mother continued to worsen, aggravated by Pauling's insistence that he wanted to go to college. Perhaps his mother's stubbornness, aided by what she saw as arrogance and snobbishness in his attitude toward her, contributed to worsening relations between them.

But Pauling would not be denied. He decided he would go to college and study to become an engineer, as this was really the main path for anyone wanting to go into science in those days. Whether his mother fought him so bitterly because of intrinsic objections against education or simply because college would prevent him from earning more money for the household is hard to say.

In any event, by the time he left Washington High in June of 1917, he was making a formidable forty dollars per month. Pauling himself recalls, with pain, one particularly bitter encounter in which his mother pleaded, "Linus, I need your help. I still have Pauline and Lucille to support. No one on the street has gone to college. Why must you?" His reply was simple, poignant, and unanswerable: "I want to learn, Mama."[10]

Even at this age, Pauling had a keen eye for practical matters, though his interest in them was hardly consuming. The Jeffress family advised him that what he was then earning was insignificant compared with what a college graduate might earn. A classic conflict had emerged, between the need for learning and the need for money. Only sixteen, Pauling gradually became obsessed with earning money, first working as a photographer's assistant, doing mostly menial jobs. Soon he was trying to enter the risky world of the entrepreneur. With the aid of some friends, he tried to start his own business, managing to get some photographic work from nearby drug stores. The effort failed within a month.

Oddly, the failure of his first business scarcely bothered him. And while the dust was still gathering over his ill-fated venture, he received news of his acceptance at Oregon Agricultural College, in September of 1917. Meanwhile, he had wandered into still one more job, in a machine shop owned by a frail, gruff, yet caring German named Schweizerhoff. Schweizerhoff told him that he could have a job there anytime he wished. The German could not have guessed how much that promise meant to the sixteen-year old Pauling, poised between adulthood and adolescence, hope and insecurity. With at least something of a financial base, Pauling returned briefly to Washington High to say goodbye to friends. His college career had begun. His mother, his friends, and his sisters now had to allow him to pursue his goals.

Septembers are temperate in Oregon and the first sure signs of winter had not yet made their appearance on the Saturday in October, 1917 when Pauling arrived in Corvallis, the home of Oregon Agricultural College, after a five-hour train ride from Portland. The very first person he saw upon stepping off the smoking and hissing Pullman was his cousin Mervyn Stephenson.

Their friendship, now re-established, did not end until Mervyn's death in 1982, though the two saw one another only occasionally during Pauling's difficult and turbulent later years.

Immediately, Pauling's genius showed itself. He glided through the difficult first-year courses in engineering, chemistry, and mathematics. His fellow students marveled and his intellect amazed the faculty.

Still, his financial problems remained. He recalls those difficult early college days: "During my freshman year I put in wood and had odd jobs; my main one was that I chopped wood for the cook stoves in the girls' dormitory and mopped out the kitchen and so on. I worked a hundred hours a month and good hard work, too. . . ."[11] Yet there was a limit to how much even Linus Pauling could neglect study for the sake of making money, and that limit showed up soon enough. For the moment, however, all went smoothly. His preparation at Washington High had more or less already covered the freshman year material. He had, among other things, probed into organic chemistry as well as qualitative analysis, by assisting a teacher named Gale in studying oil and coal samples purchased by the Portland school system. Gale was a patient and knowledgeable man. He may not have been among the greatest influences in Pauling's life, but Pauling learned much from him.

The environment buoyed Pauling as well. It was stark, functional, and working class. Yet it offered financial opportunities and the living was cheap. As Pauling explained years later:

> There was no tuition, and registration fees were only a few dollars, and books weren't very expensive. I had perhaps twenty dollars worth of books my freshman year, all second-hand. . . . I lived first . . . in a rooming house which was a boarding house, too. I got my meals there. Then I moved from there to a house on 9th Street, with another young man with whom I shared a room.

However, according to classmate Tony Schille, "Pauling rarely went in for campus activities, which bothered me, since I was in charge of many of them." Even so, Pauling did enjoy some occasional revelry. As he explained in the same interview:

> ". . . in the fall of 1917, there was a big rally with a couple of thousand of students marching down to the President's House, singing songs that had been made up for the occasion. . . . So, that was one of my memories of one of the exciting events during my first year.

At that time, engineering, home economics, forestry, and business administration were the primary schools at Oregon Agricultural College. While the vast majority of the students came from the great cattle ranches and wheat farms of eastern Oregon, others came from the coast and mountain regions. Some came from farther distances than that. The yearbook boasts of more than a few Indian and Pakistani names, in a world where India must have seemed as far away as Jupiter.

While Pauling shined in academics, he apparently had few social contacts. Even the half-social, half-business campus political activities did not arouse Pauling's interest. As classmate Tony Schille told me, he didn't like that at all: "I didn't feel he'd put in his share . . . and Linus was doing well enough; he could have spared the time." If Pauling's ability to irritate (and in later days to infuriate) others by refusing to conform was even then beginning to develop, his equally legendary and consummate faith in his own intellect was surfacing as well. C.J. Layton, in his ninetieth year when he wrote to me in 1984, echoed this theme:

> Linus and I arrived at the campus at Corvallis . . . in the fall of 1917, five months after the United States entered into World War I. . . . Some days later our [chemistry] instructor was giving us a detailed explanation of the subject when Linus cut in and corrected him. The dean thought for a minute and said, "You are absolutely right, Mr. Pauling." After class was dismissed I opined that he might have been a bit rash in interrupting the dean. He said, "Oh, no! He would not have wanted his class to be misinformed. . . ."

In later years the same faith that the world—even presidents and fellow Nobel Prize winners—would welcome his unsolicited advice, appeared over and over again. Not all welcomed it so graciously as the dean had in 1917.

While some berated Pauling about his groundhog existence and apparent indifference to the college community, he in fact saved a considerable number of academic hides. Layton remembers instances in which Pauling tutored him:

> Pauling as a young man was well-groomed, well-met and a ready conversationalist. I complained to him about not being able to understand much about chemistry. He promptly invited me over to his house that evening to go over the assignment. After hearing the explanations, I right then knew more about chemistry than at anytime prior or since.

ᴧter generations of undergraduates at Caltech and Stanford would agree with Layton without any qualification.

Even so, Pauling was far from the stereotypical bookworm. The body of folkore that has evolved over the years has it that his first and only "date" in college was Ava Helen Miller, and that he never looked at another girl. Not so, according to classmate Helen McCain:

> The . . . thing I remember is that he did date a member of my house occasionally, but she was not interested in him. Well, he was maybe just a little bit fresh; but she felt anyway that he was of too serious a nature for her and too bookish a type and so she terminated any further association.

Pauling's career as a dorm room Romeo must have ended there, for little such gossip came from other classmates. As Myrtle Williams told me, for example: "Pauling wasn't outwardly aloof or anti-social. . . . I was in college only two years and all I remember of Linus Pauling at that time was his passing the Pi Beta Phi sorority on his way to his fraternity and his smiling as he waved 'hello' to me."

Oddly, while Pauling was hardly the "big man on campus," he was not above a few pranks, even some pretty outrageous ones. And his brother-in-law Paul Emmett recalls times when Pauling was not the most careful driver: "We warned him not to drive at night during the monsoon seasons, and of course the first night he did, and had an accident, missing the side of the road, turning over and landing in a ditch."

Was Pauling a bit tipsy? It seems he was not above taking an occasional nip. Harold Granrud, who roomed with Pauling in college and who was among his closest friends in those days told me, "We had a place in college called Five Corners. . . . once in a while I'd see Linus coming out of the place with a jug of wine in one hand, and a bag of goodies in the other." The wine worked. Granrud further recalls:

> We were serenading girls one night; it was pitch dark, there were a lot of trees around, the girls were sleeping in porches upstairs.

We could hear them whispering, wondering who it was down there. Then, Linus turned to me and said, "Granny, I just confirmed a scientific fact here; the angle of incidence is greater than the angle of refraction, so I can piss against this tree without making any noise!"

There were also the "tubbings." This was a form of punishment for not having a date on Saturday night, a pretty frequent occurrence for Pauling. For a while, Pauling took it good-naturedly. Soon, however, he began to resent it. One night, he came prepared. Granrud recalls: "Linus got tubbed, but we got scared as hell because he was staying under too long. Apparently he'd hyperventilated on purpose, and was capable of holding his breath, which he did, long enough to give us all a jolt."

During everything, however, the specter of war cast shadows over the innocence of college life. It cramped Pauling's social life, but most of all his academic life. His cousin Mervyn Stephenson recalled the difficult days of Pauling's freshman year:

> This was in 1918; we were in what was called the Students Army Training Corps . . . formed by the government to keep young men in school . . . and then send them to an officers training school. We were then returned to Corvallis and Linus Pauling and I went to Tillamook . . . we immediately got a job with a shipyard . . . every morning we would take a boat out of Tillamook and go down across the bay and work all day and come back in the evening. We worked at this shipyard until it was time to return to school in the fall.[12]

The Student Army Training Corps experience was significant in another way. It was the very first experience Pauling had had with politics and the military. In future years he would have many more. Even then, however, this early experience may have influenced his future anti-military attitudes. Rita Mills recalls that

> Linus was very angry that he was not allowed to be the commander of his S.A.T.C. group, because he was not old enough. As I recall, he was not yet eighteen years old, but was already considered a

"brain." In later years, I have wondered if that had something to do with his prejudice against the Armed Services.

Perhaps it did. Frustrating events have a way of leaving their imprint on one's unconscious. However, it is just as likely that Pauling quickly forgot the whole thing. He was still haunted by financial problems. He continued working as a paving plant inspector that summer, but somehow, nothing was ever enough. For years, financial collapse had been threatening Pauling; now it had arrived. He managed to limp through his sophomore year, but out of desperation he was forced to skip classes in order to keep an assortment of jobs.

It didn't help. With his mother now gravely ill with pernicious anemia and all his money going to help her, Pauling knew that school was out of the question. He stayed out altogether during his junior year—a year which was almost completely wasted. He made little progress intellectually, nor, ironically enough, financially. Pauling has spoken freely of that trying period:

> Quantitative analysis, which I had during my sophomore year, interested me very much and at the end of my sophomore year I delivered milk for a while, . . . I didn't return to Oregon State because I didn't have enough money. I had given my mother the money that I had received . . . and at the end of the summer she told me that she just couldn't pay it back. Then along about the first of November I received an offer of an appointment as full time assistant instructor in quantitative analysis at Oregon Agricultural College to teach the sophomore course that I had just been taking the year before.[13]

Pauling's salary was to be $100 per month.

An undergraduate being offered a teaching position at a major institution of higher learning? It is true that, in those times, there really was a dearth of instructors; many young men, having left for the war, had now returned, since World War I was winding down. Classrooms were overcrowded and teachers were overworked. Even so, it was virtually unheard of for an

undergraduate to occupy the lecture podium. Pauling's enthusiasm, not unexpectedly, was considerable, though his own
words reflect the strain of the job:

> ... I accepted the job and spent the year teaching quantitative
> analysis full time. In fact I would consider now that by present
> standards it was several full time jobs. I had about forty contact
> hours per week. You know, there's a lot of laboratory [work] but
> I gave the lectures too.[14]

It is a wonder that Pauling could manage all this, especially
considering that his mother's ill-health and continuing financial
problems were burdening him as well. Still, history, with its
ardor for hero-making, may have exaggerated his faculty status.
Some have claimed that he was an "assistant instructor." Other
reports have him an "assistant professor" and virtually equal in
status to many of the regular faculty. Pauling himself claims to
have been an "assistant instructor."

What is the truth? According to an anonymous writer who
was, apparently, a classmate, he was not an assistant instructor.
In a reply to an article in *The Oregonian*, the writer claims: "I
didn't find him on any of the lists of assistant instructor. He did
assist in the lab and may have corrected exam papers for the
prof.—I did the same but we worked at student hourly pay and
were never listed as assistant instructors."

It is difficult to know what to make of all this, as not only
Pauling, but most of his classmates still refer to him as an "assistant instructor." It may all be much ado about nothing, since
the term "assistant instructor" is not the name of any normal
academic rank. Not today and not, typically, of colleges and universities in those times. More than likely, Pauling was something
like a "graduate assistant" in the modern university—helping to
grade papers, doing a little teaching, etc. This does have some
precedent, as universities (Cornell, e.g.) do occasionally use top-
notch undergraduates in this way.

Katherine Hibgy, a former student of Pauling's, told me that
when Pauling began to exercise authority, his normally taciturn
mind began to overflow with tricks and sarcasm:

One day in lab classes he played a trick on me during a lesson on acids and alkalines. I realized he was lingering near my table at one session and felt I should diligently study my lesson. After a time he confronted me with 'Katherine, is that your blue wool coat on the first hook in the hallway?' I answered, 'yes,' and glanced at it. Mercy! There was a big red splotch on the back of my hand-tailored winter, navy-blue coat I'd made the preceding summer. I felt very weak and faint. He supported me, and suggested we investigate. The entire class joined us and I was asked what I thought may have happened. I thought of the lesson and weakly replied, 'likely some one had spilled acid on my coat.' He quizzed me further and I concluded 'likely an acid had been spilled that might be neutralized by an alkaline.' As I meekly suggested that perhaps a mild soda solution might restore the color, Linus lightly moistened some soda and rubbed it into the material. Then he cleared it away and sure enough the blue color returned. Was I delighted!

Shades of the future again: With Linus Pauling, people would sometimes be vehicles to be used to make a point or as means to an end.

The most famous event in Pauling's college career is the tale of his very first meeting with Ava Helen Miller, who later became Ava Helen Pauling. In December of his senior year, he was asked by Professor Fred Allen, a burly, dour, but not un-caring man, to teach a course in chemistry for home economics majors. Pauling agreed. Talking about these years, he recalls that:

The first day that I went into class, here I was met by about twenty-five young women studying home economics. They'd been study-ing chemistry for three months and I thought they should know something about it; but I thought I'd find out. So I opened the class book and said, what do you know about ammonium hy-droxide Miss—and then I picked a name at random—Miller. [His classmates say, however, that he was naturally a bit nervous and simply picked a name he couldn't mispronounce.] Well, Miss Miller surprised me by knowing a great deal about ammonium hydroxide and I thought I'd better keep an eye on her.[15]

Ava Helen was petite and pretty. Like Linus Pauling, she too came from a sturdy and unpretentious Oregon family, though one relatively free from the grinding poverty the Paulings experienced. She was born in the country east of Oregon City, near Beavercreek, a small farm town with few amusements. It hardly mattered. Though not dangerously poor, the Millers were not wealthy either and the family needed to work almost constantly to keep things going.

Her sisters described her childhood:

She had compulsory chores to do, like all of us. But she was very feminine, not the tomboy type at all. We had to hoe in the fields, and she had her share to do; but she could be spunky, had a mind of her own. When she was a child she went to Sunday School, but later [she and Linus] were more connected to the Unitarian church than any other; but it didn't make any difference to our parents. Ava Helen never showed any disrespect for our parents' religious views.

Nor did she do so later in life, even when her own religious beliefs had waned even further. (She and her husband professed to be atheists). Invariably, she respected the religious views of others, even if she did not agree with them. On her relationship with Pauling her sisters said:

He would put notes to her in little vials, and he would give her poor grades because he was in love with her and didn't want to show favoritism. [Pauling confirmed this, saying "I was rather worried, felt that I shouldn't take of advantage of my position . . ."] . . . she resented that very much! One time in class, she questioned some theory of his, gave him an argument; he admired that tremendously.

This says much about Pauling's genuine and profound love for Ava Helen. There is little that Pauling likes more than intense debate with powerful and worthy antagonists. Arguably, that was the last time Pauling showed an opponent quite *that* much respect, but he adored her and Ava Helen adored him.

Even Ava Helen's mother loved Linus, though Pauling's mother seemed not to take to Ava Helen equally strongly. Ava Helen's sisters again recalled fondly those early and happy days.

> I remember the first time I met Linus; he was still a student. He had tremendously curly hair, very good-looking . . . and my mother loved him very much and thought he was a rising sun. But we didn't really have any indication that he'd be so famous one day. No, to this day he's like an old shoe. Comes in and makes himself at home . . . at least in our house.

Soon, however, romance made way once again for academics. A teacher named Fred J. Allen figured importantly in Pauling's life at this time. Dependable, if not a brilliant scholar, Allen taught Pauling physical chemistry in his junior year. Interestingly, Pauling was having a little trouble. A page from Allen's course book in 1921 shows that many students, Pauling included, were delinquent in handing in a particular assignment. It involved calculating the refractive index of a substance (it is unclear which substance it was). He had trouble getting the answer. The grade book shows that he changed his mind at least once.

Nobody seems to know why Pauling would maintain a correspondence with the solid and unspectacular Fred Allen. Perhaps it is because Allen was one of the few people ever to stump Linus Pauling in chemistry. Whatever the reason, they kept in touch until Allen's death forty-six years later.

Was Allen an influence on Pauling? Surely that is too strong a claim. A Millikan or an Einstein might influence Pauling, but not Fred Allen. Not only did Allen lack a doctorate, but there is evidence Pauling may have had only guarded respect for him as a scientist, as much as he valued his friendship. In a letter to Allen in 1954 he wrote with characteristic bluntness, "Thanks very much for your comments and those of Mueller, on my paper on the strength of hydrofluoric acid . . . I have decided not to add your comment about the solubility of silver fluoride."

In his later years, Pauling would usually give, at the very

least, some analysis of an offered scientific comment, even if he did not want to use it. That he passed over this simple courtesy says much. Another professor, Samuel Graf, offered Pauling more stimulation. Harold Granrud remembered Graf well when I spoke with him, as both he and Pauling were in his metallurgy class: "We took a course in the crystallography of metals, and the professor was a man named Graf; he was really one of the outstanding profs and it was that class that really got Linus started in crystal structure."

Graf's class was a catalyst, but Pauling's interest in the most fundamental architecture of nature, molecules and the links between them, and the regular polygonal patterns they form in all things in the universe dates from childhood. The rocks and stones he tossed into the streams near Grandma Adelheit Pauling's house so many years ago probably first planted the seed. In later years, with the help of highly sophisticated techniques, he unraveled the mysteries of these eerily beautiful stones. In his laboratory at the California Institute of Technology years later, he often turned his mind back to the days of his childhood and his childlike wonder at the natural world. Ernest Swift, Professor Emeritus at Caltech recalled, "Linus learned a lot as a kid; he'd sometimes say, when we were looking at some crystal or other, 'Hey, I used to see these down the valley [presumably the Willamette Valley]."

Still greater yet was the influence of Floyd Rowland. Surely he affected Pauling, Granrud, and many others as did no other member of the Oregon Agricultural College faculty. Granrud recalls, "Doc Rowland inspired many; he even helped some financially. He was a stocky, athletic guy, but not a star. But he'd get you going. He'd even help place [students] in jobs." Pauling acknowledges Rowland's influence:

> . . . He was an extreme enthusiast about graduate work and he lent money to students—he never lent any to me—I borrowed money from John Fulton, the head of the chemistry department —but he encouraged people to go on. . . . It may be that if it hadn't been for Floyd Rowland, I would not have gone on for graduate work.[16]

After the hiatus in his education, Pauling was able to return to college life. His financial problems were temporarily eased and he had begun to behave more gregariously. He had already been elected to the prestigious Scabbard and Blade, a military honorary society, by virtue of passing the qualifying exam for cadet lieutenant. Moreover, he surprised his class by tying for second place in the interclass oratorical contests held on February 3, 1921, for a talk titled "Children of the Dawn," a revealing description of his inner life and his early struggles. He even joined a fraternity, Delta Upsilon.

A new Linus Pauling had arrived. His academic prowess and the recognition gained from his victory in the oratorical contest had marked him for nomination for the recently established fledgling Rhodes scholarship. Naturally, Pauling elicited a powerful recommendation from Floyd Rowland who wrote, "Mr. Pauling possesses one of the best minds I have ever observed in a person of his age, and in many ways he is superior to his instructors."[17]

No one at Oregon Agricultural College in the closing years of Pauling's tenure would have denied this. Still, he did not get the Rhodes. In part, this was Pauling's fault. According to Hobart Vermilye, who was in Pauling's fraternity at the time of the Rhodes interview, Pauling had become a little cocky:

> At one time, Linus was called to Portland for a Rhodes scholarship interview. His first question was, how had he spent his time while waiting for the interview. Pauling's reply was, "reading *La Vie Parisienne*, which I purchased upon arriving in Portland." Sixty-some years ago that was considered as "racy" as the worst of today's magazines.

This was the brash intellectual frontiersman once more. Too confident in himself, too disdainful of authority to give a "safe" answer to what he probably and quite reasonably regarded as an inane question, Pauling may well have ruined his chances with the staid British interviewer.

Did Pauling care? Another fraternity mate, Ralph Coleman,

remembered how Pauling passed the days before the interview: "I stayed at the Delta Upsilon house, and they stuck me in a room with Linus Pauling. Well, I wasn't there too often, but when I came in, there he was reading some kind of story, a wild west magazine or mystery." Would Pauling really have wanted to leave the United States for four years? It would mean leaving Ava Helen. And despite differences with his mother, he knew she was in deteriorating health and that his sisters needed his support as well. He said himself, years later, that it was just as well that he didn't go: "I was nominated for the Rhodes . . . by Oregon State the first year that Oregon State was allowed to nominate anyone; Paul Emmett and I were the two nominees and we weren't awarded; well, I think it was just good luck."[18]

This may sound like rationalizing on Pauling's part, but it probably is not. Among other things, Pauling had already begun thinking about the California Institute of Technology, even before his senior year. He recalls that he had toyed with the idea of spending his last undergraduate years at Caltech, but had abandoned the idea when it could not promise support. Wedding plans were also on his mind. He and Ava Helen were, by now, spending virtually all their free time together. The pressure from his mother was also increasing, with Belle Pauling escalating her efforts to get her son to return home, perhaps to teach in a secondary school.

Pauling held firm throughout. He would go on to graduate school, but which? With his record, he could have gone almost anywhere. Still, Caltech was not his first choice. That honor went to Berkeley. As early as his junior year, Pauling had become interested in the nature of the chemical bond. As he explains it:

I can remember that I was asked, perhaps when I was a junior, if I would give some lectures in the evening for students who were having trouble in freshman chemistry . . . I can remember presenting chemical bond theory on the 'hook-and-eye' basis . . . [This is an old-fashioned approach to the question of how atoms combine to form molecules, based, roughly and intuitively, on the

picture of an everyday hook fitting into a hole.] . . . however . . .
I ran across the papers by Langmuir which were published that
year [his junior year] . . . I was very impressed by this work on
the electronic structure of molecules or ideas about shared electron pair bonds and it may well be that that was the start of my
interest in chemical bonding.[19]

It was an exciting concept. For the first time, Langmuir had
been able to push beyond the naive 'hook-and-eye' notion to a
profoundly more sophisticated idea. According to the new view,
the bonding between atoms consists in the fact that electrons
can be mutually held by more than one atom at a time, thereby
creating a bond in the same way that two or more people shackled to a fence are, in a sense, equally shackled to one another.

That is why Pauling made Berkeley his first choice for graduate work, since G.N. Lewis himself was the head of the Department of Chemistry. Berkeley was essentially the only
institution in the country that was actively disscusing Lewis's
and Langmuir's ideas on chemical/electronic bonding. In Germany, Kossel had been doing some work along these lines, as
had other individual scientists in Europe.

Berkeley, however, took its time about responding to his
application. Pauling also had applications pending at Harvard
and the then-fledgling California Institute of Technology. Harvard
was easy to eliminate, since, as Pauling confessed, he just wasn't
made an offer adequate to his needs. And the prospect of abandoning California for the bitter winters and crowded streets of
Massachusetts Avenue was made all the more terrible by its
proximity to the crowded and corruption-ridden city of Boston.
So it was to be Caltech.

# 2

## Probing the Structure

## of Crystals

FOR PERHAPS THE FIRST TIME IN MANY YEARS, EVERY-thing was going well for the twenty-two year old Pauling. He had at least adequate money in the form of a fellowship, and two weddings were imminent: the one to Ava Helen, and the one to Caltech.

Under the magic influence of Noyes, Millikan, and Hale, Caltech was soon to take its place among the world's great scientific research facilities. The new institution had advantages, prospects—and money. Its birth had been a near-miracle. While it is arguable who really was the prime mover in the creation of the California Institute, certainly George Ellery Hale is a good choice. Best known today for the 200-inch Hale telescope atop Mount Palomar in California, the crafty technological genius had worked for years to attract the finest minds in the world to Caltech.

Robert Andrews Millikan, by contrast, was quiet, genial, good-looking, and deeply spiritual. He earned his place among the immortals of science for his famous "oil-drop" experiment that first determined the charge on an electron. He accepted Hale's offer after an inordinate amount of soul-searching, assuming the chairmanship of the Norman Bridge Laboratory on June 2, 1921. The distinguished physical chemist A.A. Noyes had, at Hale's insistence, abandoned his post at the Massachusetts Institute of Technology in 1919.

By 1921, Hale, Millikan, and Noyes had established a vast and powerful network of friends, scientists, and many of the most wealthy people in California. Urbane and worldly, Hale glided easily through the often staid and immovable ranks of the rich and influential. He had, among other assets, close ties to Carnegie money. Millikan too, despite his religious world view and scientific genius, knew the practical realities involved in starting a new institution. He knew that the government was a far from reliable source of funds in those days, especially for an untested institution, no matter how promising. Though in later years he concerned himself little with money, he worried a great deal about it in those days. A man like Hale could be extremely useful. Endowed with great scientific ability, he could also help the new institution financially.

All this suited Pauling just fine. Pauling knew that Noyes was interested in the same problems in chemical bonding that he was. For the first time in his life, his income was high enough to allow him to seriously attack issues in abstract science. The bitter winters of Corvallis, the odd jobs, and the fraternity mayhem were finally behind him. He was able to teach one course per semester while working on his graduate courses.

Pasadena, furthermore, was as idyllic, temperate, and as pleasant a place to work and live in 1922 as it is today. Unencumbered with such "irrelevancies" as history and philosophy, not to mention political science, he could escape into his own world of chemistry, physics, and mathematics.

Part of him remained in Corvallis. Ava Helen was still only a sophomore at Oregon Agricultural College. They keenly felt the separation. Though Pauling's salary was enough for a graduate student, it scarcely allowed for many phone calls, trips, and the like.

Suddenly, the pair announced their wedding: they were to be married on June 17, 1923, in the home of Ava Helen's sisters. He was twenty-two and Ava Helen was nineteen. His attention now focused on two things—graduate work and Ava Helen.

Yet Pauling was always the self-disciplinarian. That would

be evident over and over again throughout his life: witness his single-minded efforts to solve the mysteries of the structure of protein and the secrets of molecular medicine in later years, even when doggedly pursued by a chronic battle with nephritis. Even at the time of their marriage, the attention he gave to Ava Helen was carefully measured. In later life, he would dole out attentions to his children. In everything, family included, he would not shunt science aside. Doubtless the most telling example of this tendency was the year-and-a-half-long trip he and his wife made to Europe so he could pursue post-graduate studies, leaving behind their infant son. In later life, he gave attention to his family and children only in definite portions. Professor James Bonner of the California Institute of Technology touched reluctantly on this theme when I talked with him in the summer of 1984 at Caltech: "I've heard that he and Ava Helen were so close it affected their relationship with their children, that they were less attentive than they could have been. Well, I think there's something in that, but not very much . . ." Pauling's relationships with his children appeared, however, skewed in other ways. As Gorgo Miller recalled:

> They put their father up on a pedestal; they wanted to follow in his footsteps, but it just wasn't possible and it has left its mark on them. Of course they had the advantages of a fine education. . . . Crellin told us that in growing up, he always had the feeling they expected so much of him and he always had the feeling that no matter how hard he tried, it was never good enough. Of course this was less of a problem for Linda; still, you know, I remember once when she started going out with a boy they didn't feel was her equal, they went to great lengths to break it up and they succeeded. But when she brought Barclay [Linda's husband] home, they said "He'll do, he's all right; a fine fellow."

James Bonner related similar views:

> . . . when I first knew Linus in 1929, we used to be visited by Ava Helen and a baby who they always called "Pooh," and that was their oldest son, who I really don't know. The only ones I knew [well] were Crellin and their daughter Linda; Peter and Crellin

were both sort of waywards, but they ended up OK. I remember [Peter] was talking to me about the problems of growing up and he said to me, "It took twenty-five years to settle with myself that I would never be as smart as my father."

In that, Peter, brilliant as he was in his own right (he now holds a prestigious academic post), was prophetically correct. Linus Pauling's graduate work at the California Institute was nothing if not first class. Part of this was due to Pauling's widely acknowledged brilliance, but part of it was also traceable to the unsurpassed working environment. With only seven graduate students and nine faculty members, there were opportunities for one-on-one interaction rarely seen in modern graduate school factories. A highlight of the teaching system at the California Institute of Technology in those days was the interesting innovation described by Professor Bonner:

Dr. Noyes, who I also got to know quite well, had a particular education plan for chemistry, which was that on Tuesday and Thursday, all the chemists were to meet in a nice lecture room; all profs, grad students, upperclass undergraduates all had to be there. It lasted from one to two hours and was a marvelous teaching device. The senior profs would decide on a topic, maybe statistical mechanics or whatever. You could go a lot deeper than in any course; they'd then write the meetings up and publish them in paperbound books and did this for about twenty years.

Indeed, the very greatest often attended Caltech seminars. As Professor W.K. Ferrier recollected, it was at such an event that Pauling had one of his earliest meetings with Einstein:

Einstein came over here and attended a scientific meeting and at the end of the meeting Pauling was to deliver a paper; Pauling was introduced and delivered a paper in flawless German! And after meeting him, Einstein congratulated him and asked him, "Where did you learn to speak such flawless German?" And Pauling said, "Oh, I spent a year in Germany" and Einstein said, "You learned to speak German in a year like that? Why I've been here over two years and I can't speak English yet!"

His advisor from the first days in Pasadena was the legendary Roscoe Dickinson, one of the consummate geniuses in X-ray crystallography—a technique for studying the structure of solid materials and complex molecules (the gigantic molecules found in biological structures). The fundamental principles of the technique depended on the fact that an orderly array of atoms will scatter X-rays onto a photographic plate in regular and predictable fashion. From this X-ray "footprint" on the plate, scientists can reason back to deduce what structure (arrangement of atoms) the substance must have had to have scattered the X-rays as it did. In principle, the information the technique provided was formidable and vast: distances between atoms, sizes of angles between chemical bonds and many other aspects of structure could be obtained.

Still, at this period in their careers Pauling and Dickinson were studying only inorganic substances. Anything related to organic materials and, therefore, to the very essence of life would have to wait. The research on the molecular architecture of life, the wonderful work on hemoglobin, sickle-cell anemia, orthomolecular psychiatry, the theory of anesthesia, and the structure of proteins—all were at least fifteen years in the future. The reason, in part, is that X-ray studies were difficult and time-consuming, all the more so because of the relative crudity of the equipment and novelty of the technique.

Progress did come nonetheless, as one substance after another yielded to Pauling and Dickinson's relentless probing. Microcline, labradorite, and many others all revealed their structures over the next several years. Other minerals followed quickly and memories at Caltech are strong regarding Pauling's very early work in X-ray crystallography. As Professor Edward Hughes recalled:

> Pauling did crystal structure from the very beginning as a graduate student. He would guess what the structure might be like, and then he would arrange it to fit into the other data . . . he could then calculate the intensities [of the X-ray picture] he would get from that structure and then compare it with the observed ones. . . . That was his way of doing things. Beginning in about

1924 . . . he would begin with a set of theoretical assumptions and then test them against his knowledge of chemistry. . . . So if he were doing a sulfate, he would put in a sulfur with four oxygen atoms around it tetrahedrally, and that alone restricted the possibilities a great deal.

Even as a young student, according to Hughes, "His intuition in predicting what structures were likely to be right, was unbelievable . . . he'd been trained carefully at Oregon State."

It would be wrong to suppose that Pauling somehow invented this way of doing science. What he did do was refine it, bringing it to new levels of sophistication and probing more deeply than anyone had before into the darkest secrets of structural chemistry.

Surely it was this prowess that has led some to imagine that this field was invented by Pauling, as it was also said that Pauling first applied quantum mechanics to the chemical bond. As great as Pauling's contributions doubtlessly were, Dickinson had, after all, first brought the X-ray techniques over from England, where the distinguished structural chemist W.L. Bragg and his group really *had* invented them.

The issue is troublesome, all the more so since similar issues surfaced again later in Pauling's career. In fact, Pauling never explicitly claimed credit for "inventing" these X-ray techniques. He himself admitted that:

The research that I began was on the structure of crystals by X-ray diffraction. It was a rather new technique then. CIT [Caltech] was the place where the first American work in this field was done. That was in 1917. They had continued their work there, especially Professor Dickinson, and he was the person that I worked with.[1]

Is history wrong in identifying Pauling with the field of X-ray crystallography? Yes and no. Yes, because there were too many others without whom this phase of scientific history would never have existed. No, because Pauling, more than anyone else, squeezed maximum mileage out of the crude techniques and, as Professor Hughes noted, did invent almost completely new ways of using the data obtained. He thereby left a legacy virtually unmatched in world science.

One thing is clear: whoever was responsible for crediting Pauling with inventing the new techniques, it wasn't Pauling. This is less clear, however, regarding Pauling's later scientific work. From time to time, colleagues accused him of taking more than his fair share of credit for a paper, discovery, or piece of research. That theme appeared, sometimes bitterly, throughout his DNA work, the otherwise marvelous work on sickle-cell anemia, and his bitter association with protegé Arthur Robinson in the late 1970s.

The earliest story in this vein is one that was told to me by both Jerry Donohue of the University of Pennsylvania and Art Robinson of the Oregon Institute of Science and Medicine. As Robinson related it,

> Maurice Huggins was a great physical chemist of Pauling's generation, slightly senior to Pauling; Huggins was very respected and I had a chance to talk to him a year or two just before he died. He told me he'd published one paper with Pauling, and then Huggins said he wouldn't work with Pauling once he found out what he was. He went on to say that Pauling had taken some of his ideas [and] published them as his own.

Horace Freeland Judson, in his much acclaimed book *The Eighth Day of Creation*, claims that Pauling, having visited the Bragg laboratories in England in 1930, proceeded to take three of Bragg's principles of chemical bonding and publish them as his own. Judson's assertion is interesting in the light of a statement Pauling made in a letter to physicist John Slater of the Massachusetts Institute of Technology in 1930: "We had a good crossing, and enjoyed staying in London for a week. Now we are settled in a house, living quite in the English manner. I feel that so far I haven't got very much out of coming to see Bragg. He has been very busy, however, and things may get better."

Maybe the intellectual frontiersman just didn't like living in the "English manner," particularly since, throughout his life, his visits to Europe were brief, to the point, and functional. Besides, the incident in 1930 was not the first time that Bragg and Pauling had clashed over such matters. In a 1927 letter to Bragg, Pauling wrote:

> In the absence of Professor Sommerfeld I am taking the liberty of replying to your letter concerning my recent paper in the *Proceedings of the Royal Society*. I regret that you feel that I have slighted your work on the distribution of electrons in crystals . . . It was not possible for me to give a critical review of all previous attempts to obtain information regarding electron distribution from experiments with X-rays. I attempted to give a unified treatment of the theoretical prediction of a number of properties of complicated atoms and ions; and the historical discussion of all subjects mentioned would have lengthened the paper inordinately.

It isn't clear whether Pauling's answer is sufficient. Academic journals are flexible and can accomodate papers of almost any length. Even a sentence or two would have sufficed to give credit to Bragg. It is interesting to note that Bragg himself was guilty of some of this sort of thing. The physical chemist Von Laue had an alternative theory of X-ray diffraction, in which atoms were treated as planes ("Laue Diffraction"). Though Bragg adopted some of Von Laue's ideas, he also failed to give Laue his due.

Other scientists were already starting to warn Pauling about playing fast and loose with other people's ideas. In a letter dated July 22, 1928, for example, W.A. Noyes, the Illinois scientist (who should not be confused with A.A. Noyes of Caltech), told him:

> I was very much interested . . . in your paper . . . and am quite prepared to admit that the high pressure modifications of the rubidium salts are probably of the CsCl type. . . . Several weeks ago Goldschmidt wrote me about this matter. . . . I have not yet replied to Goldschmidt, because he sent me a large number of reprints, which I had hoped to digest before writing. I shall now, however, write at once. I hope that you will publish what you sent me; it contains much more than Goldschmidt intimated in his letter to me. In view, however, of the fact that Goldschmidt may

also have been intending to publish a note on the subject, and may have been delaying until he had heard from me, I think it would be courteous to him if you would write him of your intentions.

Noyes obviously felt a need to warn Pauling of something which, under ordinary circumstances, a scientist in Pauling's position could be presumed to know.

In other respects Pauling's career was progressing smoothly. Following the pattern at Oregon Agricultural College, he both enrolled in and taught courses in science, serving throughout his graduate career as a teaching assistant for the freshman chemistry course. Like any graduate student, he developed love-hate relationships with assorted professors—avoiding the "bad" ones and sniffing out the ones to whom he related best. According to college roommate Harold Granrud, Pauling, for instance, "had no use for Millikan."

Granrud's statement, in the light of other evidence, seems to be an exaggeration. It is true, however, that there were a couple of things Pauling did dislike about the great American scientist. For one, he didn't like his lectures, and often skipped them. There was some reason for this. According to Professor Ernest Swift of the California Institute of Technology, who was a fine chemist himself and close to Pauling in those days, Millikan was disorganized. Pauling himself reminisced in an interview: "Kinetic theory—Millikan, 1923, fall. I took a course from Millikan at the very beginning of my second year and my notes begin to look a little better; I was getting neater." Interestingly, the interviewer interrupted: "You said that Millikan himself was a bit disorganized." Pauling's only reply was, "I have lots of notes that are in pretty good shape like this."[2]

Pauling occasionally dealt with an awkward question simply by not responding, changing the subject, or even ending the interview. That he doesn't dispute the interviewer's comment seems to be a way of acquiescing, at least in this case.

According to many old colleagues, the lack of harmony between Millikan and Pauling was in fact related to more important differences of opinion. Religion was a sore point. Millikan was a profoundly religious man, while Pauling was the quintessential atheist, firmly believing that an empiricist epistemology and materialist metaphysics completely refute theology. If a concept or idea could not be given a definition in terms of some assortment of laboratory procedures, Pauling thought the idea meaningless. So did most of the scientists at the California Institute of Technology in the early days. After all, logical positivism, the British version of John Dewey's instrumentalism and pragmatism (somewhat oversimplified) was beginning its ascent in British departments of philosophy and philosophy of science. Wittgenstein and A.J. Ayer were young men and their revolutionary and anti-metaphysical notions were sending shock waves through old and established religious ideologies. And while the theologians vilified the new positivism, scientists championed it.

Not every scientist or philosopher agreed with the new ideas. Certainly Robert Millikan was the most distinguished exception of that era. Only his fabled scientific genius saved him from becoming a pariah. Even so, the faculty at Caltech quietly giggled at Millikan's theology. As Professor Ernest Swift of the California Institute recalled, "Most of us laughed at Millikan, because religion and science are incompatible. Religion doesn't square with the scientific method."[3]

Swift's views are somewhat simplistic, since the interactions between philosophy, religion, and science are now known to be inordinately more complicated than this. They do, however, reflect a common scientific attitude of the day.

Pauling was no exception. True, he rejected theology intuitively, as he accepted much of science intuitively, especially his own contributions. Yet he rejected Millikan's theology just as surely and just as confidently as he had rejected a theological interpretation of that vision of Christ over his bed so many years before.

The chasm between Millikan and Pauling widened further as Pauling came to understand Millikan's politics. Millikan tilted far to the right. That too made it difficult for him to fit into the academic milieu of the California Institute of Technology. Then as now, academic thinking was strongly liberal. Indeed, contemplating an MIT appointment in a letter to John Slater a few years later, Pauling expressed the fear that attitudes in Cambridge might be too conservative for him.

Finally, Millikan and Pauling differed even over the most routine matters. Pauling recalled that "I . . gave a course once and then Dr. Noyes told me that Millikan had complained to him about physics courses being given in the division of chemistry and chemical engineering and that I shouldn't give the course anymore."[4]

Still, there was no complete break between the two. Pauling, after all, recognized Millikan's brilliance and his influence at Caltech and the two remained superficially amicable. As much as he may have wanted to say more about Millikan's disagreeable views, he was still too young and lacking in power and influence. In later years, fear of the Caltech "establishment" scarcely swayed him at all.

The influences on Pauling came from other quarters and other types of men. Religion and politics aside, it was an exciting period in the history of physical science. Sommerfeld was breaking new ground in his study of the behavior of atoms as they absorbed electromagnetic radiation, while the great Niels Bohr was refining the theory of atomic structure he'd developed barely a decade earlier. And Einstein's special theory of relativity was only twenty years old and still somewhat controversial.

Within a few years, the name of Linus Pauling would become a metaphor for all the brilliance, excitement—and controversy—that science at its best can generate.

# 3

# From Caltech to Europe

QUANTUM MECHANICS IS A CONCEPT THAT HAS IN-
spired more brilliance, more fundamental breakthroughs in science, and more humbuggery than virtually any other scientific
idea. So fundamental were its precepts and its view of the universe, that it had the most profound philosophical implications.
With its insistence on the principle of "uncertainty," it rocked
the classical philosophical thesis of a universal causal determinism. For with the new precepts, it was impossible in principle
to predict both the position and velocity of subatomic particles.
So deeply entrenched was man's faith in determinism that the
new science of quantum mechanics led even the great Einstein
to cry out that "God does not play dice with the cosmos."

In physics, men like Heisenberg and Pauli rocked conventional thinking further by insisting that motion might not be
"continuous." According to quantum mechanics, light is emitted
in discrete bundles or "quanta" of energy, rather than in continuous streams.

The development of the new concepts at precisely the time
Pauling was passing into the ranks of the world's great scientists
is testimony to the role of luck in Pauling's career. He did not
fail to notice the profound implications the new quantum mechanics might have for the problems in which he was interested.

Had Pauling come to Caltech twenty years earlier or later, he might never have performed some of his greatest work.

Pauling approached quantum mechanics from a somewhat different angle than his contemporaries. While physicists regarded it as a general tool for describing physical events on an atomic scale, and philosophers saw in it solutions to some of the classical problems in metaphysics, Pauling recognized the immense analytical power it might have in the more restricted domain of chemical problems—in particular the chemical bond.

A caveat is in order: folk wisdom, once again, has it that Pauling single-handedly linked the great problems of chemical bonding with the ideas of quantum mechanics. The mere existence of this mythology reveals Pauling's power as a publicist. The field was positively shimmering with men of genius and their revolutionary concepts. If a gulf between physics and chemistry had previously existed, there were now many trying to bridge that gulf.

One such scientist was Richard Chase Tolman, one of the great physical chemists at Caltech. In later years, Pauling admitted Tolman's influence:

> . . . Richard Chase Tolman was applying statistical mechanics and quantum theory to some chemical problems. . . . A quantum theory of the heat capacity of crystals had been formulated by Einstein and refined by Peter Debye. It was recognized that the quantum theory provided the basis for the third law, but because of the imperfections of the old [version] of quantum theory the law remained somewhat unclear. . . . Tolman and I published a paper in 1925, still based on the old quantum theory, in which we showed that a reasonable discussion of the quantum states of a crystal with use of the methods of statistical mechanics leads to the conclusion that the entropy should be zero for all perfect crystals . . .[1]

As with most scientific concepts, the fundamental idea is simple: heating a substance increases molecular randomness, so the entropy (disorder) increases as temperature increases, and vice versa.

Still, the third law was not that aspect of the new research that fascinated Pauling:

> One of the great chemical problems, however—the nature of the chemical bond—remained a puzzling one throughout this period . . . . As I recall my early life, I recognize that I was often satisfied with a very incomplete sort of understanding of the various aspects of nature . . .[2]

From about 1925 on until the mid-1930s then, the problem of the nature of the chemical bond was to virtually dominate Pauling's scientific interest. Only around 1935 did he allow his obsession with the chemical bond to be curbed by a growing fascination with molecular medicine.

Much of Pauling's interest in the chemical bond was due to Tolman's influence. Pauling would follow Tolman about the corridors of Caltech, pacing anxiously and introspectively outside his office while Tolman was discussing something or other with an eager graduate student. He even went so far as to imitate Tolman's mannerisms, his casual dress and his halting, staccato delivery in the lecture hall.

And it was Richard Tolman who was responsible for one of Pauling's most significant and earliest intellectual and psychological conversions. Many years later, Pauling recalled the event in an article published in *Daedulus* called "Fifty Years of Progress in Structural Chemistry and Molecular Biology":

> There were so many gaps in my understanding that the . . . problems mentioned above did not stand out among the hundreds that I failed to understand; often I did not know whether to attribute the failure to myself or to the existing state of development of science. . . . One episode impressed itself on my memory so strongly that I conclude that it had a significant impact on my development. In the spring of 1923 Tolman asked me a question during a seminar. My answer was "I don't know; I haven't taken a course in that subject." At the end of the seminar, Dr. Richard M. Bozorth, who had received his Ph.D. degree the year before, took me to one side and said, "Linus, you shouldn't have answered

Professor Tolman the way you did; you are a graduate student now, and you are supposed to know everything."[3]

For perhaps the very first time, Pauling really began to appreciate the depth of the probing, doubting, and understanding that first-class science demands. This was the way of Tolman, and the way of science. The approach was not new. Descartes had described this method of approach to knowledge in his *Meditations* and the *Discourse on Method*. One began by systematically doubting all that could be doubted and then rebuilding the edifice of human knowledge on absolutely certain foundations. So reconstructed, it was possible, at least in principle, to know with absolute certainty all that can be known. Tolman believed that it was literally possible to know everything there is to know. Linus Pauling thought so too, and dedicated the rest of his life to the verification of this principle. Knowledge, he now realized, could no longer be approached "mechanically"; one had to do more than wait for the right "course" to come along in order to answer all the great questions of science.

But practical matters intruded. Though his financial problems had eased somewhat, they had not vanished altogether. In spite of his teaching position, he had had to return to his old job as a paving plant inspector in 1923, the summer that he married Ava Helen. But during the second summer he was given additional grant money to be able to devote himself full time to his research in Pasadena. On the other hand, he was still supporting his mother and sisters, at least to a degree. And he owed $1000 to an uncle—a sum he was able to repay later.

In juggling his teaching, research, and odd jobs, Pauling had developed an extensive capacity for hard work. One of the ways he overcame hard times was simply to work that much harder. Further on in life, when Ava Helen fell victim to terminal stomach cancer, it was his limitless capacity for work that prevented him from plummeting into chronic depression. At Caltech he often registered for as many as forty units of classwork and twenty units of research. The university later passed a rule preventing graduate students from carrying that much of a load.

Finally, he attained his lifelong goal. He received his doc-

torate with high honors in June of 1925. His dissertation consisted of the various papers he had already published on the
atomic structure of crystals. And the Paulings had another reason to rejoice. In March of 1925, their first child, Linus, Jr., was
born. Happy and active, he often accompanied his father into
the laboratories of Crellin Hall as a boy. As Pauling had done
years before with his father, Linus Jr. absorbed the sights,
sounds, and the dazzle of science firsthand.

Even under these happy circumstances, Pauling was beginning to think about working in Europe. Caltech was unsurpassed
in America, but the great physical chemist Peter Debye and the
distinguished physicist Arnold Sommerfeld were in Europe. For
anyone interested in problems of chemical bonding, especially
as they related to quantum mechanics, Europe was the place.

G.N. Lewis, on the other hand, was pursuing his work in
the United States, practically across the yard from Pauling in
Berkeley. Lewis was as great as anyone in Europe in that field.
Where should Pauling go next? Although he had abandoned the
idea of going to Berkeley for graduate work, it wasn't a place he
could just forget about. Was it to be Berkeley or Europe, G.N.
Lewis or Sommerfeld? He fought indecision and frustration for
some time, confessing his fears and uncertainty to close friends
at the California Institute. Things had grown more complicated
when, just before receiving his Ph.D., he again had a chance to
work with Lewis. As he explained,

> . . . I applied for and got a National Research Council Fellowship
> and I put down that I wanted to work in Berkeley. I was always
> interested in Berkeley and G.N. Lewis. I had visited there a couple
> of times. Lloyd Jeffress was there in '25–26 as a graduate student
> in psychology. I saw G.N. Lewis in '25 briefly and asked if I could
> come up as a National Research Council Fellow. . . . I think Dr.
> Noyes had suggested that I ought to be a Guggenheim Fellow in
> the first batch. Well I hadn't my doctorate yet, and I wasn't in the
> first batch. I didn't apply, you know.[4]

Most likely, Pauling was just too young, especially without the
doctorate in hand. Yet he did receive it the second time around.

The lure of Europe won out. Possibly G.N. Lewis, venerable as he was, was not in the very forefront of the newest research simply because of his distance from the European centers. Also, Lewis was getting along in years, and Pauling may have felt that the newest ideas could be found only in Europe.

There was another factor as well. A.A. Noyes had been acting more or less as Pauling's mentor around this time, although he too was not completely certain what Pauling's next step should be. At first, he wanted Pauling to remain in Pasadena to finish up some of his papers on crystal structure, and go on to Berkeley around midyear. As he told the young chemist at the time, "You have quite a lot of work going on. . . . stay here and finish up those crystal structure papers and whatever else you are doing . . . then . . . you can go up to Berkeley."

The National Research Council, however, was less than pleased with that idea. The rule at the time was that National Research Fellows had to conduct their research at an institution other than the home school. Remaining in Pasadena an extra few months clearly did not satisfy that requirement. They expected Pauling to head for Berkeley and begin work with Lewis immediately.

However, just as that appeared settled, Noyes changed his mind. This time he thought Pauling should head for Europe after all. He told Pauling, "You ought to go to Europe right away. I'm sure that you'll get the Guggenheim Fellowship; and the Institute will give you $1,000. And if you run out of money, I'll advance some money to you. . . ."[5] Perhaps that was part of the attraction of Noyes; he reminded Pauling of the generosity of his earlier mentor, Floyd Rowland at Oregon Agricultural College.

Few dared to turn down A.A. Noyes. Pauling decided, after considerable soul-wrenching, that he would have to renounce the National Research Council Fellowship and take the Guggenheim. Pauling was worried about this kind of bridge-burning—the National Research Council could well have been of help later. But there was nothing to be done. His decision took effect on February 28, 1926, his twenty-fifth birthday. (The record shows, however, that Pauling actually gave up the fellowship *before* he received the Guggenheim.) True, there was little trouble getting it, especially since Noyes, and Pauling's own formidable record, were beginning to exert their weight. Still, it is an early manifestation of Pauling's staggering self-confidence. And when Pauling did receive the Guggenheim, as everyone thought he would, he was one of only thirty-five who had the honor that year.

So it was settled. The Paulings would head for Europe. As early as October 21, 1925, he had written to Sommerfeld at the University of Munich. As this was a classic moment in the history of science and a pivotal point in Pauling's career, the letter is worth quoting. Both the content and the tone of the letter show Pauling in awe of the distinguished and venerable Sommerfeld. This was not an attitude characteristic of Pauling in years to come.

> I am planning on studying in Europe during the next year, probably as a fellow of the International Education Board. I should like very much to work in your university if it is convenient for you. . . . I should like very much to have you direct my investigations.

Sommerfeld was not easily impressed—he routinely expected such deferential treatment. Still, he did reply quickly, if a bit perfunctorily, saying he would be willing to work with Pauling and making it clear that Pauling would have little trouble finding accomodations.

Pauling's talents as a self-publicist were evolving and he made sure the papers knew. ("Pauling always made sure of that," his former classmate George Payne told me.). An unidentified newspaper item (probably from the *Oregon Journal*, judging from the typeface) announced "Dr. Linus Pauling . . . will leave for Munich Germany, in March to begin study with Arnold Sommerfeld, Professor of Theoretical Physics at the University of Munich."

The Paulings, during this period, were already planning to leave for Europe without Linus Jr., who was still an infant. He would be left in the capable hands of Ava Helen's mother. A theme that emerged from my conversations with Pauling's old colleagues was how often his child had to take second place (if, indeed, a close second) to his wife, which may partially explain their "abandoning" Linus Jr. for a full year and a half. On the other hand, the Paulings were by no means well-to-do at that time, and the sheer expense of bringing him along (not to mention the possible difficulties of him adjusting to a strange environment) may have been prohibitive.

# 4

# Making Strides in Quantum Mechanics

AFTER ARRIVING AND SETTLING IN MUNICH, PAULING headed straight for Sommerfeld's cramped and parsimoniously equipped laboratory. Sommerfeld wasted no time. Immediately, he presented Pauling with a theoretical problem in quantum chemistry. It was a rough one, and Pauling spent many tortuous evenings tossing crumpled-up notebook paper on the floor. He recalls:

> Sommerfeld was accustomed of course to providing problems to young people that came, and especially, I guess, Americans; I guess the calibre of some of them there wasn't very high. . . . he said [Alexandroff] wrote a paper about the spinning electron around 1900; this is standard old electromagnetic theory. With spinning electrons of different kinds he got different values of the g-factor.[1]

Pauling only partially solved the problem given to him by Sommerfeld. A more thorough solution was later worked out by the legendary physicist Werner Heisenberg. But Sommerfeld wasn't just trying to rattle the young American and show him who was boss. The problem was a critical test of the validity of the new quantum mechanics.

In his great 1922 book, *Atombau und Spektrallinien*, Sommerfeld had rather cavalierly described the physical realities of electrons in two distinct and apparently inconsistent ways. In the old theory, there were too many arbitrary rules that did not hold together. But in the new quantum mechanics, everything came together from one equation, the Schrodinger equation and the Copenhagen interpretation of quantum mechanics. Just as in classical mechanics, everything flowed from Newtonian mechanics. The parameters physicists use to "describe" electrons are called "quantum numbers" (a sort of measuring unit, used in much the same way that carpenters talk about lumber in terms of board feet). The problem was that in the descriptions of the old versions of quantum theory, Sommerfeld and others had traditionally described an electron using not one, but two distinct quantum numbers to describe what was apparently the same property (usually called the "inner" and "outer" quantum numbers). In a way, that was about as plausible as assigning two required heights for the front door—asking the carpenter to make the same door both six feet tall and seven feet tall. As Pauling recalled:

> I tried to understand the theory as presented by Sommerfeld, but I did not try to resolve the puzzle if indeed I was even aware that there was one. . . . Later on, in 1926–27, I spent a year at Sommerfeld's Institute in Munich, and I got to know him well. It is clear that he himself knew that there was a puzzle here, and it is probable that he made his students aware of it, in particular Werner Heisenberg, who was of course responsible in part for its resolution. But in his book Sommerfeld ignored the paradox presented by his simultaneous use of two numerical values for what seemed to be the same quantity—he wrote that the reader should concentrate on the equations, not on their interpretations in terms of a model.[2]

At first glance, this seems highly illogical, but there are many occasions in science where our ordinary, everyday intuitions simply collapse. In those instances, there is often not much else to do but retreat into mathematical consistency to salvage a theory. With the relativistic concepts of Einstein, the public has become more and more used to the fact that scientific ideas sometimes will not square easily with common sense. (The notion that time slows down as you walk more rapidly across the room, for instance, is nothing if not bizarre.)

The inevitability of history was pushing harder and harder on Sommerfeld, for quantum mechanics was already changing. Sommerfeld's warning to ". . . concentrate on the equations . . . not the model" became as vacuous as the old quantum views he'd relied upon. Ultimately, nobody likes a paradox for very long. With the introduction of the concept of electron "spin," both the physics and the mathematics of atomic spectra were made consistent.

Soon, the new quantum mechanics swept through the scientific world and left Sommerfeld and even Einstein behind, but carried Pauling along with it. After 1925, advances in understanding the nature of quantum mechanics as well as its relationship to the chemical bond followed quickly. With the new version of quantum theory, scientists—Pauling among them—probed ever more deeply into the mysterious architecture of the molecular universe (which, however, is not the *whole* universe; beyond terrestrial matter, much of the matter in space is non-molecular, as is the case with black holes, neutron stars, and so forth).

Even Pauling, however, would not "buy" the whole package. At this point in his career, Pauling's anti-metaphysical attitudes were practically ossified. While scientists as a group tend, naturally, to shy away from untestable concepts, Pauling went beyond even such normal (and understandable) scientific skepticism. Some scientists take philosophical ideas seriously if such ideas either affect or are, at least, implied by some scientific principle. Not so with Pauling. Ever since the vision of Christ experience of his childhood, he cared little for anything not strictly scientific. In his zeal to avoid the dogma of religion, he succeeded only in falling victim to the dogmatism of science. Quantum theory is a good example. Though it was a scientific construct, parts of it had rather obvious philosophical implications. While Heisenberg's "uncertainty principle" (part of quantum mechanics) may not have shed as much light on the great philosophical problems of free will and determinism that its early enthusiasts had hoped, its connection to these great philosophical issues is clear.

How could it be otherwise? For the very first time, scientists were challenging the idea that, in principle, every single event in the physical universe can be strictly and completely predicted. That idea stretches as far back in time as Lucretius and the pre-Socratics in the West, and the Upanishads in the East. Given an atom and every fact in the universe about that atom, one could predict its behavior as far into the infinity of the future as you like—this had been the assumption. And if one could do that with an atom, it could be done, in principle, with any larger aggregate of atoms. Then, so goes the argument, we know that the human body is just such an aggregate. Given enough information about an individual, it will be possible to predict all that person's future actions. This was the classical, deterministic view of the cosmos.

Then along came quantum theory, and man's view of the universe was turned on its head. Heisenberg's principle stated that there will always be a degree of "uncertainty" in our predictions. Without perfect predictions, there can be no determinism and therefore there is only free choice. (Most philosophers today would agree that this is an oversimplification of the classic problem of free will and determinism, of course, though some philosophically inclined *scientists* did and still do look at the problem this way. The refutation of this kind of determinism does not, as is well-known now, solve the problem. For one thing, even if *scientific* determinism is refuted, theorists have tried to reject free will from other vantage points. Some religious philosophers, e.g., have held that the existence of a Judaeo-Christian deity would rule out free choice.)

Subtleties aside, some scientists thus took the new defense of human free choice quite seriously, believing the Heisenberg uncertainty principle derived from quantum mechanics had vindicated it.

Pauling would not even entertain these arguments, no matter who was constructing them. Even Niels Bohr could not budge him, nor touch a single philosophical nerve. Referring to Bohr's writings, Pauling said that:

I read his book on the subject and I found myself completely uninterested in the arguments. The only memories I have of that meeting are those that relate to pretty straightforward interpretations, theoretical studies, and I have no memories of philosophical questions, or interpretations of quantum mechanics going beyond the conventional or straightforward ones.[3]

The meeting he refers to was a conference on magnetism given by the famed Cornell University chemist, Peter Debye, in Zurich in 1926. Leaving aside philosophical issues, it is staggering that Pauling speaks cavalierly about "straightforward" interpretations of quantum mechanics. The many heated debates about the meaning of quantum mechanics between Bohr, Schrodinger, Einstein, and others would fill volumes.

The plainsman in Pauling, the man who had dragged himself up from poverty and was charging ahead to superstardom, felt there was no time for philosophical musings. Pauling was eminently pragmatic. Still, to be one of history's great thinkers, it is necessary at times, especially in science, to reach beyond the practical and grasp the philosophical, the moral and aesthetic dimension of science. Einstein did that, and so did Heisenberg. In Einstein's collected writings, e.g. one finds deeply thoughtful, philosophical musings on good and evil, epistemology, human rights, the abstract nature of scientific truth, and much more. Failing to reach beyond science in this way, Pauling cannot be classed as one of history's greatest thinkers in the humanist sense, though there can be little doubt as to his greatness as a scientist.

There are other philosophical paradoxes connected with quantum mechanics. Physicists still debate the apparent oddity of the fact that two electrons, having lost contact with one another, can affect one another in such a way that once one electron is determined to have an 'up' spin, the other is caused to have a 'down' spin, which is necessary to conserve angular momentum. This, of course, is the ancient "action at a distance" problem in a new guise, usually called the Einstein-Podolsky-Rosen paradox: if one is measuring electron $a$, how does electron $b$ fifty yards away "know" the effect on 'a'?

In fairness to Pauling, however, none of the above philosophical issues have any bearing on the practical *scientific* utility of quantum mechanics. However, the work at this time was again slowed by personal and scientific friction with W.L. Bragg. In March of 1927, an exchange took place between the two men. It is important to note that Pauling, just two months earlier, had published his most important paper to date, "The Theoretical Prediction of the Physical Properties of Many Electron Atoms and Ions; Mole Refraction, Diamagnetic Susceptibility, and Extension in Space." In large measure, it was a culmination of much of his recent work in applying quantum mechanics to chemical bonding. In the paper, he clearly demonstrated his progress. As he explained:

> Shortly after reaching Munich I read a paper by Gregor Wentzel in the *Zeitschrift fur Physik* on a quantum mechanical calculation of the values . . . for electrons in complex atoms. . . . Wentzel reported poor agreement between the calculated and experimental values, but I found that his calculation was incomplete and that when it was carried out correctly, it led to values . . . in good agreement with the experimental values.[4]

In short, Pauling had convincingly demonstrated that the structure of the electron orbitals in even the most complicated atoms could be described with quantum mechanics. He would go on to give ever more brilliant descriptions of a dazzling variety of atomic structures and crystals.

As mentioned before, Bragg replied, clearly indicating his displeasure with Pauling for failing to give him proper credit. This is almost certainly the source of Bragg's celebrated indifference to Pauling when he visited Bragg's laboratories a few years later.

Pauling charged ahead and by 1928, he was ready to formulate a set of principles which, according to his theoretical research, determined the structure of complicated crystals (such as the silicate minerals tourists see in any rock and mineral shop window). Of these principles, probably the most important was the one that suggested that the strength of the chemical bond between a positively charged ion (such as the sodium ion in ordinary table salt) and a negatively charged one (such as the chloride ion in table salt) was a direct function of the strength of the charge on the negative and positive ions (although this is not the only factor in bond strength). That principle, in turn, helped enormously in making theoretical predictions about the properties of ionic substances. (An "ionic" substance is anything with a number of ionic chemical bonds—an ionic bond exists if electrons are transferred between two atoms. The "covalent" bond, by contrast, exists between atoms where electrons are shared, rather than transferred.)

By this time Bragg was bristling, even spreading stories in England about Pauling's thievery and lack of professional ethics. He was very disturbed by what he perceived to be simple appropriation of theories he himself had formulated earlier. Many who have examined Pauling's early career believe that Pauling really did steal his famed principles from Bragg. One of the more neutral statements—by Horace Judson in *The Eighth Day of Creation*—reads as follows:

> [Pauling] understood that the various relations among atoms that dictate the stable forms of a crystalline substance could be stated as a set of six principles. He wrote these down. They were published the next spring. To this day, they are called the Pauling rules. The principles were not entirely original with Pauling. The first three, anyway, had been in the air among crystallographers —had, in fact, been used by Bragg. Pauling clarified them, codified them, demonstrated their generality and power.[5]

After the initial display of outrage by Bragg, the furor subsided. Pauling continued working for the remainder of his European stay, gathering more information on bond angles, crystal structure, and quantum mechanics. The visit with Sommerfeld in Munich really was the high point of the stay. After that year was over, he did spend a few weeks at Bohr's Institute, and about five months in Zurich, attending the lectures of Schrödinger and Debye. Nor was he anxious to leave, even extending his stay by six months, with a little financial assistance from A.A. Noyes. Yet his best work was done in Munich.

Then too, pressures to return home were building. Ava Helen was tiring of spending her days touring cathedrals and tending to the needs of her husband. Also, she missed their son. She pressured him to return. The strains began to cause the Paulings to bicker over assorted inconsequential matters. As long-time friend and colleague Jerry Donohue, recalled, "Linus told me later that [the trip] was hard on his wife; she'd been visiting museums and all that for too long and was getting bored; they'd fight about money lots of times and she wouldn't talk to him for days." She had not, after all, seen Linus Jr. in nearly two years. Despite Noyes' generosity, time and money, her patience was running out.

Thus it was with great relief that he returned from the lab one day to find that he'd been offered an assistant professorship at the California Institute of Technology. As they set sail for America, most of the tension between them ebbed. Pauling was also eager to see his son, and Ava Helen was positively "jumping with anticipation," according to Harold Granrud.

On reaching Pasadena, they set out to find an apartment— not an easy task in the closing days of the 1920s. The United States economy was not robust and California was scarcely an exception. During the time they were away, rents and housing prices had escalated considerably. But with the assistance of some friends at Caltech, the Paulings did find a small, wood-frame house where they could comfortably settle and raise their son.

# 5

# At Home at Caltech

BY THIS TIME IN THE PAULINGS' LIVES, MOST OF THEIR adult attitudes had crystallized. Ava Helen's commitment to the religious views of her earlier years had waned. Pauling, of course, had stopped concerning himself with religious questions years earlier. His mother had died in 1919 from pernicious anemia, and without her influence, his all-consuming passion for science had overwhelmed any residual worry that might have existed about an afterlife. As he himself declared, "I was skeptical of dogmatic religion, and had passed the period when it was a cause of worry."[1]

Despite the uneven success of his visit to Europe, his knowledge of chemistry had advanced greatly. By 1928, chemists agree, the rough outline of the nature of ionic and covalent bonding had been reasonably well worked out. Chemists also understood how the overt physical and chemical properties of substances were related to the molecular structures of such elements.

Pauling's personal difficulties with other scientists continued. Just as the troublesome relationship with Bragg receded into the background, another antagonism sprang up—one Pauling had to iron out before settling down to new work. Friction was developing between Pauling and A.A. Noyes. According to Professor Ernest Swift, himself a close friend and the beneficiary of Noyes' will, "There was something between them; it may have dated back to Linus's stay in Europe, when Noyes promised him a job he didn't get."

Swift is almost correct. It was the nature of the job that angered Pauling. Pauling referred to that period in a 1964 interview:

> When I was in Europe . . . I received a letter from A.A. Noyes saying that he was writing to offer me an appointment as "Assistant Professor of Theoretical Chemistry and Mathematical Physics," and I accepted it, but by the time I got here . . . the physics had been dropped, although Tolman was appointed jointly in chemistry and physics . . . I don't know what happened with the physics, whether Millikan objected to my having a joint appointment or whether Noyes decided. . . . He was preventing me from being given an appointment to Berkeley . . . and he may have decided that he didn't want me to be associated with the physics department in this way, that perhaps I would shift.[2]

That Tolman would garner a dual appointment, when Pauling could not rankled the young scientist. What made it worse was the fact that Pauling was just returning from a period of study with many of the greatest physicists in the world, and was obviously familiar with all the newest wrinkles. Had he not worked closely with Sommerfeld himself? Pauling had the greatest respect for Tolman, but he had equal faith in himself and his own abilities as a physicist.

There was little he could do. Though Noyes was frail and near the end of a brilliant career, what he said was law around the Pasadena campus. As brash as he was, Pauling had enough good political sense to forget the matter and accept his new title.

Very soon, he settled into a new routine as a fulltime member of the Caltech faculty. In 1928, he published his most widely discussed paper, on orbital hybridization, a notion familiar to most high school chemistry students today. It was a remarkable accomplishment. Up to that time, certain aspects of the carbon atom had thoroughly baffled investigators. Judging from observational methods like spectroscopy, researchers were forced to conclude that the four bonds of the tetrahedral carbon atom were of two kinds. The thorn was that a very well-established body of chemical theory demanded that the carbon atom bonds be of only *one* kind.

Pauling's solution was ingenious. Using concepts borrowed from quantum mechanics, he postulated that a "resonance" structure was possible where the two different kinds of bond required by observation could be hybridized or "averaged" to produce four equivalent bonds—precisely as chemical theory demanded.

In an even more important paper published in 1931, Pauling deduced, from the principles of quantum mechanics, results of even greater importance than his European work. This paper, "The Nature of the Chemical Bond," was to become, less than a decade later, the basis for his most famous scholarly book of the same title, and one which is still regarded as a classic in its field. It is Pauling's greatest scientific book, if not as widely publicized as, for example, his popular books on vitamin C. In the paper, Pauling stated for the first time his six rules for chemical bonding. The fifth rule is the most important: Pauling argued that the more an orbital of one atom can overlap the orbital of another atom, the stronger will be the bond between the two atoms. From this and other rules, researchers had a basis for predicting and describing the actual architecture of a huge number of atoms. Over the years following this paper, more and more crystals yielded their structural secrets to researchers.

But he could not rest. Great as his success was with classical technology, Linus Pauling was not satisfied. X-ray crystallography was an old and faithful technique, but it had its limitations. Pauling, eager to extend his study of molecular structure to substances other than the common solid crystals of tourist-shop windows, wanted something better. He wanted to study structure and substances in other states of matter, such as gases.

He solved that problem in 1930 when he visited Herman Mark in the quiet and picturesque German village of Ludwig-shafen. This marked the beginning of the use of *electron* diffraction, as opposed to X-ray diffraction, in research at Caltech and in the United States. The technique was ideal for the study of simpler molecules such as hydrogen—molecules that do not solidify at room temperature.

Aided by his student L.O. Brockway at the California Institute, Pauling worked obsessively with his electron diffraction apparatus for the next two years. But Brockway, though a good worker, wasn't exactly the person Pauling needed. He drove Brockway hard, but soon realized that he needed another assistant. Though Brockway remained, Pauling soon obtained the services of Verner Schomaker, a tall and amiable man, who was as accomplished as anyone in the field of experimental science. Now at the University of Washington, Schomaker essentially began his career with Pauling in 1931. Still, Pauling was uneasy. Schomaker remembers that Pauling told him electron diffraction was a prodigiously difficult technique—"too hard, and that I ought to do something easy for a year or two at first." The comment was not an evaluation of Schomaker's abilities. Pauling knew that there was no one available who was better qualified than the young scientist. Instead, it's the sort of offhand, quick decision so typical of Pauling at his best. He did not want anyone in his laboratory less than fully prepared and he didn't need much reflection or study time to decide on his action, the native abilities of his new student notwithstanding. Schomaker was nonplussed by Pauling's abrupt turnabout, and busied himself with an assortment of projects in the interim.

Eventually Pauling asked him to work on the project. Within twenty-five years, Pauling, Schomaker, and others had worked out the architectural structure of more than two hundred substances using the technique of electron diffraction.

The world did not wait long to recognize Pauling's accomplishments. On October 25, 1931, *The Oregonian, The New York Times* and scores of other newspapers around the country heralded the emergence of Linus Pauling as a world-class scientist. The American Chemical Society had already awarded him the Langmuir Prize in Buffalo, New York for "the most noteworthy work in pure science done by a man under 30 years of age." Linus Pauling had become one of the world's most distinguished authorities on the subatomic structure of matter. The prestige conferred on him was enormous, as the American Chemical

Society made the award only after the most difficult and searching thought, including consultations with the foremost authorities in the field and the most painstaking examination of the
candidate's published work. In Pauling's case, the conclusion
was inevitable, for during his tenure at the California Institute
of Technology he had worked out the structures of some of the
most recalcitrant elements in nature, including labradorite and
microcline.

Another of Pauling's great talents was coming into play more
and more often—his capacity for self-promotion. For some time
he had been working on a translation of Goudsmit's famous
book on the structure of line spectra. However, numerous scientists at Caltech, many of them long-time acquaintances of
Pauling's, seemed to believe he had actually written part of *The
Structure of Line Spectra*, and that he had contributed substantially to the ideas in the book. It was Goudsmit's work alone,
however.

Pauling had been having problems working with Goudsmit.
At one point he wrote to Slater saying: "I'm cooperating with
Goudsmit, but under difficulties."[3] He may have been tempted
to exaggerate his role in preparing the book for publication. Still,
if Goudsmit believed that a translation merited co-authorship,
so be it. However, Pauling did not, even in later years, always
take great pains to clarify his role in scientific work, often leaving
the impression that he had done quite a bit more than translate
or oversee a project.

Be that as it may, the Langmuir Prize not only cemented
his fame on the West Coast, but made the important East Coast
universities begin to notice the young wunderkind as well.
Among the scientists who were interested in Pauling was the
physicist John Slater. Not only were they of the same generation,
but their interests overlapped. Like Pauling, Slater had done
considerable work in the application of quantum mechanics to
the chemical bond, as well as on the structure of various substances. Since the Massachusetts Institute of Technology did not
then have the prestige it does today, Slater was naturally eager
to yank Pauling away from Pasadena to the courtyards of Harvard and MIT.

On January 21, then, after some efforts to gain approval from the East-Coast-minded administration, Slater was authorized to write Pauling, addressing him as "Dear Linus." (In less friendly years, decades later, he addressed him as "Dear Pauling.") The letter goes on to say, "I know it will be a hard job to induce you to come, but we are all determined to work hard." The rest of the letter contained Slater's best salesmanship, lauding the virtues of MIT, Harvard, and Cambridge over California, and promising that Pauling would be offered a full professorship at $8,000 per year, joint appointments in chemistry and physics, and so forth. He even tapped Pauling's political nerves: "Further I think you would like it better at the Institute than at Harvard. You were rather afraid of conservatism there; I do not think you will find it here."[4]

Pauling was unmoved. He didn't like snow (he made remarks many times over the years about the awful snow in Cambridge). But he was enough of a diplomat not to be so blunt with John Slater, a scientist who could be of great help to him with research grants, good graduate students, and prize nominations. In a letter dated February 9, 1931, Pauling responded as follows: "I have tried to decide whether or not the chance of my ultimately coming to MIT is great enough to justify extensive discussion . . . and now I am afraid that it is not . . . The Institute is a very pleasant place to work, and Pasadena a pleasant place to live."

While Pauling's letter settled the question of where he'd be for the next thirty-odd years, it raised a few new ones. He makes the surprising comment in the letter that: "If I were to come to MIT, I should desire an appointment in physics, or in physics and chemistry. And yet I am really not very much interested in physics, but rather in what may be called structural chemistry."

This is not altogether convincing. Having spent so much time in Europe with Schrödinger and Sommerfeld, it's hard to believe he was "not much interested in physics." According to classmates at Oregon Agricultural College, he was very interested in physics as an undergraduate. In fact, Pauling admits that he wasn't given the title of professor of physics upon returning from Europe because it was possible that the university was afraid he would move into the physics department completely. So it seems that Pauling *was* very interested in physics. Many years later he made a contribution to atomic physics, and even today he does a little work in nuclear physics. Besides, Pauling always had a synoptic vision of science, letting his mind range over virtually anything that might shed some light on the problems he was interested in. Certainly that included physics—especially the new science of quantum physics.

As became clear some twenty years later, absolutely fundamental differences existed between Pauling's way of doing science and Slater's. Those differences would later bring them to the brink of a personal war. At one level, the difference between Pauling and Slater was simple. Pauling was an intuitive, brilliant, shoot-from-the-hip theoretician. If he borrowed a few ideas from others once in a while, he nonetheless had enough of his own to fill three lifetimes. And he didn't hesitate to publish them—even when, as we shall see, they were scarcely beyond the highly speculative stage.

Slater was different. The MIT scientist was a plodder. Unwilling to make speculative leaps, he'd work a problem to its final demise before publishing or abandoning it. As Professor Sten Samson of Caltech described him to me: "As soon as Slater gets an idea he works it out to the end before he gets a new one . . . Pauling is a man that looks at the forest, but does not explore the individual trees; Slater looks at the trees, but forgets the forest."

Pauling sensed this about Slater. Possibly he thought it best not to work so closely with someone who had such a radically different approach to science, as it would be liable to cause friction. As Samson explained, Slater would take one idea and work it to death. He relied on calculation, not intuition, and he kept graduate students at work for months and years cranking out computations in these pre-computer days. In philosophical terms, Pauling was a Hindu mystic or an intuitionist in the late medieval style of philosopher Meister Eckhart. Slater, by contrast, was a Cartesian and Spinozistic formalist. Few thinkers in history have trusted the power of mathematics in solving complex physical problems as much as Slater did. Certainly his work on ferromagnetism was a typical example.

Slater, of course, did operate within an established tradition. The Pauling vs. Slater "duel" is perhaps best understood in the context of science as it developed from the 1930s onwards. During this period, physics evolved steadily. By the time the 1950s had arrived, the growth of solid-state physics was staggering. Its expansion resulted from the continuing dialogue between theory and practice. In contrast to high-energy physics, with the massive technological apparatus required to do research in the field, solid-state physics could be done with relatively small, inexpensive machinery. The growth of solid-state physics was further fueled by federal support, the administration hoping that more practical uses for the principles would yet be found (as in semiconductor electronics which, in the 1950s, was still a relatively new field).

In more recent times, however, a division between theoreticians and experimentalists arose: or, to be precise, a division which had long existed, simply accelerated. Perhaps with the advent of powerful and elegant theories in other branches of science, such as Pauling's work on protein structure, or in the rapidly growing field of cosmological physics, theoreticians began to think of their work as "real" science. If you did too many numerical calculations, like Slater, you were doing engineering rather than science. Happily, such prejudices have ebbed in recent years, although formal theory still commands powerful respect and probably still maintains an edge in prestige over experimentation and numerical calculation. Prejudices aside, however, the fact remains that Slater's methods, while valuable in the realm of solid-state physics, where one is dealing with extremely small molecules, cannot be applied to the study of the unfathomably larger molecules of life. RNA, DNA, and the giant protein molecules do not yield their secrets to a calculator, no matter how powerful and sophisticated. The calculations required are simply too vast, too formidable. All the most powerful computers in the world, working in tandem on such problems, would take virtually an eternity to solve them. That is where

Pauling's methods comes in. Pauling used the "stochastic" method, from the Greek, meaning "to divine the truth by conjecture." Having learned all that is known about the physical properties, the X-ray data, etc., Pauling could—better than anyone in the world—quite literally "guess" at the most likely structure. As will be seen, more often than not, he was correct, but sometimes he went badly awry.

Slater may have picked up on the differences between him and Pauling. In a letter dated May 9, 1931, after Pauling's decision to remain at Caltech had become final, Slater wrote Pauling again regarding a planned symposium of the American Association for the Advancement of Science, to be held in Pasadena that summer. After dealing with minor matters regarding arrangements and travel, Slater says:

> The proposal for the symposium sounds very good, and the titles look all right. My only possible question is as to the order of our two papers—I wonder if possibly yours had better come first. Since our qualitative ideas are so similar, it seemed to me that it might be better for me to go more into the mathematical details, and in that case your talk might allow me to dispense with . . . qualitative discussion.

That is an understatement. He knew very well that Pauling's mathematics would be sketchy, but that Pauling was a terrific speaker and better able to present the gist of their ideas.

Pauling must not have liked Slater's suggestion, since he took an unusually long time to reply, and then only prompted by a second letter from Slater. His reply was terse: "I have not yet been able to decide whether your or my paper should come first."[5] Perhaps Pauling felt that coming before Slater would give Slater top billing on the evening program. Much as academics deny it, there is more than a little show-business and theatrical protocol in formal symposia. Finally he acquiesced, since he realized that the tedious part—the mathematics—would be best understood by the audience once the general ideas were discussed.

There is one more factor that may have kept Pauling in

Pasadena. At Caltech, Hale and Noyes were aging, and Pauling was unquestionably the brightest young star in the firmament. Not so at MIT. There, Pauling would have had to contend with such brilliant young scientists as Schlechter in geophysics, Morse and Compton in physics and, of course, Slater. Sharing center stage was not something Pauling ever relished.

Finally Slater compromised and managed to get Pauling to accept a temporary appointment. True to form, Pauling could not and would not be hurried. Though Slater offered him the appointment in February 1931, Pauling did not accept until July 9. Even then, he did so only after some haggling over terms.

The stay itself was not the most productive period of Pauling's career. No papers comparable to his famous paper on chemical bonding emerged from his tenure at the Massachusetts Institute of Technology, just as little of importance came from the stay at the Bragg laboratories some years earlier. Ava Helen didn't care for the Cambridge climate any more than Pauling did, preferring the warmth and familiarity of Pasadena.

There was also their growing family to think about. A second child, Peter Pauling, had been born to them in February 1931, and by the end of the stay in Cambridge, Ava Helen had her hands full. Separated from her friends in Pasadena, she and Pauling had more than a few arguments about child care responsibilities and his scant attention to their two children.

After returning to Pasadena, family squabbling did ease up, probably helped also by the fact that Pauling was now working again in a climate and environment that was more familiar and comfortable. In any event, Linus and Ava Helen were expecting their third child: Linda Pauling was born about a year later, on May 31, 1932. And Pauling's research group continued to unravel the molecular mysteries of crystals.

Signs of change were in the air. The tranquillity of the post-MIT days would not last long. There were ominous and disturbing rumbles in the scientific as well as political atmosphere. A future antagonist, the Nobel-Prize-winning geneticist H.J. Müller, was about to be forced to flee the tyranny of the Stalin regime because of his opposition to Lysenko-dominated Soviet efforts to force the science of genetics into a dogmatic Marxist framework. Within a few years, Muller's hatred of the Soviets would bring him to the brink of legal conflict with Pauling. Yet it was also a good time for genetics. Thomas Hunt Morgan captured the Nobel Prize in 1933 for his work in physiology and medicine and advances were surfacing almost daily. Morgan also left a mark on Pauling. He speaks of Morgan's influence:

> My serious interest in what is now called molecular biology began about 1935. I had started to learn something about biology in 1929, when Thomas Hunt Morgan came to the California Institute of Technology. . . . My ideas about the structural basis of biological specificity were developed during the years 1936 to 1939 . . . I . . . had thought about some possible explanations of the observed self-sterility in the sea urchin, which Morgan had been studying.[6]

Physics was having up and down results. Absolutely fundamental breakthroughs had occured in the recent history of the science, such as DeBroglie's theory that electrons exist as waves as well as particles, which he suggested in his Ph.D. dissertation in 1924, as well as Chadwick's discovery of the neutron in 1932, and Anderson's discovery of the positron in the same year. The legendary Italian physicist Enrico Fermi was, in 1933, on the verge of discovering how to produce artificial radioactivity by bombarding a number of different stubstances with neutrons, resulting in a number of new isotopes of uranium. For this work he would be awarded the Nobel Prize in physics for 1938. But there were reverses as well. On August 16, 1933 star photographs were taking during a solar eclipse. The photographs rocked the scientific world, since they did not convincingly demonstrate the deflection of star light that would be expected because of the pull of the sun's gravitational field. To fail to verify this would be a setback to Einstein's general theory of relativity. In a report in the Washington publication *Science Service*, the renowned physicist E.F. Freundlich of the Einstein Institute in Potsdam reported that ". . . there exists a discrepancy between the Einstein theory and the results of total eclipse observation, since the plates obtained by the horizontal camera yielded a deviation about 25 percent higher than the theoretical value."[7]

In January of 1933, Adolph Hitler ascended to power in Germany.

Pauling was unmoved. Neither a world approaching the brink of catastrophe nor the most turbulent rumblings of war wrenched him loose from his moorings in abstract thought. Later on in his career, he responded very differently to political events. For the present, he continued his own research and his political maneuvering. He made friends with anyone and everyone in a position of power in the scientific hierarchy. These efforts, along with his admittedly stupendous scientific work, bore fruit when, at thirty-two, he was awarded membership in the National Academy of Sciences. It was the youngest appointment ever made to the Academy.

If Pauling remained unmoved by the great changes in the world, the California Institute was not. It pushed steadily to raise the level of its faculty, teaching, and research facilities. One of the great changes at Caltech—a change which helped to forever demolish its old "Throop" image as a technical and vocational college—was the institution of a series of seminars. Meeting Tuesday and Thursday mornings, all chemists, physicists, faculty, post-doctoral students, graduate students, and a few select undergraduates would normally attend. The meetings lasted anywhere from one to three hours. A senior professor discussed a specific topic, such as statistical mechanics, or the nature of the chemical bond.

According to Jack Roberts and James Bonner of the California Institute of Technology, these were "absolutely marvelous teaching devices." Topics could be investigated in far greater depth than any class would allow and issues could be minutely discussed in total freedom. The seminars lasted only until the outbreak of World War II, but their legacy remains to this day. Almost everyone was happy with the arrangement.

Noyes, however, was less than ecstatic. In the past he had been able to hold his own in debate with anyone at Caltech, including Linus Pauling. But his pre-eminence was now challenged by a relatively obscure figure named Howard Lucas. Lucas was a good teacher and pretty well liked around Caltech. But in Noyes's eyes he was beneath contempt. Lucas was an organic chemist. He had no Ph.D. Worst of all, he came to Caltech from Ohio State. Noyes spent many hours whining about the irrelevance of organic chemistry and the incompetence of those doing research in the field. So virulent was Noyes's hatred for organic chemistry that, in all the years the Tuesday and Thursday seminars existed, never once did they broach an issue in organic chemistry.

Even Pauling was affected by this attitude. As he said in a 1924 letter to his old mentor F.J. Allen: "The only graduate work [at Caltech] in chemistry is in physical, inorganic, and biochemistry. The last is interesting but I wouldn't want to do it." A good part of the reason was simply the respect he still felt for Noyes despite his growing lack of coherence. Yet it's also true that there *was* a logical basis for the hostility toward organic chemistry. For a long time, it could hardly be considered a science. There was little developed theory, only a collection of "recipes." As Pauling said years later: "Organic chemists develop a feeling for the chemical properties of the many substances with which they work which goes far beyond the systematized theoretical knowledge that they can express."[8] Neither Pauling nor Noyes, great theoreticians that they were, could accept this seeming lack of method.

Then everything changed. Out of nowhere came a textbook on organic chemistry, written by Lucas, that completely turned the field around. Almost overnight, organic chemistry became respectable. Lucas had produced not just a description of chemical reactions, but an actual theory as to how and why the reactions worked. Very soon, it displaced most other textbooks and Lucas became rich.

But Lucas did not completely convert everyone. Though Noyes and Pauling had to bend in the face of the obvious brilliance of Lucas's achievement, they could never look at his field as equal to other branches of chemistry. Their old attitudes were just too deeply entrenched. In Pauling's case, the record is consistent. For the rest of his career, his attitude toward organic chemistry remained cool and distant. On that subject he and Noyes—for the moment anyway—were of one mind.

Though eruptions of the old bad feelings between Noyes and Pauling occurred periodically, the next year was quiet. Pauling did not then and never would allow personal frictions to interfere with his single-minded pursuit of scientific truth. Between 1933 and 1935 he continued his work on valence bond theory, gathering new and important information on the structure of molecules—bond angles, bond energies, and interatomic distances—all of which helped him and his team work out the structures of an ever-increasing number of substances.

# 6

# Pauling vs. Dorothy Wrinch

AS THE MID-1930S APPROACHED, PAULING WAS BECOM-ing increasingly restless. He had been working on crystal and chemical bonding for nearly fifteen years. While there were innumerable unsolved problems in the field, the methods were sure and the theory well-established. As he explained, "By 1935, I believe I had worked out most of the fundamental problems connected with the chemical bond."[1]

At the same time, the changes in Pauling paralleled to some extent the changes at the California Institute itself. Like Pauling, Caltech had been investigating the structure of inorganic crystals almost since the days of its founding. Roscoe Dickinson had first used X-ray crystallography there, and his work influenced Caltech and Pauling. Indeed, the very earliest cardboard models of clay minerals still hang in cabinets at Caltech.

Caltech was, however, changing even more than Linus Pauling. Although Pauling was moving away from crystal structure, he stayed firmly and irrevocably within the orbit of the physical sciences. Caltech did not. The Institute was beginning to recognize the importance of the humanities, in addition to its traditional emphasis on the "hard" sciences. Undergraduates had no electives, but by 1939 they were required to take fully 25 percent of their course load per term in the humanities. And to teach them there were such men as the distinguished European historian William Monroe, newly arrived from Harvard. Entrenched in science and the scientific method as the paradigm for all knowledge, Pauling found the humanities program of little interest.

Biology was something else again. Within a short time, the California Institute of Technology acquired the services of such greats as Alfred Sturdevant, T.H. Morgan, Calvin Bridges, and Theodosius Dobzhansky. Soon, the division of biology rivalled chemistry and chemical engineering in greatness and worldwide influence. Pauling was influenced by T.H. Morgan's lectures on genetics and the phenomenon of crossing-over which he had first encountered in the biology division in 1929. According to Pauling,

> I had started to learn something about biology in 1929 when Thomas Hunt Morgan came to the California Institute of Technology . . . This division was strong in genetics, and by 1931, I had become interested enough in genetics to present a seminar describing a theory of the crossing-over of chromosomes that I had developed.

Morgan, of course, was famous for his work on the latter phenomenon.

Although the heyday of the biology division was interrupted at the beginning of the 1940s, when T.H. Morgan retired as chairman (causing Dobzhansky and Sturtevant to leave as well), Pauling's interest in biological problems continued. Though he had forever abandoned the full-time investigation of crystal structure, he grew more interested in structural problems in other areas of science. In later years, his fascination with the structure of DNA catapulted him into a much-heralded race with Watson and Crick for the Nobel prize.

Therefore, the year 1935 roughly marks the beginnings of Pauling's interest in the great new questions in the biological sciences, though the dusty and mysterious-looking bottles all neatly lined up on the clapboard shelves of his father's pharmacy probably planted the seeds of his biological interest much earlier in life. Money was a factor, as Pauling admits with unusual candor:

> The Rockefeller Foundation had started supporting my work about 1932 . . . or 1933. And they made it rather clear that if we were working on biological substances they'd be more interested. This was largely Warren Weaver's idea, that the time had come when a more basic attack ought to be made on the problem of life, in the field of biology and medicine. They put up a large amount of money for our work in Pasadena, several million dollars over a period of years . . .[3]

So an entirely new frontier opened up for Pauling. Though he may have felt he had mastered the chemical bond, he did not feel he had grasped and solved all the *biological* manifestations of chemical bonding. That was the new twist. Biological molecules present problems peculiar to them, problems not shared by inorganic molecules.

For one thing, there is the issue of size. By comparison with the ultra-minute inorganic molecules, such giants as hemoglobin, fibrin, and other proteins can reach a length of several feet. Furthermore, bonding forces other than the classical and familiar covalent bonds Pauling was used to come into play in organic molecules. There is, for example, the phenomenon of "hydrogen" bonding which Pauling himself had studied. These intermolecular links, approximately one-tenth the strength of an ordinary covalent bond, may nonetheless be the most important single connector of the molecules of life. They are necessary in order to replicate DNA molecules; without them we could neither reproduce ourselves nor cook eggs in the morning.

By the mid-1930s, these new bonds were classified into two groups, the so-called "strong" and "weak" bonds. (These are not to be confused with the "strong" and "weak" bonds in atomic nuclei, which are of essentially no importance in chemical problems.) The stronger were the chemical, covalent bonds. The weaker ones included, besides hydrogen bonding, the so-called "Van der Waals" forces (named after the Dutch scientist Johannes Diderik Van der Waals). Feebler than even the feeblest hydrogen bonds, they were important, but fleeting and evanescent —existing only as long as two groups of atoms are in close enough proximity to induce charge fluctuations in one another's electrical field. These induced opposite charges attract one another and thereby form the bond.

Even if Pauling really felt he had an "essentially complete understanding of the chemical bond," he was, in the face of all of this, a pioneer facing an as yet incompletely charted wilderness. Like the explorers in the early days of America, Pauling was there partly to push back boundaries and frontiers and partly, as long-time colleague Verner Schomaker says, for "a hell of a chance to enjoy himself."

From his growing interest in biology, Pauling found it was only a small step to an interest in medicine. In the Fall 1971 issue of the *Saturday Evening Post*, Pauling is quoted:

> In 1935, Max Mason had an office near mine at Caltech. One day we started talking about column chromatography (color measurements) and it struck me that it would be a wonderful diagnostic tool. You know, you could pass blood or urine through it and identify significant molecules quickly. I think it was my first medical suggestion.

Were visions of his father's twenty-five-cent bottles of "Dr. Pfunder's Oregon Blood Purifier" coming back to inspire him? Perhaps. When Pauling had been studying protein molecules only a short time, Noyes asked him what he'd been up to. Pauling replied, "Blood, Dr. Noyes, blood!"[4] This was a reference to his recently acquired interest in the magnetic properties of hemoglobin. Pauling had discovered that this large protein molecule, when found in arterial blood, is repelled by a magnet. In venous blood it is attracted.

By the summer of 1936 Pauling was deeply immersed in hemoglobin research with an able graduate student, Charles Coryell. It went well, and in the same year he and Coryell first described some of the minuter and subtler structural features of hemoglobin, among them the way it combines with oxygen.

If Pauling needed any further reason to continue with his hemoglobin research, bad luck provided it. An explosion rocked his laboratory in the fall of 1935, injuring several of his researchers who were doing electron-diffraction studies to work out structures of some nitrates of fluorine gas.

Pauling was upset—extremely upset. He genuinely cared for his co-workers and had always taken the greatest care to avoid any troubles of that sort. But in a chemical laboratory, such danger can never be totally eliminated. Even today, the hallways of the California Institute of Technology look almost like hospital corridors, with showers for quickly washing off dangerous chemicals that might spill on a researcher and other sophisticated first-aid equipment placed at periodic intervals to handle any sudden and unpredictable emergency. In fact, subsequent investigation showed that the fault lay with a careless graduate student. Nevertheless, Pauling was depressed for some time. On November 3, he confided in Noyes, saying:

> We have finally interpreted our electron diffraction photographs of $NO_3F$ as far as possible. They are rather poor, as the substance exploded in the apparatus. They give some information, but do not decide between the structure NOF and the tetrahedral structure. Since two of our men have been injured in explosions, each requiring stitches, we do not desire to continue the work . . .[5]

Part of his distress originated in a sense of guilt. While the fault was not his, the fact is that he had been warned of the chemical's explosive properties nearly a year before the incident. Not that the warning was needed: Pauling always took the greatest precautions anyway. Yet the mere fact that the warning had been issued probably induced a feeling of responsibility. It is a matter of history that Pauling tended to place science ahead of the welfare of any person. He knew this about himself and this personality trait created a great deal of tension within him throughout his career.

The work on inorganic compounds abruptly over, Pauling returned to hemoglobin. The result was a surprise. He had thought that oxygen would retain its unpaired electron even when bonded to hemoglobin. Through experimentation, he realized that it does not. Even more surprising, he and Coryell found that the *iron* atoms also had no unpaired electrons when oxygen fastened itself to hemoglobin to form oxyhemoglobin. Pauling and Coryell reported these discoveries in a paper published in 1936. The summary read as follows:

> It is shown by magnetic measurements that oxyhemoglobin and carbonmonoxyhemoglobin contain no unpaired electrons; the oxygen molecule, with two unpaired electrons in the free state, accordingly undergoes a profound change in electronic structure on attachment to hemoglobin . . . The magnetic susceptibility of hemoglobin itself (ferrohemoglobin) corresponds to an effective magnetic moment of 5.46 Bohr magnetons per heme, calculated for independent hemes . . .[6]

Prior to this work, scientists had believed that merely joining with one another made little difference to the magnetic properties of both oxygen and hemoglobin (magnetism being a function of the pairing of electrons). Pauling had shown this was not true—it *does* make a difference—just as leaving a child's magnet in the hot sun changes its magnetic properties.

Pauling was very excited about this work and talked about it for weeks around the Pasadena campus. His friends came back soon enough, and Pauling threw himself into the hemoglobin work with renewed vigor and gusto—the accidents with the inorganic chemicals pretty much forgotten. From hemoglobin, Pauling became more and more fascinated with larger, more complicated proteins.

Just as the previous year had been marred by failure and injury, so 1936 was blessed by some of Pauling's finest scientific work to date. In addition to the paper on hemoglobin, he published still another breakthrough on the phenomenon of protein denaturation. There are some surprisingly everyday goings-on connected with denaturation. Fry an egg and you denature proteins. When the white turns white, what is happening is that the protein is breaking down, or "denaturing." It was Pauling, along with his colleague Alfred Mirsky, who first explained this process. According to their theory, first published in that 1936 paper, all proteins are "polypeptides"—long strings of amino acids that are hooked together as well as coiled in a variety of different shapes under ordinary conditions.

Like any chain, something has to hold the links together. The links here are hydrogen bonds which Pauling himself had described so well in *The Nature of the Chemical Bond*. Much weaker than ordinary covalent chemical bonds, they are easily severed, especially by heat. The heat of the frying pan bursts apart the bonds holding the polypeptide chain together. Once made up of well-ordered, pleasingly regular geometrical figures, the molecule quickly falls into randomness and chaos. So the egg turns white.

The success of this paper soon led Pauling into a collaboration with Robert Corey, himself one of the world's leaders in protein chemistry. In contrast to Pauling, Corey was reclusive, willing and even eager to avoid interviews and shun the limelight. In an unpublished biography of Pauling, professors Mildred and Ted Goertzel of Rutgers say:

> We remember Corey as a timid slight man in a well-ordered study who was obviously upset because he feared we might identify him somehow with Pauling the dissenter.... Although he relaxed somewhat when the conversation moved away from controversial issues and talked in a friendly manner about trivialities during an extended leave-taking, we felt he was glad to have us leave.

However, Corey worked well with Pauling, and the pair planned an assault on the amino acid building blocks of the protein polypeptide chain. They worked on the problem, on and off, for quite a few years to come. The problem of proteins was immensely complicated and, of course, Pauling was still very interested in other matters, such as structural and other aspects of hemoglobin (itself a protein). So their initial progress was slow.

Just as one great scientist arrived, another departed forever. On June 3, 1936, A.A. Noyes died of pneumonia in Pasadena, barely three months before his seventieth birthday. Though long expected, his death was received with the most profound sorrow at the California Institute of Technology. Noyes, more than anyone, was Caltech, and Caltech was American science in microcosm. The Institute labored under as heavy a gloom as it had ever seen. Even Pauling, despite earlier differences, genuinely grieved at his passing. Yet Noyes's death had lingering and at times, exceedingly unpleasant consequences for Pauling. Very soon, he found himself saddled with the chairmanship of the Division of Chemistry and Chemical Engineering. Given his stellar reputation, it was inevitable that he would be chosen as chairman. According to Professor Jack Roberts, a student of the fabled Howard Lucas: "Pauling was not a naturally gifted chairman, and I doubt he was looking forward to it. When he did assume the post, he really didn't do much of the day-by-day duties, delegating [them] to others."[7]

However, the prestige of the post and the reduced teaching load that came with it did give Pauling the chance to expand his interests. Other aspects of the chemistry of life were already exerting their pull on his intellect. Besides the alpha-helix generally, he was thinking about the planarity of the peptide bond, the role of Van der Waals forces in the construction of the protein molecule, as well as the structure and function of hemoglobin. He was soon invited to give the George Fisher Baker lectures in chemistry at Cornell University in the Fall of 1937. These lectures later reappeared as *The Nature of the Chemical Bond*, generally considered to be his magnum opus.

The Cornell lectures paved the way for a meeting between Pauling and Karl Landsteiner that same year. There were few men in the world that could "honor" Linus Pauling by visiting him, but Landsteiner was one. A magical name in biological chemistry, he was born in 1868 and was therefore many years Pauling's senior. He had already captured a Nobel Prize for his epochal work in the classification of blood types. Serene and unflappable, Landsteiner was not easily impressed. He had visited with Pauling before. After hearing him lecture on hemoglobin at the Rockefeller Institute in 1936, Landsteiner had already invited Pauling to come to his laboratory to talk about issues in medicine and immunology. His belief was that Pauling's understanding of molecular structure might help develop explanations for some of the immunological reactions that had so far eluded his own analysis.

Even though little of immediate consequence emerged from this meeting, they remained friends and Pauling frequently mentioned Landsteiner in his lectures. Everyone knew that Pauling was the man to go to for ideas. Even if he was not strong in mathematical niceties (he found extensive calculation tedious, though his grasp of mathematics was not in any way defective), his ability to intuit a good idea was without peer. Great issues in chemistry, chemical bonding, quantum mechanics, crystal structure—all yielded their secrets to him.

There was one exception: the polypeptide chain. He and Corey had spent a good part of 1936 as well as the summer of 1939 worrying about the architecture of the chains—alpha keratin particularly. Still, success was nowhere in view. It was not their fault. The great British crystallographer, W.T. Astbury, had taken and interpreted some key X-ray photos of protein chains, but the interpretation was wrong, as was the mathematical information derived from his photos and interpretation. Unaware of this, Pauling had not been able to find a way of coiling a polypeptide chain in three dimensions to make his chain models consistent with the Astbury data. It would be eleven years before someone read the photos correctly. So great was Astbury's reputation, that everyone thought it impossible that he might have floundered so badly. When Pauling finally realized that it was not he, but Astbury, who was at fault, his chain theory fell into place and his first Nobel Prize followed not long afterwards, in 1954.

There were other obstacles. He first had to meet the challenge of Dorothy Wrinch, the British mathematician and biologist. If her theory had been right, he would never have received the Nobel Prize. While Pauling and Corey spent night after night in the bowels of Gates labs, trying to sort out the mistakes in their chain model, Wrinch was presenting her own conception of protein structure. Educated at Girton College, Cambridge, and at the Universities of London, Paris, and Vienna, she had the finest training in mathematics and, later on, studied biology and chemistry with such notables as the great chemist Irving

Langmuir. What stymied her in her efforts to win recognition as a scientist was her blunt and aggressive manner, for which she was almost universally disliked. Her long-time friend, Professor Marjorie Senechal of Smith College, told me simply that "she had an acid tongue," and in one of her articles wrote: "And when the intruder is a woman, not a humble woman who is eager to please and graciously accepts criticism from her betters, but a brilliant, witty, and sharp-tongued woman who does not know her place, then this is just too much. She simply had to be knocked down."[8]

Indeed, Dr. Wrinch herself provides ample evidence of this in her correspondence. In a letter in the archives of Smith College, she writes: "My opinion of FOS is confirmed. He is a facile experimentalist. His forte is making gadgets. God help biology so long as this is the type of person chosen to break new ground. . . ." Such blunt language might have been accepted from a man, but not from a woman scientist. Nor was a woman scientist supposed to challenge well-entrenched male academics such as Linus Pauling.

A classic and bitter battle in the history of structural biochemistry was beginning, between two powerful intellects, two stubborn antagonists, and, most important, two—at that moment—equally credible theories. Certainly many early reactions to Wrinch's ideas were positive. In a letter to her in 1935, the distinguished philosopher and scientist Michael Polanyi said: "When I write this down, I might add, as a piece of fortune-telling, that you will live to great recognition of your vision."[9]

In 1937, protein chemistry was both inordinately complicated and hardly out of its infancy. The emergence of conflicting and competing theories was, under the circumstances, unavoidable. Protein molecules are unfathomably large, many reaching several feet in length. As a consequence, their structure cannot be worked out by calculation, as can the structure of simpler molecules. The structure of certain hydrogen molecules, for example, can quite literally be calculated because of their small size and simplicity. Not so with proteins, with their many hundreds of thousands of atoms. Moreover, the scientists of the late 1930s did not have powerful computers available to assist their research, and more than one harried and underpaid graduate student spent many long hours doing calculations by hand.

Added to this were the very specific and baffling problems Pauling was having with the chain theory itself. The theory proposed by Dorothy Wrinch was very different. Usually called the "cyclol" theory, this unusual idea held that amino acids could be "hooked" together in far more complicated ways than had previously been supposed. In the chain theory, amino acids (the building blocks of protein) were hooked together by chemical bonds, just like cars in a train—each amino acid linking with the one in front of it and the one behind it. In the cyclol theory, by contrast, the amino acids were joined together side-by-side as well. From this, Wrinch further deduced that the amino acids would form a regular pattern of hexagons which could then fold back on themselves to form cages.

This concept did have certain advantages. Most significantly, the theory had considerable aesthetic appeal, since the protein "cages" were geometrically constructed and nicely symmetrical. Such considerations are, perhaps surprisingly, extremely important in deciding on the worth or validity of a scientific theory. The greatest scientific theoreticians in history have always taken symmetry and aesthetic simplicity seriously. Einstein's efforts to construct a unified field theory, however incomplete, reveal his assumption that physics is more elegant and beautiful to the extent that the universe of physical phenomena can be subsumed or explained by an ever smaller number of physical laws. The great appeal of the Watson and Crick "double helix" model for DNA surely lies in the elegant intertwining of its two slender strands. It is true that the allure of symmetry has faded somewhat, primarily because of the now-famous discovery of parity violations in physics, not to mention the introduction of Pauling's own alpha-helix, which violated symmetry in that the helix repeats in non-integral turns. Today, symmetry-breaking is very common.

But Pauling would not have it. As he told Wrinch many years later, "Fifteen years ago it was thought that geometry is important in crystallography. There has now been a revolution

... indeed it is now seen that geometry has no significance. Symmetry has no significance.... it enters in an incidental way."[10]

This claim is difficult to understand and evaluate. Certainly Pauling is wrong so far as the *general* importance of symmetry and beauty in science is concerned. Despite concepts such as parity violations, most practitioners of physics still place some importance on aesthetic appeal, symmetry, and simplicity, and consider these when deciding among competing theories. And among philosophers of science, symmetry and beauty are not only omnipresent features of the universe but also figure importantly in a scientist's decision whether or not to accept or reject a theory. The entire universe, from the smallest objects to great galaxies and clusters of galaxies, shows design, order, and symmetry.

On the other hand, symmetry is not such a simple matter either. It is known, for example, that there are equations which *display* symmetry, but which have solutions of *lower* symmetry! (To speak of an equation having "symmetry" means, roughly, that one can apply transformation operators to it and still leave the equation invariant.) This is true of the hydrogen atom, where the interacton looks the same with, for example, the electron on either side. However, the electron orbitals may not have this symmetry.

This sort of phenomenon is true also of planetary motion, where the *solution* to the equations, though not the equations themselves, have less symmetry, as described by classical equations. (Interestingly, the classical equations have the same symmetry as the quantum mechanical model for, e.g., the H-atom as described by the Schrödinger-like wave function. For example, the symmetry of interaction in gravity is inversely proportional to the distance and exactly the same is true in the atom itself: column interactions are also invariant, proportional to the distance. Specifically, the "s" electron wave function is highly symmetrical, but the "p" electron wave function has lower symmetry (i.e., only one axis can be changed and still preserve symmetry.) In general, much the same applies to an "s" orbital electron in a many-electron atom, though, of course, corrections for the affects of other electrons in larger atoms have to be taken into account.

Dorothy Wrinch clearly believed that high-symmetry solutions would be of lower energy and thus more stable, which, indeed, was *very* often the case in the history of science. On the other hand, Pauling postulated a solution with *low* symmetry, believing that high-symmetry solutions would have higher energies and, therefore be less stable. As it turned out, Pauling was right: the low symmetry solution was more stable, contrary to Wrinch's predictions. In a way, Pauling's discovery of low-symmetry, low energy solutions in chemistry is analogous to the discovery of parity violations in physics. (Though not exactly: the parity/symmetry violations in physics involve a slightly different kind of symmetry, for reasons beyond the scope of this discussion. This is one of the reasons for the great importance, despite its failure, of Einstein's work on a Unified Field Theory later in life; a completely unified field theory would have a great deal of symmetry, although parity violations would have to be preserved.

It is hard to believe that Pauling could be entirely sure of what he was saying. Surely he knew, for example, that aesthetic and symmetry considerations play an important role in physics.) But what is true of physics is, *a fortiori*, true of chemistry, since chemistry is a special case or special application of the laws and principles of physics. The final test of any theory is whether, of course, it squares with experimental evidence. At that time, the evidence did not conclusively support one theory over the other. History might lead in either direction, towards Pauling's chains or Wrinch's cyclol hypothesis.

So Pauling needed a plan, a master blueprint that would vanquish both the cyclol theory and Dorothy Wrinch. In the absence of sufficient data to tip the scales in favor of his chain theory, he planned a smaller-scale assault. In his most ingenious style, he and Corey decided to try solving some smaller problems before tackling the much more abstract and difficult features of proteins. Their idea was that by first solving the structures of key amino acids, the grosser features of protein structure would eventually reveal themselves.

Their logic was impeccable. Given the simplicity of the amino acids (compared with entire strands of protein), results came immediately. By 1938, Corey had already solved some of the simpler dipeptides (protein "chains" of only two amino acids in length). The most important of these was diketopiperazine. Its structure showed evidence of resonance in even this simplest of amino acids. Perhaps more importantly, these studies showed that the peptide bond had to be *planar* (i.e., there could be no "free rotation"—the atoms could not turn and twist in an indefinite number of possible ways.) As philosopher Robert Olby explains, in his excellent work, *The Path to the Double Helix*: "If one accepted that diketopiperazine was equivalent to an open chain dipeptide *this would mean the planarity of the peptide bond*." Professor James Bonner confirmed this in his interview with me:

> Linus started out on crystal structure of proteins, getting crystals of amino acids and dipeptides and studying the peptide bond, and that was the great insight he gained from this, that the atoms arranged in the peptide bond are coplanar; so this immediately led him to start making models of how you could patch amino acids together to make peptide bonds between two amino acids, all being co-planar. The alpha-helix was one possible structure, where the peptide bonds are all stacked above one another; the planarity limited the possible configurations very much.

Given this critical information Pauling soon realized that the alpha-helix had only a few possible structures, since the planarity of the peptide bond limited them in the way described above. That being the case, the structure of the complete protein molecule could not remain hidden much longer. Pauling then attacked the problem by his "stochastic" method. (Pauling used this term in a special sense, meaning a sophisticated and educated "guessing" at the structure based on known features of the substance in question. The term "stochastic" has, however, a technical use among physicists, referring to any random process. For example, the so-called Monte Carlo method involves an algorithm having to do with random numbers. In order to mimic random processes in nature, one uses random numbers generated on a computer. Brownian motion is another example of a random process in this sense. When I use the term "stochastic" in this book, I use it in Pauling's sense.)

Pauling and Corey then attacked the problem of building the complete polypeptide chain in such a way that it would square with the raw X-ray data on proteins already studied. (It is a virtually inviolable rule of X-ray studies, that any proposed molecular structure *cannot* contradict the X-ray data.) The path to the alpha-helix was emerging from the shadows.

As a result of this work, Pauling obtained a grant in 1937 from the Rockefeller Foundation. Since Dorothy Wrinch was already there, the chances of a collision between Pauling and Wrinch were greater than ever. In 1935, Wrinch's reputation was such that the Foundation saw fit to give her a grant of $12,500 for a five-year period. Not only was her cyclol work brilliant, but she had already published some forty papers of great scientific importance. Within the next few years, she incoporated much of this information, as well as considerable new data, into her classic books, *Fourier Transforms and Structure Factors, Chemical Aspects of the Structure of Small Peptides* and *Chemical Aspects of Polypeptide Chain Structures and the Cyclol Theory*. She was also the first woman ever appointed to Oxford as a full-time faculty member. (Oddly, she had tried for a meeting with Pauling to discuss their theories at about the time of her grant. But at the time, Pauling's own work on proteins was probably going too smoothly for him to worry about Wrinch. She did not, for all her work, have Pauling's prestige.) Her achievement is all the more impressive because it was difficult for scientists to get grants in the 1930s; the depression and crash of 1929 were still too vivid in people's memories.

But the Rockefeller Foundation was different. For one thing, Warren Weaver was at its helm. Despite the economy, Weaver wanted the best for science, particularly biological science, which had always fascinated him, although he had been trained as a physicist.

Weaver's reputation as a scientist as such was modest at best, but he was a skilled and enthusiastic administrator and organizer. His arrival at the Rockefeller Foundation was a turning point for the institution. Though it had functioned adequately for many years, it had fallen into disarray, confusion, and mismanagement by the late 1920's. Along with the inexorably decaying economy, the Foundation was choking amid its own internal chaos.

The Foundation consisted of a number of "boards" which received funds. These boards, in turn, were supposed to dispense money for a variety of scientific projects. The boards, however, were themselves plagued by the disorganization that characterized the Foundation as a whole.

In 1937, under Weaver's guidance (he had taken over in 1931) the Foundation embarked on a massive reorganizational campaign, trying to alleviate confusion by eliminating the boards and replacing them with several "divisions." Each of the divisions was to concentrate on one area of human knowledge. The new division system did appear more logical, since all research and goings-on within the new divisions had to fall into the area of knowledge for which the division was responsible. Also, a single director was now in charge of what went on within any given division.

One more factor was finally responsible for Wrinch's appearance within the Foundation. The new organizational system was to be *interdisciplinary*. Though each division was responsible for only one area of human knowledge, anyone could contribute. Weaver was determined not to tolerate elitism and academic territorialism in the "new" Rockefeller Foundation. In that, he followed the philosophy of the distinguished historian and philosopher of science, Karl Popper. It was Popper's view that: "we are not students of some subject matter but students of problems . . . And problems may cut right across the borders of any subject matter or discipline." Unwilling to be stymied by divisions between the various branches of learning, Weaver wanted to draw upon the expertise of whomever might have something to say about the solution of a problem.

Dorothy Wrinch had expertise in both mathematics and biology and knew as much about both as anyone. Thus it is no surprise that Weaver snatched her up at the first opportunity. He spoke about his interdisciplinary philosophy in a letter to *Science* in 1938. Talking about the Foundation's report for that year, he said it was necessary to develop new research into "those borderline areas in which physics and chemistry merge with biology. . . ." How well Dorothy Wrinch fit Weaver's vision may be understood by quoting from a paper presented in 1983 at the National History of Science meeting by Sibilla E. Kennedy of the State University of New York at Stonybrook:

> Weaver's object specifically was to quantify biology; to follow the trends indicated by the discovery of the gene, to discover the structure of proteins and other macromolecules and, in short, to initiate a revolution in biology which would be comparable to the quantum revolution in physics.[11]

Nonetheless, trouble began surfacing almost from the beginning of Wrinch's association with the Rockefeller Foundation. While her scientific genius was undeniable, her personality offended many. Her powerful ego and stubborn determination to prove to the world that she was right eventually led her into personal collisions. She was as merciless and skilled in verbal jousting as she was in the chemistry laboratory. Nor did she hesitate to demand anything she thought she ought to have, whether it was permitted to others or not. Soon she demanded an assistant. Weaver, mild-mannered though he was, was quickly running out of patience. Complaints began drifting into his office on a nearly regular basis. By 1936, he described her in ambivalent terms:

> Wrinch is a queer fish, with a kaleidoscopic pattern of ideas, ever shifting and somewhat dizzying. . . . There is no question but that she has already entered deeply into the wide variety of topics that bear on the general problem of protein structure: and she has

obviously impressed a number of critics, like Astbury . . . whose competence cannot be questioned. She continually raises the question of direct assistance under her supervision—"Oh, Dr. Weaver: If only I had a handsome young man to twiddle the test-tubes for me!"—but repeated discouragement of this idea . . . should convince her we are not prepared to furnish funds for this purpose."[12]

If Wrinch did make the comment about the "handsome young man," it was probably an expression of professional frustration more than anything else. The fact is that Weaver continually stood in her way, alienated by what he saw as her abrasive manner.

Still—was this the only problem? At a symposium at Smith College some years ago, her close friend of many years, Elizabeth Moore, said, "She was very dynamic. She was the bulldozer type, wasn't she? She'd tend to bowl you over with her energy, her ideas. It was hard to get a word in edgewise."[13] David Harker, another supporter and friend, compared Wrinch with Nobelist Francis Crick. "The same dominance of the conversation, and insisting on talking about *their* interests, not your interests, and the same combinatorial minds, brains. . . ." (Harker was incidentally one of Pauling's earliest graduate students as well as a distinguished biologist in his own right.)

Perhaps this is one of the sources of her later friction with Pauling. Insults are one thing. They can be handled, skirted, turned back, or ignored. They are specific and localized. The sort of egocentrism Harker describes is subtler, harder to get a grip on. One cannot "rebut" it. Surely these observations applied equally to Pauling, for whom conversation always had to be about his interests or subjects *he* believed worthy. His sister-in-law Gorgo told me: "If you weren't talking about things he liked, he'd just curl up in a corner and ignore people." That sentiment was echoed by Professor Ted Goertzel, in an article about Pauling in the *Antioch Review*: "In social situations, he will discuss his own work, or other scientific and intellectual topics, but shows no interest in the people around him as personalities."[14]

Despite the problems, Weaver knew very well that the Foundation needed Wrinch. And given the collaboration expected among the various scientists working at the Rockefeller Foundation, and the fact that both Pauling and Wrinch were interested in structural problems in biology, Pauling knew that he would have to deal with her.

A meeting between the two would have provided a great opportunity for Wrinch of course, but one that was fraught with peril. Pauling's reputation was so formidable, his clout so far-reaching, that she knew she was risking her career by disagreeing with him. A word from Pauling in certain circles could do incalculable damage.

Nor was the Foundation about to let either of them avoid a confrontation. They were becoming anxious to know Pauling's views on the cyclol theory, since it was gaining important support. Niels Bohr himself liked it, as did Irving Langmuir and David Harker. All believed the theory could account for many of the experimentally observed properties and behavior of protein in a simple, elegant, and comprehensive way. Langmuir, for example, wrote a long letter to Pauling in 1939, urging that one important virtue of the cyclol hypothesis over Pauling's polypeptide chain theory was that it was in accord with the principle of the philosophy of science that the fewer assumptions involved in a theory, the better. As he explained:

> With the polypeptide chain theory, however, you have to assume first that the polypeptide chain is folded into a structure having trigonal symmetry and second that the side chains are arranged in this structure also with trigonal symmetry. You have to make thus two *ad hoc* assumptions, whereas Dr. Wrinch needs only one.[15]

Thus, Weaver did not hesitate when Dorothy Wrinch herself asked him for a meeting with Pauling. He wrote to Pauling immediately. Pauling was doubtless in a good frame of mind, for his fourth child, Edward Crellin, was soon to be born, on June 4, 1937. Weaver received an O.K. from Pauling in March. The meeting would take place in Ithaca in January of 1938.

The meeting was a turning point in the ill-fated history of

cyclols and marked the end of any polite relationship there may have been between Pauling and Wrinch.

Prior to the meeting with Wrinch, he was torn: he genuinely worried that she might be right. Yet his sense of caution was keeping him in check. He was not ready to challenge her theory without more evidence. He spent many hours agonizing with Ava Helen, whom he often credited with sparking his best ideas. She did her best to provide moral support and scientific inspiration. If Dorothy Wrinch turned out to be correct, Pauling might lose his place as the greatest protein chemist in history.

It took actual face-to-face contact with Wrinch to drive Pauling to a substantial change in attitude. After their meeting, his skepticism was converted into blatant hostility. The long-deferred encounter squashed any residual sympathies he may have had.

In the Dorothy Wrinch collection at Smith College, there is a document bearing the title, "Notes on the talks between Dr. Doroth Wrinch and Linus Pauling." Wrinch had traveled from England especially for this meeting and, according to Claire Sullivan, a participant in a symposium held at Smith on Wrinch's work some years back, "it wasn't too friendly." In the collection there is also a letter from Pauling to Warren Weaver, which says:

> A number of years ago I made a thorough study of Mrs. Wrinch's ideas. The Rockefeller Foundation had asked her to come to talk with me. . . . The conclusion that I reached then was that the ideas that she had at that time were in considerable part self-contradictory. When I discussed her theories with her, especially the self-contradictions and the contradictions with experiments, she abandoned item after item until at the end there was almost nothing left. The contrast between the extensive claims that she had made in her papers and the . . . small amount that she was willing to defend caused me to decide not to make an effort to find the reliable parts of her later publications. There is, as far as I know, nothing wrong with her mathematical work on Fourier transforms.[16]

The meeting was difficult for Wrinch. Professor Edward Hughes recalls one of the days Wrinch was in Ithaca:

In 1937, when Pauling was Baker lecturer at Cornell, I was his assistant and we got a telegram from a British steamer, from Dorothy Wrinch, saying that she was going to be in Ithaca on a certain date and would like to see Pauling; . . . he was very upset, saying: "I do not want to give a seminar in the presence of that woman," because she had the reputation of going around quoting people without saying where she heard [the statements]; and so we decided to invite her to give a seminar. It turned out that he [Pauling] didn't say a word. But there were two professors . . . interested in protein structure who took her on! . . . she would get up there and pound on the table with this model and change the subject. Finally, Pauling intervened. But then the next morning he laughed at her in the presence of those post-docs and graduate students; [later] he really turned on her and massacred her, but *not* in public.

The meeting left Dorothy Wrinch very bitter. In a note composed soon after the fateful encounter, Wrinch wrote: "The fact that they are against cyclols in any fundamental and a priori way in itself rather gives the show away. . . . it is undeniable that the theory has NOT [sic] yet been shown to be false, and therefore only fools or men of evil wishes towards me will be against it a priori . . ."

As Professor Marjorie Senechal of Smith College summed up the meeting and its effect on Wrinch: "Dorothy just never would talk about it, and I was one of her best friends . . . But she never went near Pauling again and even boycotted talks Pauling gave [at Smith]."

Pauling had to report back. In April he wrote to Weaver and the Rockefeller Foundation:

I am sympathetic to the application of physical and mathematical methods to chemical and biological problems, and I began the interview with Dr. Wrinch with the hope that the unsatisfactory aspects of her published work would be removed in the discussion. I found, however, that her methods and results are still less scientific than they had appeared to be from her papers. I doubt that her attack on the problem of protein structure will lead directly to any valuable results, and I think that it would not be worthwhile to have her working in our laboratories in Pasadena.

Probably Pauling was trusting his intuition. Despite a lack of hard evidence, Pauling had always "felt" that the cyclol theory was seriously flawed. Many times, that intuitive way of handling problems worked. It had worked with the alpha-helix and with the notion that sickle-cell anemia was a disease of the hemoglobin molecule, and it had worked in countless other less monumental ways. He had little reason to doubt it now.

Whatever the state of Pauling's mind, Dorothy Wrinch was clearly upset by the meeting. Shortly afterwards (in a letter to Eric Neville in October, 1940) she wrote:

> I don't mind telling you that often I would like to quit. The fact that I can't makes me hold on of course, but if only I had the opportunity to do so, I easily might. I get absolutely in despair, for I see the whole set up as a power syndicate just like Hitler's and only the strong and powerful can survive. . . . I don't know how anyone of probity can survive in this world. Even decent people hesitate to stand up to Linus Pauling. He is bright and quick and merciless in repartee when he likes and I think people just are afraid of him. It takes poor Dorothy to point out where he is wrong . . .

Of course, Pauling is a strong, charismatic man, but his manner can at times be very abrupt and intimidating. It is not always easy to talk to him, especially when the conversation turns to touchy issues. Marjorie Senechal recalled a talk Pauling once gave at Smith: "After his talk I went up to him and asked him a question. Apparently he didn't think much of my question, because his only reaction was to turn to his wife and ask, 'Where's my coat?' I thought I deserved better than that."[17] Nor was Marjorie Senechal the strident, abrasive Dorothy Wrinch. Under the circumstances it is hardly a surprise that Pauling and Wrinch did not become fast friends. These personality factors could well have influenced Pauling's and Wrinch's judgments of one another's scientific abilities.

On March 6, 1939, Pauling confidently wrote to the Rockefeller Foundation:

> Some fifteen years ago, a number of people indulged in extensive speculations regarding the structure of crystals, using the self-consistency of their systems as criteria rather than test by experimental methods.
> Despite the nicely symmetrical structures which they proposed, these speculations have turned out to be wrong. I feel that Dr. Wrinch's work suffers a little bit from being similarly too speculative and from being based too largely on the assumption that nicely symmetrical structures are the right ones. On the other hand, she seems to be conversant with what facts there are, and it is quite possible that her attempts to coordinate them with structural ideas will ultimately be of value in the solution of the greater problem of protein structure.

Pauling was never clear on exactly why her methods and results weren't "scientific." The reference may have had to do with his old prejudices against aesthetics as a criterion of scientific validity, reinforced, perhaps by the fact that she was a competitor. He did fear she might be getting results. Later he felt free to publish a paper on protein structure even though he and his team did not have rigorous proof of the correctness of his own theory of protein structure. Self-consistency is in fact a formidable and sophisticated position. The Hegelians and the American philosopher Brand Blanshard defended the idea ably for many years. (By self-consistency, they mean that the ultimate test of a theory is whether the statements within the theory are consistent with one another and with all that is known about the physical universe at the time). In this, Dorothy Wrinch was only following an honored tradition.

Then on July 19, 1939, Pauling dealt the cyclol theory a crushing blow. On this date, he and his associate Carl Nieman submitted their paper entitled "The Structure of Proteins" to the prestigious *Journal of the American Chemical Society*. Fundamentally, their argument was that the cyclol structure was just too unstable to exist in nature. If it could appear in some protein, it would soon fall apart. As a result of this paper, innumerable scientists interested in proteins—many of whom were wavering and uncertain as to whether chains or cyclols were the true model for protein structure—turned quickly against her. Predictably, all this met with a vigorous defense by many of the advocates of the cyclol theory, including Dorothy Wrinch.

A delicate issue is raised by Pauling's decision to publish the protein paper. Although it is true that most of his anti-cyclol work was founded on sound, objective judgment, is it possible that Pauling here went far beyond the call of scientific duty? While a scientist has the option to attack any view for which the scientific evidence is shaky, did Pauling go further than a mere rebuttal of Wrinch's views? Rebuttal and argument are, naturally, part of the free-wheeling dialectic of scientific research and academic progress generally. Even so, there are some esteemed scientists, such as Dr. David Harker, who feel Pauling exceeded these bounds—that he was out to crush Dorothy Wrinch by thoroughly discrediting her as a serious scientist. As Harker explained to me: "Pauling wasn't all gold; I think he used his influence with journals to keep her from publishing her work."[18] (On the other hand, Harker could not actually cite a specific example.)

Marjorie Senechal reflected on the "competition" between Pauling's chain theory and the cyclol idea, as well as the relationship between Pauling and Wrinch:

> When the appeal to experiment does not produce a clear answer, then the choice among theories may be deferred . . . Or a consensus may be reached among scientists on other grounds. For example, one theory may seem more plausible than another, or may be preferable because it involves fewer assumptions. In the minds of most scientists the cyclol controversy was settled in favor of the chains years before the techniques became available which could decide the matter . . . But it is not only this that makes the cyclol controversy interesting. Even more important, its creator was subjected to cruel and unusual punishment. She was virtually blacklisted by most of the scientific community.[19]

Although Senechal would not, as she told me, put the point quite so stridently today, she feels that her view is basically correct. And she is right. Most scientists did shut their minds to cyclols long before they had any grounds for doing so. Their scorn persists very visibly even today. Pauling is in this group, but this by itself does not prove Senechal's assertion.

There is, however, more testimony. The chemist Irving Langmuir, in a 1940 letter to the JACS and its editor A.B. Lamb (who had originally sent Langmuir a copy of the Pauling-Nieman paper), wrote "I think that Pauling and Niemann's article was extremely unfair and that the JACS should never have accepted the paper for publication in that form." True, this sort of comment is hard to defend. One can argue that all papers submitted to academic journals are screened by referees and that it is unlikely that a grossly unbalanced or poorly defended paper will be published. However, many are screened by only one referee. Of course, some, like the prestigious *Physical Review Letters* do demand at least two referees. In practice, however, many academic journals are "clubby" and tend to publish papers of friends and friends of friends. But it is hard to see how there is anything unfair about simply attacking someone else's views, unless *ad hominem* attacks are involved. But Pauling did not go that far. Later, in a letter to David Harker, Pauling responded to Harker's charge that he had been treating Wrinch unfairly:

> I have decided that, although the casual reader might be misled by your letter into thinking that it represents some small contribution to knowledge, I shall not trouble to set him straight by publishing a reply . . . I shall now say that I think that you could be about better business and in better company.[20]

The best that can be said for Langmuir's indignation is that, at the time, hard scientific fact did not clearly favor Pauling's views. Pauling himself, in a letter to Langmuir, on May 12, 1938 admits as much:

> The principal reason which led Dr. Nieman and me to prepare our manuscript is that there has been a great deal of material published in support of the cyclol theory, and very little in support

of the polypeptide chain theory. Dr. Nieman and I *feel* [emphasis mine] that the latter . . . is right, and although we are unable at present to advance any rigorous argument in proof of this, it seemed worthwhile for us to state our beliefs.

Evidently, the Pauling–Nieman attack was very premature. Wrinch immediately wrote Lamb, listing a number of reasons why she believed the paper was unfair. Apparently, the most important of these had to do with Pauling's mathematics. She urges that: ". . . there is a serious arithmetical error: in addition the argument it contains is fallacious, the equations constructed by Pauling and Nieman when correctly interpreted amounting simply to my original calculation."[21]

Pauling eventually admitted that she was right. On January 31, 1940, he replied: "I wish to thank you for writing to me about the error in the calculation of the heat of formation of diketopiperazine from its heat of combustion." Oddly, Pauling refused to publicly acknowledge the point, going on to say: "It has not seemed to us worthwhile to correct the error in print, since the discrepancy of 18,000 calories per mole of residue is just about as serious as a discrepancy of 28,000." That doesn't ring true. Why not correct the error, no matter how trivial? Is not science supposed to be "exact"? Nor is science epistemically sealed. A "trivial" error one day may turn out to be a colossal error later on with a different theory, or in the light of new knowledge. In addition, the reader is entitled to know that errors have crept into a paper, as this says something about the credibility and reliability of its authors. It is interesting to note that the highly respected physicist John Slater later on similarly faulted a theory of Pauling's on grounds of mathematical deficiency. And, according to physicist Dr. Roy Benedek, "In Slater's case, the mathematical problem caused by wrong physical assumptions was great enough to completely refute Pauling's entire theory."[22]

All this quarreling about mathematics revolved around the stability of the cyclol structure. Pauling had been arguing that it was just too unstable to exist while Wrinch, pointing to that error, claimed it wasn't quite as rickety as Pauling thought.

Then came David Harker, bristling and fuming over the treatment of Wrinch by his old mentor and thesis advisor. In a letter on July 16, 1940, he wrote:

> Dear Dr. Pauling . . . I think that some of your remarks concerning the letter . . . by Dr. Wrinch and myself are not justified and I should like to present my arguments . . . I have heard rumors from time to time concerning your allegedly unfair attitude toward Dr. Wrinch and her right to discuss her theories in print. I have invariably thought—and said—that such an attitude on your part was impossible. I have always considered these criticisms of you as due to misunderstanding of your statements and unworthy professional jealousy. I should be most unhappy to be forced to believe otherwise.

Harker himself claims to have been shabbily treated by Pauling, who, he says, has used his name without permission and misused funds Harker intended as a gift to (The Linus) Pauling Institute of Science and Medicine. More importantly, Harker is a formidable scientist himself, having contributed much to the theory of ribonuclease and its action in breaking down ribonucleic acids. To this day, Harker believes Pauling did not treat Dorothy Wrinch fairly.

What are we to think? Harker, Senechal, Langmuir and others all feel strongly that Pauling unfairly demolished Wrinch's career. Of course, history must record that Dorothy Wrinch had made indisputable contributions. Even Verner Schomaker said, ". . . she was credited with seeing that if you had a Patterson function that was resolved into a set of points, instead of having to leave it as a mess, as they usually are, you *could* solve it . . ."

Others, regarding cyclols at least, were not so sure. The most distinguished biochemist, Dorothy Hodgkin, for example, remained more or less neutral, perhaps also because she was friendly with both Pauling and Wrinch. She wrote me on May 14, 1986:

> I knew Dorothy Wrinch well but I agreed with Pauling in his view of the cyclol theory. Because Dorothy . . . and I had been

close friends in the early stage of the protein work—1934, 1935 —I said rather less than others in writing, but our friendly relations were somewhat strained until the structure of myoglobin was established.

Part of the problem is conceptual: What, exactly, constitutes "unethical" behavior in science? There are so many actual and possible degrees of unethical behavior, that it is difficult to draw the line. Sometimes, of course, the case is clear, as when James Watson made use of Rosalind Franklin's data without crediting her in the famed DNA race.

Yet, despite the plethora of general claims by reputable people, no one can actually point to a clear and specific example of Pauling's "unfairness" to Wrinch. Harker alludes to Pauling using his great influence with journal editors to prevent her from publishing her views and getting grants, but could not name specific events. Marjorie Senechal speaks of an "atmosphere" of distrust and ridicule conjured up by Pauling that rebounded against Dorothy Wrinch. She also describes a sort of "bandwagon" mentality that developed, partially engineered by Pauling. Again, there is nothing tangible or concrete in these claims.

Normally, therefore, statements like this would be meaningless. Still, it is vexing. There are, after all, so many first-rate, reputable people who believe similar things about Pauling. Their best evidence is circumstantial. Pauling admits (in the 1938 letter to Langmuir) that he was worried about Wrinch receiving too much publicity. There is, as well, the business of his refusal to correct his mathematical errors. This does sound like "professional jealousy," as Harker suggested. Wrinch had even appeared in *Time* holding a model of her cyclol structure. Pauling, who was a master showman and self-promoter, was being out-promoted.

It is worth keeping in mind that Pauling's own protein studies were in disarray. Despite a small-scale success in 1938 with the dipeptides, Pauling had been staggeringly unsuccessful in developing any *general* theory of protein structure. He was very worried that Wrinch might be right. He had spent hour after hour, night after night, running his polypeptide chain theory to the data and the two just would not fit. Conversations with Nieman and others, occasionally lasting for hours, did not produce hard proof for the claims that his "chain" theory was a better explanation of the known properties of proteins than the cyclol theory of Dorothy Wrinch. Thus, Pauling might well have felt threatened.

Although Pauling probably did speak disparagingly of Wrinch on occasion (as in the letter to Harker), it is important to avoid the tempting conclusion that Pauling was motivated by sexist bias. Even Ruth Hubbard, the highly respected Harvard scientist, known for her stand against recombinant DNA research, did not take that idea seriously.[23] Marjorie Senechal dismissed it also.

In fact, Pauling on one occasion at least gave proof of his fairness toward women. Professor Jack Roberts of the California Institute of Technology tells the story of a young graduate student, Dorothy Seminol, who had applied to Caltech, but had initially been rejected. Undaunted, she appealed to Pauling and his liberal sympathies. Pauling promptly cracked a hole in Caltech's long-standing barrier against women. Though he had not given the issue much thought previously, he was very moved by her plight and did persuade Caltech to change Institute policy long enough to let her in. According to Professor Jack Roberts, "it was a remarkable performance on his and Caltech's part."[24]

In addition, Pauling's attitude toward his wife demonstrates the respect he has always had for intelligence and professional competence—sex notwithstanding.

Others did not follow Pauling's example. In fact, attitudes towards women in science hadn't changed much since the time of Newton and Tycho Brahe. Many times, Dorothy Wrinch was horribly and viciously patronized. Francis Schmitt, an MIT academic, wrote in March 1941 to a colleague at Washington University:

> I have a very high regard for Dr. Wrinch . . . Her originality is most refreshing and I enjoy chatting with her on biological and chemical matters. I can foresee difficulties, however, in fitting her

. . . in a department of biology . . . at MIT. It may be that she will
eventually find a solution to her problem by taking a position in
a mathematics department which will permit her to devote considerable time to her investigations on protein structure . . .

The double-talk is obvious. Schmitt doesn't think she knows
much biology and ought to stick to mathematics. The word
"chatting" is demeaning, clearly intended as a put-down.

Wrinch did not hesitate to make a few comments of her
own. In a note appended to the back of Schmitt's letter—a note
which was apparently never sent—she wrote:

> He enjoys chatting with me on biological and chemical matters.
> This is very nice. Why do I chat with such creatures . . . A solution
> to *her* problem. Apparently, the question is how to get a living for
> a woman who after all has the right to live. It never occurs to him
> that I may have a contribution to make or may even have made
> one and that it is *their* problem to see that I have the opportunity
> to do my best work under the best conditions, for the sake of the
> progress of science.

While it is clear that Pauling was not motivated by sexism,
he was doubtless influenced by academic "territorialism." Anyone
with academic experience is familiar with this phenomenon.
Academics tend to be clannish and protective of their own turf.
There is no reason to suppose that Pauling is an exception. His
lack of respect for humanistic studies such as philosophy and
his hostility toward organic chemistry are merely two examples.
(Ironically, Pauling found himself on the other side of the table
later on when the medical community, blinded by its own territorialism, refused to listen to anything he said on vitamin C
on the grounds that he was not a physician.)

After all, Dorothy Wrinch had been trained as a mathematician. Not only was mathematics a relatively weak point with
Pauling, but worse, Wrinch was studying issues outside her field.
Never mind that she had learned more than enough biology on
her own to present a major scientific challenge to Linus Pauling.

After the Pauling-Nieman paper came out, Dorothy

Wrinch's career eventually faded, as interest in the cyclol theory dwindled away in the face of further research and the gradual accumulation of evidence for Pauling's chain theory. By 1940, she was teaching chemistry at Johns Hopkins and had divorced her husband, John Nicholson.

Her best work was behind her. Eventually, she moved permanently to Amherst and did some research and lecturing at the University of Massachusetts, which was very far from being a leading center of activity in her field, unlike institutions as Johns Hopkins, Cornell, and Oxford.

History decided in favor of the chain theory rather than the cyclol model. Pauling won the battle with Wrinch. However, in 1951, to the incredulity of the scientific community and Wrinch's great delight, the cyclol structure was indeed found in a class of primitive proteins called the ergot alkaloids. Naturally Pauling was not happy with the news and called everyone he knew in order to have further details of the discovery. The furor, however, quieted as quickly as it had begun. The ergot alkaloids were not an important sub-class of proteins and did not necessitate any basic change in Pauling's chain theory. The most important proteins were neither alkaloids nor cyclols.

Even when the initial fires had died down, Pauling found himself having to deal with Wrinch intermittently for years afterward. When someone sent him new findings regarding the cyclol theory years later, Pauling replied:

> The papers that Mrs. Wrinch has published during the last few years and that I have read have not been convincing; I remember in particular a paper in which she presented an argument to show that the alpha helix could not be present in some globular proteins—hemoglobin, I think. I remember that there was a serious flaw in her argument.

But this is the sort of diffuse, vague claim that riddles the entire controversy between Wrinch and Pauling. Where was Pauling's objectivity now? Why did he refuse even the courtesy of calling her "Dr." Wrinch? It is shocking that he goes on to say "there was a serious flaw in her argument," without giving any explanation at all. Nor does he explain why her papers were "unconvincing."

Speaking *ex cathedra* is fine in speculative theology, but it has yet to be incorporated into the scientific method. Scientists, like most of us, often fail to measure up to science's standards of "objectivity." They are subject to prejudice, whimsy and caprice just as are those in other fields.

Underlying the Pauling-Wrinch dispute is the thorny philosophical issue of the epistemological status of scientific theory. In the absence of unambiguous experimental evidence, scientists do not usually speak of the "correctness" of their theories, but of the relative simplicity, elegance, or explanatory power of one theory over another. The late, cantankerous Oxford philosopher Gilbert Ryle has said that scientific laws do not represent true statements about the world, but simply rules for conducting scientific observations and drawing scientific inferences. The chain theory of protein structure, regarded in this light, draws its strength less from being "true" than from being useful.

# 7

# Molecular Medicine

AS THE DOROTHY WRINCH AFFAIR WAS WINDING DOWN, Pauling was already on the trail of other things. He was beginning to get excited about medicine. His mind wandered back to his successes with hemoglobin. He became ever more fascinated with what is now called molecular medicine.

One of the problems that had interested Landsteiner and a host of other pioneers in medicine was the vexing matter of antigen–antibody reactions, one of the prime protective mechanisms in the body and the biological basis for resisting disease. According to established knowledge, an invading organism, the antigen, can combine with a protective protein called an antibody. An antigen can be almost anything—bacteria, viruses or even dust—that will induce the formation of antibodies. For the health of the organism, the body must rid itself of the invader.

Though the nature and mechanisms involved in antigen–antibody reactions are well known today, this was not so in 1939. The information and theory of the day said that forces existed between antigens and antibodies that caused them to come together and neutralize the dangerous antigens. According to the data, these forces were the so-called "weak" forces (not related to the weak forces in nuclear theory) acting normally between molecules. They included such well-known forces as the Van der

Waals attractions, hydrogen bonds, and weak electrostatic forces.

Yet the forces Pauling had already studied and become famous for were the bonds existing between atoms *within* a molecule. These "weak" forces were a step up the architectural ladder: the bonds that hold molecules themselves together.

The problem was that the forces were not strong enough to do the work the theory required of them. They were so weak, in fact, that scientists realized that there had to be something else to help cement the bonds between molecules—something to make the antigen–antibody link more durable.

This is where Pauling began to attack the problem. There was already a notion called "complementariness" in the air. The idea had been effective in other areas of science and seemed promising here as well. Still, no one could quite make it work. The theory was logical enough: an antigen and antibody could "stick" together because their shapes fit or "complemented" one another, in much the same way that a lock fits or "complements" the key for which it has been designed. The surfaces of both antigen and antibody would remain in very close proximity at all points. That way, the weak forces would at least all be pulling the molecules together with equal efficacy. (In noncomplementary molecules, by contrast, the surfaces would be very close together at one point, but much farther apart at another. As a result, where the surfaces were far apart, the weak forces would be acting at too great a distance to help very much.).

When Pauling got hold of the idea he ran with it: he studied the nature of molecular interactions in far greater depth than anyone previously had. Gradually, he and his researchers ironed out some of the contradictions, supported the ideas with data, and convinced the scientific world that "complementariness" was indeed the answer to certain kinds of molecular combinations. Between 1940 and 1948, Pauling and his assistants studied the chemical reactions of hundreds of substances to garner additional support for the complementariness hypothesis.

With Landsteiner's moral and theoretical knowledge and support, Pauling prepared a preliminary paper on the topic. In the July 1940 issue of *Science*, he published a paper titled "The Nature of the Intermolecular Forces Operative in Biological Processes." Yet it appeared that Pauling was still in a combative mood after the conflicts with Wrinch. The paper contributed relatively little that was positive and new. Instead, it was an all-out assault on some ideas of the German physicist Pascual Jordan, whose incursions into chemistry Pauling resented, much as he resented Dorothy Wrinch's crossing over from mathematics into his territory.

A few years earlier, Jordan had published some initially attractive ideas about biological specificity—the notion that certain things, antibodies for example, are intended for one and only one purpose. One of his ideas was that resonance would explain how chromosomes line up in the process of cell division. Pauling's sometime collaborator Max Delbruck recalled the episode:

> That was the summer of 1940. I was already at Vanderbilt, but came back to Pasadena for a few weeks . . . I met Pauling in the corridor and told him about Jordan's paper, and he went over with me to the library and we looked at it together; and he decided within five minutes that it was baloney. . . . A couple of days afterwards, I met Pauling again in the corridor, and he said, "I have written a note to *Science* about this Jordan thing and would you like to sign it too?" I was astonished. I succeeded in mitigating some of the rudest comments! I have never written a paper in which I had less part.[1]

So Pauling quickly vanquished another struggling idea, shooting from the hip as always. Pauling and Delbruck were already arguing successfully that molecular reproduction and cell division could be explained by the notion of complementariness, but there ought to have been room for a competing theory.

Yet in theorizing about cellular reproduction, Pauling was already edging from one area of medicine into another. The Pauling–Delbruck paper was an early stab into genetics. It could be considered the first of Pauling's publications to suggest that the gene was composed of two mutually complementary molecules. His fascination with the gene deepened throughout the war years and only increased in its intensity in peacetime. Pauling was already quite completely and irreversibly embroiled in medicine—a path that would lead him to the greatest controversy and most consuming frustration of his career.

It was at about this time that Pauling got one of his occasional bad ideas. It revolved around some of his newer speculations about antigen–antibody reactions. Part of the work involved the notion that antibodies are "fastened" to antigens by proteins curling up around them. Yet this idea was faulty. Pauling had assumed, in his research, that the area of an antibody that combines with an antigen had the same sequence of amino acid residues. But as he explained it later, in the article "Fifty Years of Progress In Structural Chemistry and Molecular Biology":

> It is now known, of course, that antibodies with different specificities have different sequences of amino-acid residues in the chains that produce the combining regions, so that my assumption that antibodies have the same sequence of amino-acid residues is known to be wrong.[2]

And he soon had to retreat to the notion of complementariness to explain antigen reactions. As James Bonner of the California Institute of Technology recalled:

> Linus's bad ideas are better than most people's good ones. But it took him a long time to let go of this one though; he had a feeling, I think, that something was not right about this whole antigen–antibody business . . . Linus then got the chemistry division to appoint someone from the University of Chicago who was an immunologist, specifically to work on this matter, to see if antibodies are held to antigens in this way. They got nowhere, though the fellow was around here another thirty years or so. I recall about seven or eight years ago, I walked in on Dan [Campbell] and there they were, arms around each other's necks consoling each other about something—maybe the fact that the antigen–antibody business did not work![3]

Soon, even the nature of the gene was not enough to satisfy Pauling's restless intellect. He wanted to know more than its gross structure. He wanted to understand the molecule on its finest level. That led to his all-consuming attention to the nature of the deoxyribonucleic acid (DNA) molecule. Coupled with his growing thirst for the Nobel Prize, his entry into the legendary DNA "race" was now inevitable (the question of whether it can correctly be described as a "race" will be dealt with in Chapter 10).

Yet he was not quite ready to abandon his work on the chemical bond. Unquestionably, his most important single publication in this period and, arguably, in his entire career, was a reworking of the paper "The Nature of the Chemical Bond," first published ten years earlier. By adding six more essays, Pauling turned a brilliant early study into an epochal book. It immediately became a classic, eventually being translated into every important scientific language on earth. Though many of his ideas have naturally been superceded by newer research, the book is still referred to today and a substantial part of the theory remains valid.

Many of the concepts Pauling added to the book developed out of conversations and correspondence with students and colleagues. He had, by 1935, begun to better understand, for example, the structure of the nitrogenous compounds when his studies of $NO_3F$ produced some evidence that the compound could have a tetrahedral structure. Also, his understanding of the phenomenon of hydrogen bonding (where a hydrogen atom is shared between two oxygen atoms in water, thereby forming a feeble link between adjoining molecules) grew, as he began to realize that such bonding was critically important in the architecture of protein molecules. Along with his colleague Alfred Mirsky at Caltech, he was now able to theorize that the phenomenon of protein denaturation was due to the breakdown of the polypeptide chain which, in turn, was caused by the rupture of hydrogen bonds. (Not to imply that Pauling "discovered" the hydrogen bond: in fact, the great physical chemist Maurice Huggins had come to that notion years earlier. Pauling and others further developed the idea.) Also, under the influence of other chemists, such as Sidgwick and W.A. Noyes, he began to appreciate the fact that the hydrogen bond is not exclusively ionic, but resonates between several structures (i.e., between $F - H +$ $F -$ , $F - H \ F -$ and $F - H - F$) all of which was reflected in *The Nature of the Chemical Bond.*

He formulated many of these ideas out of contact with faculty and students at Cornell University, where he had given the George Fisher Baker lectures in 1937. With the inspiration of the awesomely beautiful Cascadilla Gorge and Buttermilk Falls of Cornell and its environs, Pauling poured himself into work on *The Nature of the Chemical Bond.* After the failure of his antigen–antibody research, he needed to return to the least controversial and most consistently satisfying and successful work of his career. The result was vintage Pauling: little mathematics and dollops of raw, intuitive genius. He admitted this in the preface:

> For a long time I have been planning to write a book on the structure of molecules and crystals and the nature of the chemical bond. . . . I formed the opinion that, even though much of the recent progress in structural chemistry has been due to quantum mechanics, it should be possible to describe the new developments in a thorough-going and satisfactory manner without the use of advanced mathematics.[4]

He succeeded masterfully. The chapter on hydrogen bonding, for example, is accessible to those with just the most basic training in science and chemistry. It is the most successful exposition of Pauling's approach to structural chemistry: make a guess at what the structure might be, and then test that guess against the experimental evidence. It is ironic that in so describing his methods, Pauling gave hope and direction to the then very young Watson and Crick in their quest for the structure of the DNA molecule. To unravel the structure of the most important molecule in the universe, the scientists merely had to follow the methods laid out by Pauling.

The reviews of the book were good, if not unequivocal in their praise. Professor Joe Mayer of the University of Chicago, for example, commended Pauling's presentation of the material for its "lucidity." And while Mayer applauds "the skillful method by which the author avoids mathematical complications . . . ,"[5] he does raise some serious problems—problems that have always plagued Pauling's approach to science. Mayer's chief complaint was that Pauling promoted his own views at the expense of other approaches, even though the corpus of evidence had not yet decided in his favor.

One controversy had to do with the way chemical bonding was treated. In the book, Pauling favored his own approach, the "valence bond" theory. In doing that, he neglected the alternative "molecular orbital" approach. As Mayer wrote:

> The author has definitely limited the discussion to only one, namely the "Heitler–London–Slater–Pauling" approach to the problem. It is entirely possible that this H–L–S–P method is the best and most powerful single viewpoint for the self-consistent discussion of the variety of problems treated. . . . [however] various examples appear in which a recourse to the Hund–Huckel–Mulliken method [the molecular orbital approach] would have clarified certain points considerably.[6]

The suggestion is heard now and again that Pauling didn't know the molecular orbital approach. It is a tempting speculation, since this approach was mathematically far more complicated than valence bond theory. Pauling had done wonderful things with the valence bond approach with little more than a slide rule. However, Professor Jack Roberts of Caltech says, "Linus certainly knew molecular orbital theory. In fact he even made his own contributions during the war years, though they were less important than some of his other work and aren't much talked about today."[7]

In all likelihood, this tendency toward bias and self-promotion in *The Nature of the Chemical Bond* got in Pauling's way. Had he treated the alternatives more even-handedly, the book would have been an even greater testimony to his genius. Underneath Mayer's praise we can hear a note of gentle criticism: "It appears likely that the H–L–S–P method will entirely eclipse, in the minds of chemists, the single electron molecular orbital picture, not primarily by virtue of its great applicability or usefulness, but solely by the brilliance of its presentation."[8] In other words, Pauling's showmanship, erudition, and clarity might serve to keep one approach in the limelight while obscuring other, possibly better approaches. (In retrospect the molecular orbital method has proven to be the more useful approach particularly after the advent of high-speed computers in the 1960s. Interesting, however, the valence-bond approach still has its advocates in the chemistry department at Caltech, where the noted quantum chemist, William Goddard, is applying the method to study the new high-temperature superconductors.) This side of Pauling was evident early on when as a graduate student he failed to give Maurice Huggins proper credit for the one paper they published together; it surfaced again in his treatment of Dorothy Wrinch.

Criticisms of his methods notwithstanding, Pauling's eminence as a chemist continued to grow, as did the reputation of the chemistry division of the California Institute of Technology. Students, scientists, and post-doctoral candidates flocked to the department from all over the world. Data accumulated rapidly in Pauling's laboratory. He was beginning to look into the literature on sickle-cell anemia—a natural offshoot of his fascination with blood and hemoglobin as the vehicles of life.

The sickle-cell work began during a dinner held in the early 1940s at which Pauling met with a number of physicians who were frustrated by their inability to cope with the disease. One physician had recently lost a patient afflicted with it. Knowing of Pauling's earlier work with hemoglobin, he hoped that Pauling might come up with a treatment. Pauling said he would look into it.

Scarcely had he begun, however, when all work ceased because the United States entered into World War II.

LINUS PAULING, in his
Oregon Agricultural College
yearbook, 1922. Pauling
tied for second place in the
Interclass Oratorical
Contest.

ARNOLD SOMMERFIELD with Niels Bohr, Lund, Sweden, 1919. As early as 1925, Pauling impressed Sommerfield, and Pauling and his wife of two years journeyed to Munich so that he could study at Sommerfield's Institute of Theoretical Physics. *Photo courtesy of the Margrethe Bohr Collection, the Niels Bohr Library, the American Institute of Physics.*

LINUS PAULING with his son, Peter, 1931. Pauling is probably wearing his Lang-muir Prize medal, bestowed on him by the American Chemical Society. *Photo courtesy of the Goudsmit Collection, the Niels Bohr Library, the American In-stitute of Physics.*

LINUS PAULING with his wife, Ava Helen, and their son, Linus, Jr., after their trip to Europe. *Photo courtesy of the Uhlenbeck Collection, the Niels Bohr Library, the American Institute of Physics.*

LINUS AND AVA HELEN PAULING with Linus, Jr. and Peter, 1931. *An Associated Press photo, courtesy of the Oregon Historical Society.*

DOROTHY WRINCH (*far right*) shows a model of her cyclol structure to Dr. Katherine Blodgett (*far left*) of the G.E. Research Laboratory and Dr. Wanda K. Farr of the Boyd Thompson Institute at the G.E. Research Laboratory, Schenectady, New York, November 1936. This photograph was taken in the midst of the "competition" between Pauling and Wrinch over the nature of the chemical bond. *Photo courtesy of the Dorothy Wrinch Papers, the Sophia Smith Collection, Smith College, and Joseph Schenkman of Schenkman Books.*

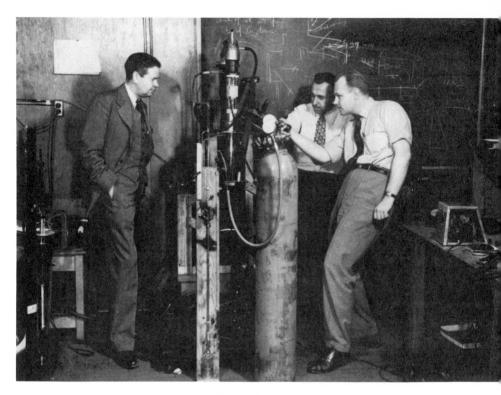

JOHN SLATER *(far right)*, 1948. Slater tried to lure Pauling to the Massachusetts Institute of Technology in early 1931. After some consideration, Pauling accepted only a temporary appointment from 1931–1932, and then returned to the California Institute of Technology. *Photo courtesy of the MIT Museum.*

HERMAN J. MULLER working with two lab assistants, preparing fly flood, 1949. Muller was a Noble Prize winning geneticist. He and Pauling had been on friendly terms, but gradually, political differences created a rift between them, and they began criticizing each other in print. *Photo courtesy of the Lilly Library, Indiana University, Bloomington, Indiana.*

LINUS PAULING in 1949, at the height of his groundbreaking work on hemoglobin and sickle cell anemia. *Photo courtesy of the Oregon Historical Society.*

Linus Pauling with his daughter, Linda, and Dr. Ballantine, President of Reed College, 1954. Pauling gave the commencement address at his daughter's graduation. *Photo courtesy of the Oregon Historical Society.*

ALBERT EINSTEIN, 1936. Einstein came to Pauling's defense when Pauling was denied a passport in 1952. *Photo courtesy of the Niels Bohr Library, the American Institute of Physics.*

LINUS PAULING with one of his structural models, 1954, just days before he was awarded the Nobel Prize for Chemistry. *Photo courtesy of the Oregon Historical Society.*

Five of the seven Nobel Prize winners, Stockholm, Sweden, 1954. Left to right, Dr. Thomas Weller, Dr. Max Born, Dr. Frederick C. Robbins, Dr. John Enders, Dr. Linus Pauling. *Photo courtesy of the Oregon Historical Society.*

# *8*

# The War Years

THE WAR YEARS MAY HAVE BEEN THE MOST IMPORTANT years of Pauling's life. For one thing, his interest in molecular medicine and biology escalated sharply. For another, he became deeply interested in politics for the first time in his life. Explanations of the birth of Pauling the politician have been varied and bewildering. Certainly Ava Helen played some role—she had always been at least marginally interested in politics. She had been particularly impressed with Franklin Roosevelt when, soon after taking office in 1933, he began formulating laws to help the unemployed.

With Ava Helen's influence and support—and she could be a most formidable and convincing spokesman for any cause— Pauling could not resist the lure of politics.

Caring deeply for the nation and for the suffering and injustice he saw about him, he volunteered his services and his laboratory to the government. In his patriotic fervor and consummate hatred of fascism, he did not discourage his students from going off to war. Many never returned. His son Linus, not yet eighteen, enlisted in the Air Corps, which naturally caused Pauling and Ava Helen a great deal of worry.

Increasingly, Ava Helen's energy and passion had and would effect Pauling. Almost invariably, she voted for candidates closest to a socialist philosophy. This liberal spirit had been aroused in her early in life, by a mother and father who were outspoken themselves and who sympathized with the poor and oppressed. Even today, two of her sisters still retain the critical, questioning intellects and liberal sympathies bred into the Miller family early in life.

Often, she had felt the assaults on Pauling as deeply as Pauling himself. On the occasion of his "Meet the Press" interview, she had, according to Rae Goodell in *The Visible Scientists* ". . . become very irritated with Lawrence Spivak . . . after the show was over . . . got out of her chair and started after Spivak. "He could run faster than she could, so she didn't succeed in catching up with him. He got down . . . and out the door." For years, also, she corresponded and worked closely with the noted peace activist, the Reverend A.J. Muste. She sympathized with the Pacific League (later accused of being a "communist front"), devoted years to the Women's International League for Peace and Freedom and dedicated much of her time and energies to the American Civil Liberties Union, serving as a board member in the Los Angeles branch for several years. She had also given lectures on peace and human rights in the United States and nearly forty foreign nations. In recognition of her work with the ACLU she was honored, on November 1, 1981 at the Santa Catalina School in Monterey. The ACLU spokesperson described her as one

> whose concern for justice and freedom has spanned the era from the Sacco/Vanzetti case in the 1920s to the present time . . . who spoke out against the internment of Japanese-Americans in 1942 . . . challenged the inquisitorial committees of Congress in the 1950s and . . . who has remained steadfast despite the harassment of bigots and witch hunters through the hot and cold wars of her time.

As Ava Helen and Pauling became more politically active, Pauling virtually abandoned his most interesting scientific work for the duration of the war. The sickle-cell research, the quest for the alpha-helix, and the ultimate solution to protein architecture languished in limbo for ten years. He became a vocal supporter of the New Deal—so much so that he made speeches supporting FDR during his re-election campaign in 1937. They were the first genuinely political speeches of his career.

Pauling's plunge into the miasma of politics amazed everyone. Edward Hughes of the Caltech faculty didn't hesitate to say how he felt about Pauling and the numerous journalists who so cavalierly accused Pauling of leftist leanings.

> I had really never seen Linus talk much about politics at all before this, but then it took as much of his time as science did; I became curious enough that one day I finally asked him his registration. As far as I know, no newspaperman ever bothered to look that up. Pauling's answer was, "You know, I'm ashamed of it, but the first time I registered to vote, I registered as a Republican, and I voted for Hoover in 1932."[1]

This is accurate, but the allegiance did not last long. In 1929, with the advent of the Stock Market crash, economic depression had set in throughout the world. Businesses failed, many people were homeless and many others committed suicide. But with the election of Franklin D. Roosevelt in 1933, laws were passed to provide at least some employment—in government hospitals, theaters, on construction crews, anywhere work could be found. That was the so-called "New Deal." Up to this point, though Ava Helen had been active politically, Pauling himself was immersed in science. But under his wife's influence, and in reaction to the obvious suffering he saw about him, his political allegiances began to swing. By the end of Roosevelt's first year in office, Pauling was a Rooseveltian Democrat. When he changed his affiliation, he was fervid about it and his drift toward the left had begun. Soon, Pauling and Millikan were to be seen in the hallways of Crellin, locked in debate over various political conundrums. Presidential candidates were often the topic of their discussions. The legendary Tuesday and Thursday morning meetings had virtually dissolved by this point because of the war, but the Pauling-Millikan debates provided a small compensation. The sight of these apostles of science battling furiously, armed with data, studies, and frequent jibes, was not a spectacle anyone at Caltech was liable to miss.

But Pauling's leap into politics can, in the final analysis, be traced to a private rather than a public upheaval. He probably never would have become involved had it not been for a disease that nearly cost him his life, and the devotion of the doctor who saved him. Here lies the real seed of Pauling's political awakening. In the fall of 1940, he became terribly ill with glomerulo nephritis, commonly called Bright's Disease. It began insidiously. He complained, on and off, of feeling "tired" and "washed out." Ava Helen immediately became concerned, but Pauling dismissed his symptoms as merely due to "overwork." Soon, coworkers began to notice a change in his complexion. His usual ruddiness was gone and he was moving and working more slowly than usual. Pauling finally agreed to an examination, only to hear the gloomy diagnosis.

Though it is manageable these days, nephritis was considered a dangerous disease in 1941. Everyone expected Pauling to die; his kidneys were highly inflamed. Pauling's old friend and reviewer Joe Mayer tried to sound an encouraging note in a July 16 letter to Ava Helen: "Since Linus wrote me about three months ago that he had nephritis, we have not heard directly how he is. Several people have been asked here and we hope that his recovery has been rapid."

Ava Helen's reply on August 12 was cautiously optimistic, although family friends said she was desperately worried. She told Mayer:

> This is a very slow business, you know, and we can't expect any very rapid change. He stays in bed a good bit but manages to get a good amount of work done. He lectured in Chicago for a month during the summer term and didn't seem to suffer any ill effect. He will have to remain on this restricted salt-free diet and remain as physically quiet as possible.

His physician, Dr. Addis, did put a lot of weight on nutrition. Certainly this influenced Pauling to head in the direction of nutritional research later on. Thirty years later, he acknowledged his debt to his physician and the regimen that saved his life: "I was essentially put on a low-protein diet with no meat, to rest the kidney. The physician [Addis] also said that I should take supplementary vitamins, one of which was vitamin C. I don't know really how much I took, but it was probably 100 grams per day."[2]

Addis was considered an extremely good man in his field, Pauling having heard of him through his vast network of contacts in science. Addis was also a great admirer of Pauling and devoted himself assiduously to his patient for the next four or five years. He came by train to Pasadena once a week at least, just to check on Pauling's progress. Professor Koepfli of the University of California, Pauling's old friend and confidante, observed, "It was an incredible relationship and it probably saved Linus' life, there's little question about it."[3]

Addis was also a communist. Because of his leftist politics, he had been having difficulties for years, being declared a security risk by the State Department even before the anti-communist fervor of the 1950s. His influence on Pauling was unmistakable: the psychological shock of witnessing the abuse, vilification, and ostracism of the man who, quite literally, had saved his life was too much for Pauling to bear. Pauling took a quantum leap in his political commitments: Rooseveltian principles were now too far to the right for him.

One incident during the early 1940s seems to have confirmed Pauling in his new leftist leanings. The internment of Japanese-Americans had begun around this time. Ever the dissenter and crusader, Ava Helen adamantly determined to retain their Japanese-American gardener. Pauling offered no resistance to the idea, which, given the circumstances, could be seen as a political gesture. But in 1943, with Pearl Harbor fresh in people's minds, trouble came in the form of a hate note. Peter Pauling had just fed the rabbits: suddenly, he burst through the back door in terror; written in red on the garage door was the sentence "Americans die, but we love japs."

That was hardly the end of it. Anonymous phone calls and threatening letters followed. The family was torn with fear and rage, yet the Paulings stood firm. Undaunted, they kept the gardener on until he left on his own, when he was called back to Fort Shelby as a U.S. Army inductee. Nonetheless, the episode left its mark.

So affected was Pauling that, for a while, he considered a radical restructuring of his life. Certainly this trauma escalated his interest in politics. Pauling himself says that up to that time he had been far less politically active than his wife. He involved himself more with Ava Helen's efforts, via the ACLU, to prevent the internment of Japanese-Americans. For the time being he also continued his scientific work, even garnering the William H. Nichols prize of the New York section of the American Chemical Society in 1941, "for his distinguished and pioneer work on the application of quantum mechanics to chemistry and on the size and shape of molecules."[4] Such prizes are given not for any one discovery or piece of research, but for laudable patterns of consistent, first-class work. Still, Professor Arthur Hixson of Columbia, chairman of the committee which bestowed the prize, saw fit to note his work on interatomic distances, and the forces operating in that domain. In the committee's words:

> It was Dr. Pauling who discovered that a radius of activity could be assigned to each atom; that is, there is a definite amount of space "filled" by each atom with its force . . . Dr. Pauling has originated methods of accounting for such forces and consequently of explaining in part some of the erratic properties of atoms.[5]

Nevertheless, Pauling's anger over the incident of the gardener and the lukewarm support from the authorities continued to gnaw at him. He felt they could have done more, could have been more supportive. As Ava Helen explained years later, "The authorities wouldn't do anything about it, although my husband was doing war work at the time."[6] (Actually, the local sheriff did place a guard, but the Paulings felt that not enough had been done to apprehend the culprit.)

While his interest in politics was growing, Pauling still kept an eye on the practical side of life. In the fall of 1941, he began a series of discussions with the Shell Oil Company. They, in turn, were impressed with the Nichols Prize and decided to make an attempt to convince Pauling to work in their laboratories. Pauling seriously considered the offer. On October 13, J.F. Taylor of Shell wrote Pauling:

> I quite understand the importance you attach to your prior engagement for October 25 . . . I think your decision as to whether or not you wish to accept my offer is going to hinge almost entirely on your own estimate of the interest and challenge of the job at Emeryville, and will hardly be swayed . . . by meeting some more Shell executives at lunch.

It was not an offer he could easily spurn. For one thing, considerable money was involved. Secondly, he would be granted virtually everything he wanted in terms of research facilities, an issue about which Millikan had not been overly generous. Wrestling mightily with the decision, he wrote Millikan on October 2:

> . . . I must decide within a few weeks whether or not to accept appointment as Director of Research of the Shell Development Company. The position has many attractive features. . . . In order that I may have knowledge of my probable future at the Institute, if I remain here, I would like to have the Board of Trustees consider the following three questions. (1) The discrepancy between my present salary, $9,000, and that offered, $25,000 weighs heavily with me. (2) The future support of our work needs consideration. (3) I have hoped to expand our work toward the field of medicine.

Pauling was trying, reasonably enough, to write his own ticket. In the end he decided against the offer. Millikan, though not pleased, eventually granted most of what Pauling wanted. More research money appeared although, according to Ernest Swift of the Caltech faculty, it never quite matched the Emeryville offer.

Most likely, Pauling was just not the industrial type. Professor Edward Hughes of Caltech indicated that the decision to abandon the Shell offer appeared less difficult to Pauling once he really thought about it:

> The scientific environment [at Shell] simply wasn't right for Linus, and he knew it. For one thing, you don't have much freedom to do what you want in those places, your own research and all that; there were pretty severe restrictions on publication too. Anything that was patentable couldn't be published until it was patented, since they didn't want their competitors to know what they were working on.[7]

Although the salary may initially have tempted him, Pauling was not so concerned about money as to make that his deciding factor. Besides, he could not stomach the idea that corporate bigwigs would tell him what and where he should research. In later years, his famed distaste for authority would be his very best defense against the charge that he was, as Louis Budenz put it, a "disciplined member of the Communist Party."

It may be, however, that Pauling came as close as he did to accepting the Shell offer only because he wasn't getting his "real" scientific work done anyway. As the war effort expanded, Pauling and the California Institute jettisoned project after project to devote all their energies to defeating fascism. As James Bonner of Caltech said tersely, "The war sure raised hell with this place." Almost daily, memos flooded Millikan's office in 1942, urging the faculty and staff to tackle this or that practical military problem.

Everyone was behind the effort, including Linus Pauling. In a document entitled "Memorandum on National Defense," the faculty of Caltech declared that "we have volunteered [our] personal services to assist the government in the present world emergency to the utmost of [our] abilities . . . Every member of the Institute is exploring where his special knowledge and training can be useful."

So, instead of examining chemical bonding and molecular architecture, Pauling was concentrating his energies on improving gunpowder, measuring oxygen pressure in submarines, and devising better liquid propellants. Caltech even found itself devoting its resources to making better scrambled eggs for troops in the field. But some non-military research continued: a new nutrition program was developed by the renowned biochemist Henry Borsook. In a short time, such industrial giants as Lockheed and North America Aviation had contributed upwards of $60,000 to study the dietary habits of the American people. Though Pauling was not directly involved in this nutrition program, it did interest him and probably contributed to his later interest in nutritional research. Borsook made quite a fuss over the role of vitamin C in human nutrition. In the archives of the program, Borsook claimed at one point that vitamin C was "the most serious deficiency in the . . . diet. It is difficult to obtain enough vitamin C when the consumption of citrus fruit or tomatoes is low."[8]

Still, it would be a mistake to suppose that Pauling totally abandoned his theoretical interests during the war years. In fact, he had done a nice little piece of scientific legerdemain in attempting to create a synthetic antibody against a particularly virulent type of pneumonia, the so-called "type III" pneumonia virus. A public announcement of this work first appeared in the August 1942 issue of the *Journal of Experimental Medicine*. This project again involved the idea of "complementariness"—the notion that two dissimilarly shaped molecules could alter their form and fit together, thereby altering chemical reactions in the body.

The result was supposed to be a man-made antibody. This was the really striking part of the theory. As far back as 1911, Russian scientists had made some horse serum which stimulated antibodies for diptheria, and the Germans subsequently patented the Russian concept, though the idea of synthetic antibodies had never reached the practical stage.

Pauling thought he had made a breakthrough. He thought he had, for the first time in history, made antibodies outside an animal body. It didn't work, any more than some of his earlier ideas about antigen–antibody reactions had. As Verner Schomaker of the University of Washington summed it up: "He thought he had made antibodies in vitro, but it was all pretty much on the wrong track."[9]

Pauling was profoundly and deeply disappointed. This was the most interesting work he had done since the beginning of the war effort. However, it was a consolation that the idea of complementariness *generally*—if not this specific application—was sound, and survived to play numerous and varied roles in medicine and molecular biology.

Stung by the uneven course of this project, he confined his research during the remainder of the war years to the oxygen meter, rocket explosives, and other hum-drum technological innovations.

Though his scientific work ambled along dryly and unspectacularly, his political awareness was growing. One important influence was the great physicist J. Robert Oppenheimer. The relationship between Pauling and Oppenheimer, whose work on the Manhattan Project forever changed the world, has always been mysterious. Both were home-grown American scientists and each had fought his way out of a humble background to the very summit of world science. Both were stubborn and had strong leftist inclinations.

Despite these similarities, tensions existed between the two men periodically throughout their careers. Although Oppenheimer had actually invited Pauling to join his group and run the chemistry section of the legendary Manhattan Project early on during the war years, Pauling had declined. Why he did so is not completely clear. In a documentary aired on "Nova" in 1977, the narrator, Robert Vaughn, suggested that Pauling had "his own work to do."[10] Pauling has never wished to talk about it.

Certainly he would not have let the routine scientific work of the war years keep him from participating in the Manhattan Project. There had to be another reason. Most likely, his suspicions of the atomic bomb were a factor—a speculation later confirmed by his famous activism for a nuclear test-ban treaty in the 1950s.

Most of the time, however the two men were on good terms. In fact, Pauling's most prized mineral collection was given him by Oppenheimer. In a letter to Oppenheimer on the 3rd of November, 1954, when Oppenheimer was at MIT, Pauling's colleague at Caltech, Charles Coryell, wrote, thanking Oppenheimer for his assistance in formulating a petition in support of Pauling's Nobel Prize:

> Thank you for your help in supporting Pauling. I doubt that many Nobel Prizes have been so popular with the masses . . . Out of 86 approached, 86 signed without hesitation and almost all are delighted that this Nobel Prize embarrasses the State Department. Your moral victory raised spirits in the Universities and the National Labs, and Pauling gets some of the fruits for the beating he has had to take since 1948.

Pauling himself returned this favor when Oppenheimer's "loyalty" to the United States was questioned. In 1954 the Atomic Energy Commission found that Oppenheimer should not be retained as a consultant to the commission. Pauling spoke out about the case:

> I am deeply concerned by the lack of clear thinking shown in the report . . . If it were not for the fact that I discern in the statements and actions of many of our leaders in Washington a similar inability to think clearly, I would say that the people who appointed the committee had just had bad luck in their appointments.[11]

To better understand Pauling's (and Caltech's) complex relationships with Oppenheimer, it is necessary to look back a few years. Caltech itself had, early on, been friendly toward Oppenheimer, at least for a while. Oppenheimer had been at Caltech in the 1927–1928 academic year as a Fellow of the Institute and, after studying at the University of Leiden in the Netherlands and in Zurich in the 1928–1929 academic year, returned again to Caltech. He left in the early 1940s to join the Manhattan Project.

Yet, scarcely had he left when Caltech, with Pauling's moral support, began trying to lure Oppenheimer back. Thus as early as August 31, 1941, Millikan wrote Oppenheimer and offered

him a position at Caltech, arguing that ". . . at the last meeting
. . . I was authorized to go up to a salary for you of $10,000, the
same as the offer made to Thomas Hunt Morgan when he left
Columbia to come here."[12]

Of course, phrases like that are diplomatically disastrous.
In effect, Millikan was saying that what was good enough for
Morgan should be good enough for Oppenheimer. Oppenheimer, however, was not renowned for his humility, and may well
have resented the implication that he was not worth more than
Morgan. However, Millikan really did want him, and he used
Pauling's presence as an inducement: "Pauling, Yost, Borsook
and their helpers want to add their talents to a joint program
with physics on the applications of nuclear changes to chemical
and biological research developments. . . ."

But by 1945, all bets were cancelled. It was not until later
in that year, after the first atom-bomb exploded at Alamagordo,
New Mexico in July of 1945, that Caltech was finally able to
snare Oppenheimer with the offer of a fulltime professorship.
Since he doubtless sensed his importance, Oppenheimer's commitment to the California Institute of Technology was less than
total, and he spent much class time discussing leftist politics.
The historian Jamie Sayen, in his excellent work, *Einstein in
America* points out that, in fact, several members of Oppenheimer's family also were involved with leftist politics, including
his brother Frank and his wife Kitty, who had been a "fellow
traveler" during the Spanish Civil War. Furthermore, Oppenheimer spent most of his year at Caltech in Washington since
he continued to serve as a government adviser on the use of
nuclear weaponry. In this capacity, he co-authored the Acheson-
Lilienthal Report on control of nuclear weapons.

Such activity proved to be a growing irritant for Millikan.
He may have been able to tolerate Oppenheimer's politics, as he
tolerated Pauling's. But there was, in addition to his continual
absence from Pasadena, some question about his approach to
research and teaching, which was raised by Pauling. Pauling's
feelings toward Oppenheimer cooled, despite their good relationship earlier. In a June 1945 letter by Millikan to Pauling's

old mentor, Richard Tolman, then at the National Defense Research Committee in Washington, Millikan describes Pauling as objecting both scientifically and pedagogically to Oppenheimer:

> ... although the theoretical physicist in cosmic rays is becoming something of a nuisance because he strings out interminable articles in the *Physical Review* and may start with incorrect ... postulates, Oppenheimer is at least one of the good men in that field ... The negative side is that he is not a good teacher, was charged in Berkeley with holding extreme views, and according to Pauling has not exerted a wholesome influence on some of his younger co-workers. Pauling told me that both he himself and Ernest Lawrence had at times harbored doubts of the character of his influence on younger associates.

It was a disappointing time for Pauling, and the gift of a mineral collection hardly compensated for his disillusionment and disappointment with Oppenheimer. This is difficult to understand, since the tone of Pauling's objections to Oppenheimer appear political, even though Pauling's own politics seem to have been in line with Oppenheimer's (even at this point in his career, Oppenheimer's politics were definitely left of center.), However, this is not necessarily true of Pauling at this early point in his career. There is some evidence that in his early years, he was primarily apolitical; to the extent that politics interested him, he actually leaned slightly to the right (e.g., he voted for Hoover). It was really after Pearl Harbor that Pauling, with the influence of Ava Helen, became involved in politics and began to move toward the political left.

However, there is still another hypothesis which may explain his objection to Oppenheimer. The latter was always a mysterious man and by no means the archetypical specialist. He was well-read in literature, philosophy, the classics, and could even read Sanskrit, thus enabling him to study Hindu literature in its original language. Such matters were alien to Pauling, and he had little regard for them.

There is still a more specific theory: Oppenheimer was well

known to have close relationships with his students. Often, he would take long walks with them, reciting from Hindu classics such as the Bhagavad-Gita. The students were mesmerized by Oppenheimer to the extent that they, like the followers of Ludwig Wittgenstein in the same time period, would adopt his mannerisms and speech inflections and even follow him to Caltech after he left Berkeley.

Pauling, by contrast, though he had, in his own way, a captivating effect on students, kept considerable professional distance from them. It is quite possible that his objections to Oppenheimer were thus more methodological than political: he simply felt that Oppenheimer's methods were not suited to effective, dispassionate teaching. In spite of Pauling's own leftist sympathies later in life, he did make it a point, throughout his career, to keep his political and scientific work separate, and certainly to keep his politics out of the classroom.

In any case, Pauling clearly had serious doubts about Oppenheimer's value to a university community. It is conceivable that he had such doubts when he declined Oppenheimer's offer to work on the Manhattan Project.

As we have seen Pauling was relatively inactive politically at this point, compared to Oppenheimer and conservative physicist Edward Teller (the "father of the hydrogen bomb"), but he would begin to catch up very soon. New forces, visible and extremely important, were at work in postwar America—forces which would soon radically change Pauling's political consciousness and catapult him and Ava Helen directly onto the political scene. Foremost among these was the Scientists Movement, whose aims and goals are inexorably intertwined with the name of Leo Szilard, who was then at the Met Lab in Chicago. It is a testimony to the far-sightedness of the leading scientists of the day that even before the cataclysms in Europe had officially died, they were already beginning to worry about the ominous threat of atomic annihilation.

As with so many of these scientists, Szilard's position had shifted. He had, on the one hand, been one of the small group of scientists who persuaded Einstein to write his fateful letter to Roosevelt urging the establishment of the Manhattan Project and ultimately, the atomic bomb. After the war, however, Szilard became a zealot in the effort to halt any further use of atomic weapons, a quest he pursued until the day of his death in 1964.

While Szilard was busy trying to set up this or that ad hoc committee in his pursuit of control over nuclear power, the Scientists Movement was certainly his brainchild. If any official date can be assigned to its birth, we might give it as 1944, at the famed Met Lab, which was under the direction of Physicist Arthur H. Compton, another colleague of Pauling's. The Movement advocated: "the necessity for all nations to make every effort to cooperate now in setting up an international administration with police powers which can effectively control at least the means of nucleonic warfare."

Also, in 1944, physicist Zay Jeffries headed a committee to study the uses of nuclear physics. Once this important report was released, scientists at the Lab devoted increasingly larger amounts of time to the implications of atomic energy for the future of mankind. According to John Simpson, a scientist and member of the group, many of the staff "became very concerned with formulating ideas on the use of the bomb and its influence upon the attainment of international control of the weapon." Soon, many of the most heralded scientists of the world were attracted to the movement with, of course, the exception of the politically conservative Edward Teller. Oppenheimer, Hans Bethe, Harold Urey, Eugene Wigner, and the wily physicist and presidential advisor, Robert Bacher, were all sympathetic. In addition to academic supporters, the movement also included such government luminaries as Vannevar Bush and James Conant.

Pauling, too, was drawn to the spirit of the movement. The presence of Bethe and Bacher probably influenced him: Bethe, because his genius was so great, and Bacher, brilliant too, who was also from the California Institute of Technology.

Of all these men, certainly the one who loomed most menacingly over Pauling's public life throughout the 1950s was Vannevar Bush. His initial relations with Bush were cordial and uncomplicated. On January 4, 1945, Bush wrote Pauling to tell him his President needed him:

A short time ago the President called upon me for reports upon several subjects . . . One of these questions has to do with the entire future of medical research in this country. . . . . it has been decided that the best possible way is to create a special committee to devote its attention to the matter . . . The committee on Medical Research has given me a list of suggestions for the constitution of the committee, including the chairman. Your name is in this group and I am therefore writing to you at once to ask you to serve as a member of this committee.

Pauling was thoroughly and completely delighted. He immediately dropped what he was doing to race down the hall and tell the news to his old friend Ernest Swift; he then ran back to his office to phone Ava Helen. His war work was now pretty much finished and his interest in medicine had been given new life by his rapidly growing fascination with molecular disease. On January 11, just six days later, Pauling dashed off a reply: "I am very pleased to accept the appointment mentioned in your letter of January 5 as a member of the special committee which will devote its attention to the question of the future of medical research in this country."

It was a new frontier—a perfect complement to the frontiersman in Linus Pauling. Responding within a week was unusual for Pauling. He often answered letters in a leisurely fashion, perhaps in order to demonstrate nonchalance and indifference. There were no games this time. Pauling had been fighting for money and power in the area of medical research ever since he'd asked Millikan to improve his position at Caltech, at the time of the offer from Shell Oil. Here was his chance.

Critics did not overlook the political overtones of Pauling's appointment. They charged the presence of a hidden agenda— that concern over the future of medicine was not the only thing on his mind. To many, the appointment merely afforded Pauling a chance to enhance his own prestige. In later years, of course, when his political involvements had deepened, the charges of self-glorification and power-seeking grew to thunderous levels. At worst, he was called a dupe of the Communist Party. The less extreme of his critics called him an overly moralistic showman.

# 9

# Politics and the
# Postwar Years

THE SPELL WOVEN BY VANNEVAR BUSH AND THE GLAM-
our of national politics were immensely attractive to Pauling.
He continued to involve himself in quasi-political matters. Some
of the same committees that had prepared the medical research
report for Bush also suggested, in 1945, that a National Science
Foundation be set up, and that funds up to a quarter of a billion
dollars per year be earmarked for fundamental research in the
sciences. Pauling was beginning to see that scientific clout could
dovetail with political power. He championed the proposal, realizing what influence he might have as a voice known to members
of Congress. On April 19, 1983, he spoke at a meeting of the
American Chemical Society: "I urged that Congress act by setting
up [the] NSF and giving it a suitable appropriation. I also urged
that a counter-balancing fund to support basic research be set
up by the industry of the U.S., so that the field of research would
not be dominated by the federal government." This is a strikingly
conservative view for one who would be so loudly attacked in
later years as a "fellow traveler."

Yet even as he swam in the waters of national politics and
his fascination with political power deepened, Pauling could
display the greatest compassion for the ordinary man. It has
been said of Pauling that no matter how much he professed to
care for Man, he cared little for any particular man. Certain

critics have expressed the opinion that while he campaigned tirelessly to change ideas about nuclear power, while he and Ava Helen circled the globe in the vain quest for world peace, the problems and the natural rights of the individual mattered little to him. They see him engaged in a quest for immortality and power, willing to step ruthlessly over whomever gets in his way.

But there is one man, at least, who would have denied all of this: a glassblower at the California Institute of Technology whose name was Clancy. In 1945, Clancy was about to face a gloomy retirement, with little money and few friends. The faculty of the California Institute wanted to help him, and appealed to Pauling, for he alone had enough clout with Millikan to obtain results. Pauling agreed that something more should be done for Clancy and wrote Millikan on May 1:

> I am . . . taking the liberty of communicating to you an opinion which has been expressed to me by members of the Division of Chemistry and Chemical Engineering, and to which I subscribe. This opinion is that, in view of the many years of able and faithful service to the California Institute of Technology which Mr. Clancy has rendered, it would be appropriate for the California Institute to provide him with a modest annuity, to be paid throughout the period of life remaining to him.

This was Pauling at his most caring and compassionate. His colleagues took little time to back him up; on May 8, Millikan received another letter signed jointly by several members of the faculty and containing the same request. Thanks to Pauling, the suffering of Clancy's final years was to a great extent alleviated.

But while Pauling can be immensely friendly and generous to non-academics, he behaves quite differently toward his scientific opponents and political nemeses. As Pauling scholars Mildred and Victor Goertzel point out,

> Pauling may have a tendency to judge others by how completely they admire him and to withdraw from those who do very well but are not given to effusive admiration. Does Pauling have wounds too deep to heal? . . . Does he unconsciously think of

himself as a "crackpot?" As the perpetual pariah? And identify
with them? Does anyone who does well threaten him?[1]

And when threatened, he may shoot first and do more conclusive
and exhaustive research later. This is the way Pauling reacts to
criticism. As with so many scientists, or academics generally,
for that matter, once he forms an opinion, it takes a good deal
to change it. Jack Roberts of the Chemistry and Chemical Engineering Division of Caltech told me one such tale:

> [While] I was revising my book, *Basic Principles of Organic Chem-
> istry*, Verner Schomaker and I got into a problem on resonance
> . . . At the same time, Linus was revising *The Nature of the Chemical
> Bond*; so we buttonholed Linus in his office one day and said "this
> is the way we can talk about resonance without hassles." He lis-
> tened attentively and finally said, "You know, I don't like to change
> anything in *The Nature of the Chemical Bond*." That was the end
> of that session.

This is not to say that Pauling was habitually uncooperative.
As long as his personal views were not at stake he could go to
great lengths to aid in causes, even causes not directly tied to
his own work. With the war essentially over, Caltech was busy
trying to rebuild the graduate school, and Pauling helped in every
way he could. He was instrumental in persuading Millikan to
reinstitute Dr. W.V. Houston as Dean of the Graduate School.
Houston had been Dean three years earlier before leaving to
fulfill wartime responsibilities. Pauling thought highly of him
both as a scientist and an administrator. The day he realized
that Millikan was vacillating on Houston's reappointment, he
immediately barged into Millikan's office to bombard him with
innumerable reasons why Houston should be reappointed. Millikan quickly got off the fence.

Later in the summer, Pauling endorsed the idea of massive
increases in funding for medical research on a national scale.
Hardly very significant in itself, this opinion does indicate the
direction of Pauling's social and political thinking. He was not
yet close to communism, but the seed was taking root. Ava Helen

was moving closer to a Marxist position in the mid-1940s, and in a few years Pauling too would move decisively to the left (though it appears that Ava Helen was always much more radical than her husband). For example, in 1959, Cushing Strout, the E.I. White Professor of American Studies at Cornell University, shared a membership in the ACLU with Pauling and was also teaching at Caltech. At that time, the influential John Birch Society was charging that disloyal underground political activities were taking place in Pauling's laboratory.

Although politically liberal himself, Strout was an anti-communist in the spirit of the *Partisan Review* and *Commentary*. He believed, for example, with the ACLU, that communists (and other totalitarians) ought to be kept off the national policy-making board, because they tended to reject the concept of civil liberties for those who disagreed with them (e.g., they supported the Smith Law against the Trotskyites in 1941). At this point, Pauling voiced his disagreement, saying that no restrictions on membership could be made, in the name of tolerance. Thus far, the discussion had been reasonably civil and polite.

Then, Ava Helen leaped into the conversation. As Professor Strout wrote me, in July 1984:

> . . . Mrs. Pauling, something of a Madame La Farge, in my sense of her, was increasingly scornful and called my position reactionary. (In fact, the California branch of the ACLU had never accepted the national board's policy of excluding communists.) I said Norman Thomas held the same position. "He's nothing but a bourgeois reactionary!" she insisted. My wife and I soon left; the tension was rising and the impasse was clear. Pauling himself remained perfectly civil.

Despite her disagreement with its national board, Ava Helen remained an active member of the ACLU for half a century and, in fact, helped found the southern California branch. She also worked with the Women's International League for Peace and Freedom and gave lectures on human rights, peace, and nuclear testing at home and in many foreign nations.

Pauling began to suffer some ominous physical symptoms

during this period. He was having trouble working; weakness and a feeling of general malaise became more frequent. Ava Helen's greatest fear was being realized: his bout with Bright's Disease was *not* a thing of the past as she had so desperately hoped.

The disease was only simmering, however, and Pauling kept it far from his mind. He even accelerated his pace, perhaps in an unconscious attempt to outrun the disease. By 1946, theoretical science was reasserting itself in universities all over the world. The war was over and scientists could happily return to pre-war pursuits. Pauling went to one meeting after another, as scientists worked furiously to re-establish old links, tidy up research alliances, and catch up on what each other had been doing before the long interruption.

Within a few months, Pauling attended the Pacific Division meeting of the American Association for the Advancement of Science, the Chicago meeting of the American Chemical Society, and various other minor conclaves. He even found time to renew very old acquaintances, visiting with his old undergraduate professor, Dr. Fred Allen, who was then at Purdue. As W. Seagers, a graduate student at Purdue at the time recalled: "Whenever Dr. Pauling was in the vicinity he would drop in and was easily persuaded to address the graduate students on his latest research results. It was always a fascinating give-and-take session."[2]

By 1947, Pauling was still busily putting his scientific house in order—renewing contacts, getting promising graduate students into solid academic positions, and the like. He was thinking relatively little about science—much as a novelist, long away from the typewriter, might spend a few days cleaning and arranging a study. On February 17, for example, he wrote to Niels Bohr to recommend his student David Shoemaker (currently at the University of Oregon) for a position. But while he did tell Bohr about his upcoming professorship at Oxford, there was not a word about theoretical science.

Another reason for Pauling's relative standstill in science during 1947 was a complex, tedious, and not terribly profitable correspondence with the brilliant and stubborn chemist Kasmir Fajans. Fajans lit the fires when he questioned some of the conclusions in Pauling's *The Nature of the Chemical Bond*. Perhaps the only interesting aspect of this correspondence is the discussion of certain philosophical issues. Fajans charged, over and over again, that Pauling had made claims that were "metaphysical"—not based on scientific observation. In a review of Fritz Ephraim's *Inorganic Chemistry*, he says:

> In what way Pauling obtained for one equation with two unknowns the values $X = 0.15$ and $Y = 0.24$ is not said. It was probably based on the additional intuition claimed as necessary also for many other quantitative conclusions of the resonance theory. However, since none of these resonating forms has any reality, it does not make much difference.

Pauling did not wait to reply. On April 14, he wrote Fajans:

> The remarks which you make seem to me to be the result of an unrealistic and strained effort to force the discussion of molecular structure into an oversimplified pattern, with exaggerated emphasis on ionic configuration. A qualitative discussion of molecular structure is, of course, necessarily somewhat artificial.

The disagreement continued for some time, with neither side satisfying the other. On June 19, Fajans reinforced his view.

> . . . in the case of $H_2O$, one finds on p. 71 of Pauling's book a description based on the resonance viewpoint that is more detailed than it is possible to arrive at otherwise. My doubts in this respect were based on the fact that Pauling admits the arbitrariness in the use of the concept of resonance and is of the opinion (p. 12) that this is of little significance. I can hardly agree with this attitude.

Today, most chemists accept Fajans' view that resonating forms are merely "convenient" fictions which allow scientists to explain otherwise unexplainable physical behaviors of various substances. In that sense, Fajans is correct in describing them as having "no reality." However, Fajans assumes a rather naive metaphysics, maintaining that anything that cannot be immediately detected with the five senses has "no reality." It is true that one cannot open the dresser drawer and see a "resonance form" or a "chemical bond." But the fact is that scientists talk all the time about things that don't "exist" in the usual sense. Pauling was merely postulating the existence of "resonance forms" as theoretical constructs. Thus, Pauling *was* correct.

Eventually, the tedious exchange abated and Pauling entered more profitable waters. In April 1947, he and the famed biologist George Wald Beadle obtained a $300,000 grant for a five-year program of research into the structure of proteins. With that grant, he would finally crack the secret of the alpha-helix, taking a giant step towards solving the vexing problem of how proteins are constructed.

Inspired by the grant and filled with hope and enthusiasm for the future, Pauling renewed contacts with one of the men whose scientific genius had first inspired him. On August 10, he wrote to Arnold Sommerfeld. His former European mentor was still working and in good health, despite advancing years. The letter was unusually long and chatty for Pauling, full of reminiscence rather than shop-talk:

> We hope that you and Frau Sommerfeld are not suffering too much under the difficult circumstances of the post-war period. The young man Mr. Merrill who visited you over a year ago and took a photograph of you was good enough to send a print of the photograph to us. We were very glad to see your familiar faces again.

This renewed acquaintance with Sommerfeld certainly reminded Pauling of the terrible importance of students working with good teachers. So it was that in November, he wrote to Niels Bohr again, recommending that Verner Schomaker study at the Institute for Theoretical Physics the following year. On November 20, Bohr responded postively, indicating that other Pauling students had been getting on well:

> Professor Verner Schomaker shall be very welcome indeed to work in this Institute for a time next spring . . . We have been very glad

to have Dr. David Shoemaker with us and I hope he will have a profitable time here. It was a great pleasure to learn that you intend yourself to make a longer visit to Europe and on this occasion also plan to come to Copenhagen.

All of Pauling's friends had survived the war years well, including his own family. Linus Jr. was twenty-two and a junior at Pomona College (his progress had been delayed by three years' army service) and was on the verge of entering Harvard Medical School. Peter Pauling, who was later to gain a measure of fame for his much-publicized but ineffective defense of his father from the charge that he was "racing" to find the structure of DNA, was then just sixteen. He was hoping to become a physicist, but finally entered biology, trying to match his father's expectations. In this he did not quite reach the mark.

Linda had turned fifteen and was evolving into a young woman, regularly enjoying her interests in classical music, as well as painting, reading, and dancing. Crellin was ten and feeling the weight of the Paulings' expectations. Though not a behavior problem, he very much had a mind of his own. (Later in life, he is reputed to have temporarily changed his name, but I could not verify this for certain). As Pauling's sisters-in-law told me:

His sons did put their father on a pedestal; they wanted to follow in his footsteps, but it just isn't possible and it's left its mark on them. Crellin's been up here many times. He told us that in growing up, he always had the feeling they expected so much of him and he always had the feeling that no matter how much he did, no matter how hard he tried, it was never good enough.

He is reputed to be the most brilliant and stubborn of the Pauling brood.

Pauling experienced a loss at this time. Near the end of 1947, his good friend and teacher Roscoe G. Dickinson passed away from colon cancer, while still comparatively young. His death devastated Pauling. It was caused by precisely the sort of cancer that would figure so importantly in his later studies of vitamin

C. It isn't unimaginable that Dickinson's death influenced the direction of Pauling's later work, inasmuch as Dickinson was the closest friend that Pauling had lost to cancer up to that point. Like Sommerfeld, Roscoe Dickinson had been a very early influence on Pauling; they had worked together on the X-ray studies of crystal structure at the California Institute of Technology. For weeks, Pauling was inconsolable. Nor was his mood aided by the death of Millikan's second son, Glen Millikan, who had been killed just two months before Pauling's second letter to Sommerfeld.

Yet there were happier developments as well. Max Delbruck returned to the California Institute as a professor of biology, after many years at Vanderbilt University Medical School. This pleased Pauling and helped lift him from the doldrums. There is little doubt that with his renewed inspiration, Pauling was even further stimulated to attack protein structure again. By 1948 Pauling was again on an even keel, buoyed by the Presidential Medal of Merit awarded him for his already staggering contributions to science and humanity. The work on crystal structure, profound new insights on the nature of the chemical bond, relentless efforts to bring about world peace—all were noted by President Truman.

Pauling and Corey were getting closer to solving the mysteries of the polypeptide chain. According to Pauling,

> ... we carried out that investigation over a period of years, and by 1948 it was evident that there were no surprises about these molecules, really. We had made our information more precise but hadn't changed our understanding in any qualitative sense. The dimensions I had taken eleven years before for the polypeptide chain were shown to be correct. So in the spring of 1948 I again attacked the problem of coiling the peptide chain.[4]

But his health was becoming an issue and the old problems with nephritis were about to flare up again. In the spring of 1948, Pauling went to Oxford as a visiting professor. Always sensitive to climatic changes, and already slightly weakened by the reemerging nephritis, he soon caught cold. He spent several days in bed, quite bored and tired of reading detective novels and westerns. Soon he began tinkering with some folded pieces of paper. On them he had drawn atoms and the chemical bonds between them. He folded the paper at the bonds and continued this process until a helix emerged. In an instant, he knew how to form the bonds between one turn of the helix and the next. He jumped from the bed, walked about the room and began folding and refolding the paper to check his conclusions. He completely forgot his illness. Now he had the alpha-helix, at least conceptually. Pauling described the moment in a "Nova" broadcast:

> Eleven years earlier I had worked one summer with molecular models of the sort, the string and the rod-and-ball molecular models, and with my ideas about the structure of compounds of that sort, that I thought would give the right answer, and I had failed. Well I tried again—I didn't have any molecular models with me in Oxford but I took a sheet of paper and sketched the atoms with the bonds between them and then folded the paper to bend one bond at the right angle, what I thought it should be relative to the other, and kept doing this, making a helix, until I could form hydrogen bonds between one turn of the helix and the next turn of the helix, and it only took a few hours of doing that to discover the alpha-helix.[5]

In that instant, Pauling had discovered one of the great secrets of life. Protein chemists now had a greater working grasp of the structure of biological tissue. The most immediate results of this discovery came when the Paulings returned to Pasadena. With his long-time collaborator, Corey, Pauling worked out the structures of such fibrous proteins as muscle, fingernail, and hair. They soon realized that all proteins exist as helices. The helical shape was found to be a basic configuration of protein molecules in many life forms. Using Pauling's methods and discoveries, the path lay open for Watson and Crick, in a few short years, to map the structure of DNA.

Still, while Pauling may have discovered the alpha-helix in theory, he still had to prove its existence with data. The visit to England gave him the chance to see some really good X-ray photos of proteins. Although the inconsistency between his own expectations and the Astbury data still bothered him, his conversations with Perutz and with Jerry Donohue, also distinguished protein chemists, convinced him that the existence of the alpha-helix would soon be verified.

A breakthrough in one area of science often suggests new directions for research. Pauling had already spent some time thinking about hemoglobin because it was a typical and easily studied protein molecule. Always interested in any problem relating to molecular structure, he had become particularly fascinated by one aspect of the structure of hemoglobin:

> The Rockefeller Foundation had started supporting my work about 1932, I believe it was. . . . They put up a large amount of money for our work in Pasadena, several million dollars over a period of years . . . My first work in this field [molecular biology] was on hemoglobin in 1935—a theoretical job. I asked what the structure of the hemoglobin molecule should be in order to account for the way it takes up oxygen.[6]

But soon another dimension of the hemoglobin molecule captured Pauling's attention, taking him almost completely away from proteins and the alpha-helix. The catalyst for this new research was a dinner with several physicians who were members of a committee on medical research that later contributed a section to the Bush Report, "Science, the Endless Frontier." One of the members of the group, Dr. William B. Castle, described some work that he was doing on the disease, sickle-cell anemia.

Common among American blacks, sickle-cell anemia causes dramatic and obvious changes in blood cells. At one point Castle mentioned that the red cells of patients with the disease appeared deformed, or "sickled," when the blood examined was taken from the venous circulation, but they retained their normal disc-like shape in blood from arterial circulation. The disc-like shape of normal blood cells allows them to pass easily through the blood vessels. By contrast, the sickled cells are rigid;

they clump together and have great difficulty in moving through the blood vessels.

After some discussion, the idea occurred to Pauling that sickle-cell anemia could be a "molecular" disease—a disorder traceable to and directly caused by an abnormality of the hemoglobin molecule. The deformity in the molecule could itself, in turn, be caused by a mutated gene. Soon afterwards, Pauling had the idea that the abnormal hemoglobin molecules he thought existed in the red cells of these patients would have mutually complementary regions on their surfaces, which would cause them to "clump" together. These collections of molecules would be attracted to one another by very weak intermolecular forces called Van der Waals forces, causing the formation of a quasi-crystalline mass which, as it grew, would distort the red cell to the "sickled" shape characteristic of the disease. Thus deformed, their oxygen-carrying ability would be drastically reduced, thereby producing the clinical symptoms of the disease.

Although the concept of a molecular disorder was Pauling's original idea, like most new ideas in science, it did not arise *ex nihilo*. Pauling had been interested in the structure of molecules, and the hemoglobin molecule in particular, for some time, and he had been influenced by several great molecular biologist and geneticists. As Professor James Bonner of Caltech explained, "Pauling started worrying about sickle-cell anemia after 1946. I think he wouldn't have worried about it had it not been for George Wall Beadle's influence; Beadle was very interested in human mutations and defects in enzyme formation caused by mutation."

Since Pauling had, as explained above, the idea that the defect in the hemoglobin might be traceable to mutation, Beadle's work on mutations and their relation to disease provided the theoretical context for Pauling's own application of the ideas.

There remained the practical task of experimentally proving his theories. To tackle the problem, Pauling assembled a group of three researchers. Pauling asked one of these men, Dr. Harvey Itano, who had already received his M.D. and had recently started on a Ph.D in chemistry, to acquire blood cells from a sickle-cell anemia patient. The team needed to determine whether the hemoglobin from ordinary blood differs from that in diseased blood. If it did not, Pauling's theory would collapse. The problem was difficult. A complex apparatus had to be designed to separate diseased cells from normal ones, since standard techniques like ultracentrifugation did not work. By 1949, Dr. Itano, with the assistance of Dr. S.J. Singer, had solved that problem. The new technique was dubbed "electrophoresis" (they did not, however, invent the technique—Swedish scientists had done so earlier—they adopted it for the problem at hand) and, with the skilled guidance of Itano and Singer, worked nearly perfectly. The hemoglobin was found to differ in its electromagnetic properties from normal adult hemoglobin. The theoretical issue had been confirmed: the abnormality did indeed involve a mutation in the gene responsible for the synthesis of the beta chains of hemoglobin, which, in turn, leads to the substitution of one of the 146 amino-acid residues in the chain by a residue of a different type. As Pauling explained years later:

> This was, I think, the first time that the expression "molecular disease" had been used. Dr. Itano and his co-workers soon discovered other abnormal human hemoglobins, and over one hundred are now known. Abnormal proteins of other sorts manufactured by certain human beings, as well as other animals, have also been discovered. . . . I also knew, from the work of Brown and Reichart on the crystallographic form of crystals of hemoglobin from animals of different species and from the work of Landsteiner on the serological properties of the hems., that there are a great number of kinds of hem. molecules, presumably one for each animal species, and I was sure that the different kinds of hem. molecules are manufactured under genetic control.

The experimentation took place from 1945 to 1948, and led to the publication of the classic paper, "Sickle-Cell Anemia: A Molecular Disease." There is, however, a controversy over the work. As mentioned above, Singer and Itano designed the apparatus and carried out the actual experimentation. Yet, in addition to Pauling, Singer, and Itano, Ibert Wells's name also appears on the paper. Two of the distinguished scientists with whom I discussed the work, Bonner and Schomaker, never mentioned Wells. What exactly was Wells's role? Paper co-author Jonathan Singer says: "I have no idea where Bert Wells might be, but his contribution was miniscule: I think it was wrong of Linus to put his name on as he did."[7]

Dr. Arthur Robinson, of the Oregon Institute of Science and Medicine, states that Pauling had less-than-honorable reasons for adding Wells's name. With only three authors, the tendency in scientific periodicals of the time would be to list all three. But with a fourth, the paper's authors would be referred to as *"Pauling et. al,"* with just the principal author mentioned. Thus, Pauling's name alone would gradually become associated with the research.

But what, precisely, *did* Pauling do? That he did not get involved in the day-to-day experimentation is completely consistent with his history. Pauling never went to extraordinary lengths to actually verify theories mathematically and experimentally. If he liked a theory and had preliminary supporting data, his tendency was to rush to publish it. And even if Pauling did little of the "nuts and bolts" work, it certainly was not fraudulent for him to include his name on the paper. He was doing nothing more than following standard practice. Scientific papers often appear in which the "principal author" has done no "leg work" at all besides obtaining a research grant. Pauling, in this case, did much more than that; in 1946 he wrote Itano as follows:

> I think that we can postpone the discussion of the research problem in which you might work until your arrival here. I am very much interested in having a study carried out of the relation of the sickling of red cells in sickle-cell anemia to the chemical nature of hemoglobin in the cells, and perhaps this would be a suitable problem.

Pauling was the orchestrator, the mastermind behind the work. In an abstract sense, Pauling may have been wrong to list himself as first author of the 1949 paper. But from the perspective of day-to-day science, Pauling was more ethical than many of his peers. Scientific papers often list "first authors" who have done far less than Pauling did in this case. Without his ideas and influence, there would have been no breakthrough in the study of this terrible disease in 1949.

# *10*

# The McCarthy Era and the "Race" for DNA

AS PAULING APPROACHED FIFTY, PROFOUND AND FAR-reaching changes were occurring at the California Institute of Technology. Just as he began immersing himself in no-nonsense medical research, the California Institute moved in a more spiritual and philosophical direction, both in atmosphere and course content. Although Millikan had formally retired in 1945, he was the primary influence behind these changes. On December 20, he wrote to a trustee named Honnold about the addition of a scholar in theology and philosophy to the faculty:

> It is generally recognized that the greatest *values* in life lie quite outside the field of physical measurements and have to do not with the acquisition of knowledge about the physical world, but rather with ideas suggested by the words "conscience," "morality," "religion," etc. . . . in other words with what is usually spoken of as the higher or spiritual, as distinct from the material, side of life.[1]

Millikan had built his entire life on that assumption, but had become increasingly disturbed over the years by anti-theological attitudes among the faculty, Pauling included. When he retired he worried that whatever spiritual thread he had been able to weave into undergraduate education would soon vanish.

137

That was why he appointed a minister, Dr. Theodore Soares, as Professor of Ethics and Philosophy. He further explained to Honnold that "it was the motivation, also, behind our action—unique among technical schools—of requiring every boy who went through our four-year course to spend at least one-fourth of his time in the field of the humanities."

Soares was not enthusiastically received, as Millikan had feared. The extent of his influence on the undergraduate population is difficult to measure, but he had no influence on Pauling, or on most of the other members of the Caltech faculty. As Professor Ernest Swift told me, "Millikan brought Soares here, because [Soares'] views were like his. But religion just isn't based on close reasoning of the facts, and we just didn't put much weight on what Soares and Millikan thought, when it came to religion."

In the end, Millikan triumphed. In spite of philosophic neanderthalism among some of the faculty at the California Institute of Technology, he succeeded in his goal. The humanities eventually became an integral part of the Caltech curriculum—and became so far earlier than in other technical schools in the country. Though it was a gradual process, by the late 1940s, the role and value of the humanities at the California Institute of Technology was widely accepted among most of the faculty. This was to Millikan's credit.

Though Pauling spurned the ideas and judgments of men like Soares, he began the 1950s with one of the most philosophic meetings of his life—his first visit with Einstein. Einstein had formally studied the great philosophers and he had written many technical articles on the classic problems in philosophy including free will and determinism, natural rights, the nature of space and time, the meaning of life, and many others. In fact, the discussion between Einstein and Pauling in January 1950 centered around ethics, politics, and world peace, rather than science—a timely education for Pauling. The tone of the meeting was expected, since both Pauling and Einstein were already beginning to become concerned with the growing threat of nuclear annihilation.

Following that, and filled with hope and excitement about

his plans for future peace crusades, Pauling wrote the physicist Leo Szilard on February 20:

... I went to see Einstein on the twelfth, and had a good talk with him. . . . When I get an extra copy of my speech, I shall send it to you. The principal point that I made in my talk is that the question of peace or war has now become so important as to overshadow all other questions—it is of a far greater order of magnitude than anything else.

Pauling's deep concern over the prospect of war was already becoming evident to the California Institute of Technology. Faculty and friends saw less of him in the laboratory, though he always kept one foot in research. Although his concern was genuine, his activism was also self-aggrandizing—he always loved the limelight, as his frequent personal appearances on national television attest. As his colleague Jonathan Singer put it:

What Linus did, with his ego drive, was to insist that from his data on crystal structures . . . he could extrapolate. . . . But what was astonishing about Pauling, and what makes him great, was that he was willing to move to a concept on the basis of certain data whose relevance was not clear to others. Only Linus was willing to take the inductive leap. . . . The history of science shows that that, in itself, is perfectly justified—yet it's the same egocentricity that led him to collect thousands of signatures of scientists on a petition to ban atomic testing.[2]

Almost immediately, however, Pauling's political machinations started to get him into trouble. On November 14, 1950 he released a statement saying he had been subpoenaed to appear as a witness before the Senate Investigating Committee on Education of the State of California. As he wrote on November 15:

... I testified for over two hours, mainly about my reasons for objecting to special loyalty oaths involving inquiry into political beliefs. I also emphasized my convictions about the importance of security regulations for workers on classified projects, to be applied, however, in such a way as to do the minimum of harm to those who are considered to be poor security risks. My own political views are well known. I am not a Communist. I have never been a Communist. I have never been involved with the Communist Party. I am a Rooseveltian Democrat. I believe that it is of the greatest importance that citizens take political action, in order that our Nation not deteriorate.[3]

Pauling was most worried about the zeal of California politicians in imposing "loyalty affirmations" on any employee of the state. Anyone wanting to work for the University of California, for example, had to take whatever oath the Regents required.

Was Pauling a communist? He was not—despite all the charges of "fellow-traveling" that were leveled at him throughout the 1950s and into the 1960s. He certainly was not a communist in the official sense of the word, which is to say he was not a member of the party "under discipline." Later, Louis Budenz, an ex-communist, would declare that Pauling was in fact under discipline. However, Budenz was relying on hearsay evidence, and his testimony was later discredited.

Pauling also notes in his press release that while he was not a communist, he would not, on principal, testify to this before any committees. He believed that no citizen ought to be required to announce his or her political beliefs. McCarthyism, while hardly at its frenzied peak, was beginning to gather steam. The crackdown began early in California, home to the movie industry as well as an active communist party.

In fact, McCarthyism was stronger in California than anywhere else in 1950. Pauling's run-in with the California State Senate Un-American Activities Committee was his first major political battle. Robert Bacher of the California Institute of Technology recalls those days well:

Through a series of circumstances, I was chair of . . . an elected committee [on academic freedom and tenure at Caltech] . . . during that period there was a great attack on Linus, made locally in California and Linus was attacked unfairly and very viciously. Here is the fifth report of the Un-American Activities in California, 1949. . . . it's a big, thick book. They insisted Linus testify before them as to whether he had ever been or was a member of the

Communist Party . . . this caused trouble for Linus and was something that caused the Institute very much pain.

James Bonner also confirmed the great consternation Pauling was causing in the Caltech community. As he described it,

> Pauling's way of outmaneuvering the California Senate committee was . . . Machiavellian. . . . They'd originally planned on having the hearings . . . on the Caltech campus. But, realizing the indelicacy of that, they retreated to Pasadena City College. And when they first summoned Pauling on November 13 of 1950, he refused to answer on the grounds that their questions were improper, much as he immediately explained in his subsequent press release.

Finally the committee threatened to cite him for contempt. Pauling wrote to Lee DuBridge saying he had no objection to stating his political views; he merely objected to the circumstances. He did not wish to be forced to say anything before the committee.

Robert Bacher was worried. The night before Pauling's second appearance before the California committee, he called Charles Lorenson at the Institute, whose judgment he trusted. He told Lorenson that he believed they should pay Pauling a visit the first thing in the morning. Lorenson quickly agreed and, on the morning of the 14th, they corralled Linus. Bacher recalled telling Pauling: "Linus, they're going to cite you for contempt in that committee." Pauling was non-plussed. He thought this was unlikely, and responded by downplaying the importance of the committee and the credentials of its members. Bacher and Lorenson were not completely reassured when they left. Yet on that day Pauling displayed a surprising aptitude for politics. He arranged to have a public interview with reporters on the steps of the administration building (the old Throop building, eventually flattened by the earthquake of 1971). He flatly told the press that he was not and never had been a member of the Communist Party.

With the committee attacking in the center, Pauling won from the flank. When he went back before the committee the next day, the members of the committee asked him if he had, in fact, made that statement to reporters. Pauling answered in the affirmative. The attorney for the committee continued asking the same question that Pauling had refused to answer the previous day: "Well, now tell me, are you now or have you ever been a member of the Communist Party?" Pauling's answer was the same: "I can't answer that because that's an improper question."

The committee was in a vise. Given Pauling's public declaration which he confirmed to them on that day, the committee had no legal grounds for a citation of contempt. He had, after all, stated that he was not a communist. He just wouldn't state it when asked. The episode reveals much about Pauling's nature. Just as Caltech had had trouble disciplining him, this incident, along with numerous others throughout his career, indicates a maverick streak in Pauling that renders it implausible that he could have ever been a communist "under discipline." Beyond that, the unlikelihood of Pauling's being under discipline to any institution or party is all the more evident considering the fact that he knew such an allegiance would displease many older members of the Caltech community.

Still, if Pauling was not a communist under discipline he would, in the days to come, move steadily towards the left. He created controversy by endorsing the Rosenbergs, the Institute for Pacific Relations, the Hollywood 10, and other such groups. His many speeches also drew criticism. Typical was a February 17 talk at Carnegie Hall where he declared that "the world now stands at a branch in the road, leading to a glorious future for all humanity or to the complete destruction of civilization."[4] In those days, phrases like "glorious future" and "peace" were considered "communist talk."

Not everyone at Caltech was, as suggested above, happy with the outcome of the investigations. The younger faculty members tended to be on his side, but many of the older faculty wanted him to leave the Institute for good. At this time Lee Du Bridge, though nervous, still supported Pauling. Some of the trustees did not. Within days after the November 14 fiasco, the trustees requested a series of meetings with Bacher's committee. According to Bacher, "Some of the trustees wanted to discharge Linus—terminate his professorship. . . . I think, however, that though the trustees, many of them, had different views from Linus, many had more sympathy with his right to speak than is commonly recognized." According to Bacher, the trustees worked very hard on the issue, realizing that it was a matter of the gravest importance for the Institute as well as for Pauling. In the end, Pauling was not asked to resign his professorship, and no statement about it remained on file.

Nevertheless, a statement remained on file in the hearts and minds of many, and Pauling never again held the exalted position he was used to at Caltech. The trustees were not mollified by efforts at conciliation from Bacher, Du Bridge, and others. Several who felt some statement should have been placed on file or even that Pauling should have left Caltech may have resigned in protest. (The evidence is unclear on this point.) Even Lee Du Bridge's support was not to last forever. When political pressures got to be too great in the early 1960s, Du Bridge also abandoned Pauling.

Still, his closest allies did put the matter aside, perhaps because there was a feeling that Pauling was on the slicing edge of important discoveries. In their eyes, his political activism was insignificant and irrelevant in light of his brilliance as a scientist.

Their trust was well-grounded. Setting politics aside for the time being, Pauling again turned his energies to the problem in protein study whose solution had eluded him since 1937. Success came quickly. In October of 1950, he and Corey sent a letter to the *Journal of the American Chemical Society* announcing that they had devised a "two hydrogen-bonded spiral configuration" that was in conformity with all empirical data. At a lecture at Caltech in February of that year, he gave one of his famous "baby toy" lectures, where he used soft plastic bubbles in a variety of colors and shapes to demonstrate his latest theories. In a matter of weeks, he christened his new model the alpha-helix. The concept that had emerged from his toying with folded paper in 1948 was now a reality. He formally presented it in Stockholm at an international congress in crystallography in 1951. It was a single helical structure (in contrast to Watson & Crick's famous *double helix*) conceptualizing the manner in which proteins and protein chains are folded in space.

This contribution was of vast importance. In essence, Pauling and Corey had shown, for the very first time, that many of the basic materials of life were spiral, single-helical staircases. Indirectly, he also contributed much to the *way* stuctural biochemistry was done. Indeed, in an ironic twist, Watson and Crick later needed only to imitate the intuitive methods devised by Pauling—to make a theoretical guess at the structure of a molecule, and then test the structure against all known data.

Pauling and Corey were also working on the structures of hair, muscle, silk, horn, quill, collagen, and other biological substances. Collagen, a more complex protein that is found primarily in bone and the cornea of the eye, proved to be troublesome. Their model, a three-stranded helix, was completely incorrect.

But the three-stranded helix was, in a way, merely a small extrapolation in concept from the single, alpha-helix, which by no means enjoyed wide acceptance. Professor Edward Hughes, at eighty still a most animated and energetic man, spoke quite frankly to me in 1984 about Pauling's problems during the DNA period.

> Actually, most of the people in England didn't believe the alpha-helix for a year or two, Perutz especially. . . . Corey gave a twenty-minute paper on the amino acids of peptides, and there was no controversy. I had thirty minutes for Pauling's paper, and then all of the rest of the afternoon, maybe three or four hours, these Englishmen got up and said why they did or did not believe in the alpha-helix. Perutz was one of them.

Why did Perutz and the others have so many doubts about Hughes' presentation of the alpha-helix?[5] The fundamental reason was that it contradicted the view held by many scientists that nature tends to organize itself into simple, symmetrical patterns. This belief was not, in fact, based on established scientific principles, but instead reflected the aesthetic tastes of leading chemists and physicists at the time. After the discovery, in the mid-1950s, of nonconservation of parity in certain radioactive processes, the concept of symmetry, formerly sacrosanct, was considerably weakened. Indeed, examples of "broken symmetry" have become crucial to understanding in fields as diverse as cosmology and solid-state physics. That Pauling realized that the structure of proteins did not have to be symmetrical *before* the discovery of parity violations is, of course, a testimony to his genius. In the late 1930s Pauling had already dealt a severe blow to Wrinch's symmetrical model of the cyclol structure, so it is ironic that the question of symmetry was now coming back to haunt him with respect to one of his own models.

For years, Pauling had been wrestling with experimental results that contradicted Astbury's data with regard to where, precisely, the helix should repeat. In a perfectly symmetrical universe, all steps should be integral ones. Thus the British biological community attacked the alpha-helix for violating symmetry, while Pauling alone of all the world's biochemists theorized that the helix could have an asymmetrical, nonintegral number of turns or repetitions of each amino acid along the helical chain. This idea was unacceptable to many. Bragg and Perutz were following the classical principles of crystallography. From the regularity of the X-ray patterns, they had assumed that the number of amino acids had to come out exactly even along each turn of the helix. A complete helical turn, they thought, could not end in the middle of an amino acid—an idea as counterintuitive as the suggestion that a man could have 3.6 children. Only Pauling saw that this assumption was not necessarily true.

On the other hand, there were aspects of the alpha-helix that didn't run into controversy, such as Pauling's discovery that the peptide links between the amino acids in the protein chain all had to be in one plane. That, in turn, limited the number of ways the helix could twist and turn in three-dimensional space.

At the meeting, Bragg and Perutz grew more belligerent as Corey tried to defend Pauling's conception. To make matters worse, Pauling's paper had to be compressed into a space of thirty minutes when it really should have been given a full hour.

Besides having to shorten his presentation, Hughes had to

fend off several hours of not always civilized attack. Even so, he had every expectation that he and Corey would have enough time to rebut Perutz, Astbury, and the others. Instead, they found themselves limited to five minutes. Hughes was almost as furious as Pauling and wrote him to say so.

What had gone wrong? Pauling had been unable to take advantage of the first real chance to publicly defend his theory. The reasons were political. On January 14, 1952 he had requested a passport to attend the meeting. He and his intimates had been worried about this request, given the tenor of the times and his political activities. Still, he had behaved nonchalantly, speaking animatedly about the alpha-helix and, on occasion, chatting optimistically about DNA. He was ready for a showdown. Indeed Astbury had written him as early as September 20, 1951, implying that it was high noon for the alpha-helix:

> The Royal Society had asked me to try and arrange a discussion, "The Structure of Proteins," probably towards the end of April. . . . There is no need for me to tell you that the chief catalyst for this current protein excitement is to be found in your recent paper with Corey and Branson, which means we can hardly hold such a discussion without one or more of you people taking part—and I almost said defending yourselves!

For a while, all seemed well for the April 28 conference. Then Ruth Shipley of the passport office informed Pauling, on February 14, that a passport for him ". . . would not be in the best interest of the United States." Of course he applied again, on the very same day, writing President Eisenhower: "I am now writing to you, as president of the United States, to rectify this action and to arrange for the issuance of a passport to me. I am a loyal citizen of the United States. I have never been guilty of any unpatriotic or criminal act . . ."

Pauling did not receive a direct reply from Eisenhower, but received a bland and noncommittal reply from the Assistant to the President, Sherman Adams, which promised only to "look into the matter," if Pauling would provide the State Department with some evidence supporting his claims. Thus, he sent the

State Department a statement, made under oath, declaring that he was not a communist, had never been a communist, and had never been involved with the Communist Party.

But the state department, on the grounds that his "anti-communist statements were not sufficiently strong," again denied him a passport, this time by telephone on April 28—the very day he was to leave for the conference.

Pauling was beyond fury. He immediately wrote his British contact, Astbury: "I regret very much to have to inform you that I shall not be able to take part in the in Discussion Meeting of the Royal Society . . . I have received a letter from the Department of State saying that a passport is not being issued to me."

The McCarran Act (intended to restrict the foreign travel of any Americans with suspect political sympathies, on the grounds that secrets might be passed to enemy agents abroad) had been used as the theoretical basis for the denial of Pauling's passport, setting an extremely dangerous precedent. Even worse, Louis Budenz, a rabid ex-communist, had, on June 29, 1950, identified Pauling as a communist "under discipline," before a House Select Committee to investigate tax-exempt foundations. He would do so again on December 23, 1952. Later, in 1970, the Budenz testimony was correctly and summarily dismissed, since it was "in the nature of hearsay," according to a letter from Richard Ichord, Chairman of the Committee on Internal Security, to an unknown inquirer from Missouri. (Though hearsay has some epistemic value, it could not support the charge that Pauling was a party member.)

Of course, this came too late for the protein conference. Shunned by official Washington, Pauling was depressed, relying on colleagues and friends for solace. Astbury forgot his contempt for the alpha-helix and wrote a sympathetic letter to Pauling on May 13:

> I had already written to you to say how disappointed, and indeed indignant, we were to learn this at the last moment, and I must say that reading your documents only intensifies these feelings. I am no communist, and in fact I find most manifestations of Communism loathsome and dishonest—witness the utterly fantastic

Soviet attack recently reported in *Nature* on your own resonance theory.

The resonance theory clashed with Soviet ideology since it is based on quantum mechanics and therefore allows an element of indeterminism in the universe: in Marxist theory, the universe is 100% predictable.

Clearly, Astbury was angry. Yet he was helpless to do much about it, despite his firm conviction that politics should not intrude into scientific conferences. Pauling turned to Einstein —the one scientist likely to have influence. Pauling wrote him on May 14: "In case that you have not seen reference to it in the papers . . . I was prevented from making a trip to England by the refusal of the Department of State to issue a passport to me." Interestingly, this letter contained no direct appeal for assistance from Einstein, and Pauling apparently wished only to inform him. A few days later, however, Pauling wrote Einstein again— this time directly asking for his intervention:

> On thinking over the matter of my visit to England and my work on the structure of proteins, I have decided that it is of sufficient importance for me to make the trip that I should apply again for a passport. I have accordingly done so. I enclose copies of my letters to the Secretary of State and to the President. I think that it would without doubt be of significant aid to me if you were to write, perhaps to the President or possibly to the Secretary of State, saying that you know me, that you think that my scientific contributions are of some importance, and also that you have confidence in my loyalty and integrity—as I trust you have.[6]

Einstein wasted no time in dispatching a strong defense of Pauling to the Secretary of State:

> From my distinguished colleague, Professor Linus Pauling of the California Institute of Technology in Pasadena, California, I have received the following information: (1) He has twice been refused a passport which he needed for a visit to England to attend a scientific conference. (2) He has now renewed his request for a passport for a third time. I feel it to be my duty to testify that

Professor Pauling is one of the most prominent and inventive scientists in this country. I have the highest esteem for his character and for his reliability as a man and as a citizen. To make it impossible for him by governmental action to travel abroad would—according to my conviction—be seriously detrimental to the interest and reputation of this country.[7]

Einstein's reply to Pauling is as interesting as the letter to the government—both for its historical value and for his view of the state of the world:

It is very meritorious of you to fight for the right to travel. The attitude of the government corresponds, of course, to the state of transition toward a kind of totalitarian state in which we find ourselves. The simple means to make this possible is the uninterrupted repetition of the lie that the country is in mortal danger. Behind this attitude is the intention to crush the Soviet Union by war. As long as this tendency prevails the fight for the conservation of the democratic rights seems to me not promising. But not to fight is still worse. My hope is that the stalemate in Korea and the resistance of Europe will slowly change the mentality of the influential people in this country. There are signs which justify such hope . . . the fact that the very subtle diplomat, Mr. George Kenna, has already expressed himself against this tendency and has nevertheless been made Ambassador to the Soviet Union. The fact that independent minds like you are being rebuked equally by official America and official Russia is insignificant and to a certain degree also amusing . . .[8]

There is hardly a better comment on the absurdity and illogic of those days than the fact that both the United States and the Soviet Union would brand Pauling an "enemy"—the United States for his leftist views, the Soviet Union for his resonance theory (see chapter 13).

Pauling's battle continued unabated through the spring and summer of 1952. The next step was a letter, drafted by Joe Mayer of the University of Chicago, which was signed by a number of other famous scientists, including the great Enrico Fermi, Harold Urey, and even Edward Teller. On May 22, the letter was dispatched to Dean Acheson. The now monotonous theme was repeated:

> But even aside from our interest in the principle of freedom, we are incredulous of the reason given for witholding [sic] the passport: that it is "not in the best interests of the United States" to grant the passport. We cannot believe, with the greatest stretch of our imagination, that any reason can exist which would make the granting of a passport of so great harm to this country as its withdrawal . . . What harm, what information, what tales could Professor Pauling take with him to England, even were he so inclined, that can compare in damage to the incredible advertisement that this country forbids one of its most illustrious citizens to travel?

This letter too was of no avail. Washington and Dean Acheson were digging in their heels. The only faintly hopeful reply was a short letter from Senator Douglas on May 29: "If the authority to deny passports is to be exercised in some cases, the citizen involved should be able to secure some review of the decision in order to protect against arbitrary or misinformed action."

Eventually, the pressure did have some effect. Pauling was able to get some limited duration passports for conferences in the Middle East and Paris—good only for those trips. So far, however, he really had not had his showdown with the English scientists. He continued to pursue the opportunity amidst a number of bizarre twists and turns. For one, Pauling flagrantly disregarded the wishes of the Italian genius Enrico Fermi. The Mayer letter had been sent to Fermi for his signature. Fermi eventually agreed, but he was always uneasy about political imbroglios. He insisted on an express proviso that his signature could be used only if it were not sent to the *New York Times* for publication. Despite that proviso, Pauling allowed the Mayer letter to be published by the *Times*. He sent it first to Senator Wayne Morse from his home state of Oregon. Pauling liked Morse, in part because Morse had, sometime earlier, given a speech attacking the passport division. That, in turn, led to

Morse being vilified by Senator McCarran. Morse then made another speech, in which he included the letter along with Fermi's name. The papers, including the *Times*, picked it up. The incident infuriated Fermi and affected his relations with Pauling for the rest of his life. Yet the letter was helpful to Pauling. When his professional interests were at stake, he never allowed anyone else's needs to interfere.

Physicist Leo Szilard made the odd suggestion that Pauling travel *without* a passport. The legal grounds for doing so were shaky, although Szilard tried to convince Pauling otherwise. The idea was to get a "visum" from the government of the country he wished to visit. While the idea tantalized Pauling, he nonetheless wrote his friend Mayer on July 7, saying "I understand that it is against American law to leave the country without a passport, and that I would be liable to prosecution if I were to go . . ."

One result of the denial of Pauling's passport extends far beyond other matters in historical importance. Had he been able to travel to England in 1952, he might well have beaten Watson and Crick in the legendary and much publicized race to unravel the structure of the DNA molecule. Pauling's earlier (May 28, 1948) Nottingham lecture, "Molecular Architecture and the Processes of Life," had already shown that his interest in the biological molecules of reproduction was reaching its fullest vigor. At one point in the paper he says:

> The detailed mechanism by means of which a gene or virus molecule produces replicas of itself is not yet known. In general, the use of a gene or virus as a template would lead to the formation of a molecule not with identical structure but with complementary structure. . . . If the structure that serves as a template (the gene or virus molecule) consists of, say, two parts, which are themselves complementary in structure, then each of these parts can serve as the mold for the reproduction of a replica of the other part . . .[9]

In other words, a virus or gene might reproduce in two stages: The original might split in two pieces, with each piece producing a replica of the other piece. The two reproduced halves would then constitute an entirely new molecule which would be a complete and exact copy of the original one. Pauling was pleased with this new work and rightly so: while many of the details had to be revised later on, history has accepted his general ideas as correct.

It is difficult to say for certain, however, where and when the world's greatest protein chemists began the DNA odyssey in earnest. Ostwald's great paper of 1944 demonstrated for the very first time what others had only suspected: molecules of deoxyribonucleic acid could transfer genetic information. That inspired still others to continue the quest for the molecule of life. In the words of Robert Olby, in *The Path to the Double Helix*:

> With the passage of time the work of Avery, MacLeod and McCarthy looks, if anything, more significant than in 1953; perhaps it was the most important discovery in the path to the double helix. It marked the culmination of a series of achievements which established the chemical basis to enzyme action, antigenicity and finally transformation . . . In short, Avery's work on bacterial transformation was not neglected. It did lead directly to further chemical and genetic studies, the outcome of which was crucial for Watson & Crick.[10]

One of the reasons Avery's work was so significant is that it demanded a radical rethinking of what was sometimes called the "central dogma." One of the versions of this theory suggested that genetic transfer was located in proteins, not in nucleic acids. This was right in line with Pauling's own intuitions. Pauling was one of that small group of scientists who firmly believed that proteins, rather than a nucleic acid such as DNA, carried the essential messages of life from one generation to the next. In his own words:

> During the war I was doing some work with pneumococcus polysaccharide and antibodies to pneumococcus polysaccharide and I knew the contention that DNA was the hereditary material. But I didn't accept it, I was so pleased with proteins . . . that I thought that proteins probably are the hereditary material, rather than nucleic acids.[11]

His reaction was not surprising. As Maslow quipped, if the only thing you have is a hammer, you treat everything as if it were a nail. Pauling's hammer was protein. Since so much of the biochemistry of life was related to it, he supposed absolutely everything having to do with life was so related.

Even so, the quest for DNA accelerated only slowly. In the mid-1940s, for example, it was still relatively slow-paced. Maurice Wilkins was still in Berkeley, working as a physicist on the Manhattan Project. Though Wilkins eventually spurned physics because of the threats posed by atomic research, and turned instead to molecular biology and the famed Cavendish Laboratory in England, he was—at that time—still interested in war research.

But by the early 1950s, the scientists in Wilkins's laboratory in England, principally Rosalind Franklin, had been making tremendous progress with DNA. Between 1951 and 1952, Rosalind Franklin had taken some of the sharpest and most detailed photos of DNA so far seen. Certainly Watson and Crick would not have gotten the Nobel Prize had they not stolen her data, as Watson himself admits in *The Double Helix*. Even the venerable Caltech chemist Edward Hughes admitted that "Rosalind should have gotten far more credit than she did get. She was a nice girl and a brilliant scientist." He further added:

> You know, I never understood something about Watson's book to begin with. What bothered me was that he criticized Franklin so severely through the course of the book, and then in an epilogue took it all back. My theory of this is that W. L. Bragg, a real gentleman, knew what was going on and made a deal with him: "I will write the foreword," as he did, "if you put this epilogue in." That's the only way I can understand it.

It is hard to confirm this particular theory (James Watson declined to be interviewed for this book). However, the theory does appear plausible; Hughes could be right in supposing that someone like Bragg could have insisted on such an action.

Pauling, because of his problems in getting a passport for travel to England, did not see the new photos. Possibly because of this, he lost the Nobel Prize awarded for the solution of the DNA puzzle. (In addition, his prospects for his first Nobel for protein work might have been temporarily endangered, though this is not clear, since the price was still far in the future.) Pauling was approaching desperation. He felt he had to confront the British scientists who were so skeptical of the alpha-helix. In one of his most virtuosic displays of creativity and showmanship, Pauling solved the problem by deciding to hold another protein conference, in Pasadena in September of 1953.

All the major figures in the field of protein chemistry came: Perutz, Astbury, Kendrew, Bragg. . . . Professor Edward Hughes described the meeting to me amidst his panoramic array of tinkertoy chemical structures in his office at the California Institute of Technology:

> . . . We had a big conference in the Athenaeum that lasted all week; we paid the airfare of all these Englishmen, and all the Americans too. It was in the Hall of Associations in the Athenaeum; the papers were to be an hour long, with unlimited discussion; the only time off was Wednesday afternoon, when we had a big picnic up at the Paulings'.

The expected battle between Pauling and his English adversaries didn't really materialize. Hughes conjectures that Max Perutz, the dean of British protein scientists, had come to the conclusion that Pauling was right and that the alpha-helix was correct. In the time lost since the original conference in England, Perutz had been studying Pauling's data more closely than ever and had realized that the Astbury data was wrong and that symmetry was not, just as Pauling had claimed, a necessary feature of protein structure. Doubtless part of the low-key tone of the meeting was also due to residual sympathy over Pauling's difficulties with the passport office, but the logic of Pauling's arguments could not be ignored.

Then, too, scientific attention was now being redirected from the study of proteins to the quest for DNA. In the beginning of 1953, the British scientists working on DNA—including most of the protein chemists—were already becoming concerned that Pauling had discovered the structure of DNA. Watson spoke candidly about the race: "We always worried, of course that maybe Linus Pauling would start thinking about it . . . But then in December, we heard, via his son Peter, who was then a student in the Cavendish, that his father had a structure for DNA. And that made us very, very curious."[12] "Curious" is hardly the word. They were terrified. They soon learned that the Pauling-Corey paper, "A Proposed Structure for the Nucleic Acids" was to appear in the February issue of the *Proceedings of the National Academy of Sciences*. However, they soon realized that Pauling had made a number of basic errors in his eagerness to get the solution before Watson and Crick. For one, he had the structure inside out, with its backbone on the inside instead of the outside. More importantly, because of other structural problems involving the position of the hydrogen atoms it was not, technically, even an acid. Perhaps most significantly, it did not have the explanatory power that the facts or, indeed, any good scientific hypothesis requires. It could not, for example, show how either cells or whole organisms could perpetuate themselves. Professor Verner Schomaker explained his objections to me:

> . . . he was intensely interested, hoping to solve that structural problem . . . he and Corey rushed their paper off . . . even though I'd said, "Look here, there's something wrong." There was a minor feature I could see when I was next door and I looked at the drawings Bob Corey was making. If they did something a little differently, the distances and angles would be more suitable. I made a model with the Pauling-Corey ideas . . . Linus was interested and set some young fellow working out the details of the thing, and that's after he'd sent the other paper in. Indeed, even after Watson and Crick's paper had appeared, he still wasn't convinced he was entirely wrong. The main thing about it was that it was inside out compared to the right model. Well he'd apparently just made up his mind on it . . . his conviction that he was on the right track was so great that he wouldn't listen to what hindsight shows were good reasons . . .[13]

This issue is puzzling: certainly Pauling *was* aware of possible structural problems—even to the point of communicating with Watson himself about them. In a historic letter dated March 5, 1953, Pauling wrote:

> I am writing to remind you about the protein conference . . .
> I think that we might as well discuss the structure of nucleic acids,
> as well as of proteins . . . and I hope accordingly that you will
> arrive in time. . . . Also, Delbruck said that you had found a beau-
> tiful new structure for the nucleic acids . . . Professor Corey and
> I do not feel that our structure has been proved to be right, al-
> though we incline to think that it is right. I may mention that we
> have made a small revision in it . . . Professor Verner Schomaker
> . . . pointed out that a significant improvement could be effected
> by rotating the phosphate tetrahedron about their vertical axes,
> through 45 degrees. . . . At the present time I think that this small
> change in our proposed structure needs to be made. I am still
> checking to see whether any other change needs to be made.

Pauling may have been simply fishing, since, as indicated above, Pauling really did not listen to Schomaker, as the latter explained to me.

Of course the most publicized aspect of Pauling's involvement with DNA research is whether or not he actually participated in a "race" to unravel the mysteries of the DNA molecule. There have been many, including Pauling himself, who have denied the existence of a race.[14] Most historians of science deny it, as do most scientists. Typical of them is Anne Sayre, author of *Rosalind Franklin and DNA*, the only biography so far published of Franklin. According to her, "the 'race' existed only in Watson's mind." She says:

> Apart from Watson's assertion that it was so, there is no proof
> whatever that Pauling was losing sleep over DNA, or was imme-
> diately prepared to make the quest after its structure a full-time
> pursuit . . . What it all comes down to is that the suggestion of
> Pauling's imminent rivalry, though presented in the terms of a
> suspense thriller, is a red herring. It is no more and no less than
> a splendid, and only slightly transparent rationalization, one that

fits in neatly with the other rationalization which implies that Rosalind [Franklin] as an impediment standing squarely in the path of scientific progress, deserved to be pushed aside . . .[15]

Sayre is wrong in what she asserts though right in what she implies. She implies that Watson used the rivalry with Pauling to justify some of his shabby treatment of Rosalind Franklin. That may well be true. The above-mentioned book by Anne Sayre argues convincingly that it was her photography and her distinction between two previously unseen forms of DNA (the hydrated and dry forms) that allowed Watson and Crick to obtain the structure. It is probably true that Rosalind Franklin should have at least shared in the Nobel Prize. Yet it does not follow that Pauling was only mildly interested in solving the DNA puzzle.

Despite the efforts of Sayre and others to establish otherwise, those closest to Pauling claim that he was, in fact, engaged in a DNA race. Verner Schomaker, Pauling's former student and long-time friend from the "electron diffraction" days at Caltech, said, "He was intensely interested and was really hoping to solve the structural problem of DNA; he worked hard on it through the summer and fall and then he and Corey rushed it off into publication . . . he was really excited about that problem and wanted badly to solve it." Peter Pauling has published another heroic effort to destroy the notion that there was a battle between Pauling and the English group. This was a piece called "DNA— the Race that Never Was?," which appeared in the May 1973 issue of *New Scientist*. He vehemently denies the existence of any such race, claiming that nucleic acids and their structure just formed another interesting set of problems for his father. Verner Schomaker commented, "Peter Pauling was not viewing it as being as intensely important as it was, probably because Pauling's concern lasted only a short while. But I remember clearly telling them that there was something wrong. . . . There was a problem I could see when I went next door." But Pauling was riding high. He was not about to fuss over angle measurements. He had drawn a bead on the structure of DNA and he was heading into print as fast as he could.

Edward Hughes seemed to agree with Schomaker about the

existence of a race: "Of course they published the structure that was wrong, and this scared the living daylights out of the English people." Why would Pauling rush into print when everybody was telling him there was trouble unless he saw the DNA problem as a race? Then, of course, there are universal truths about the human ego: the idea that any academic, within distance of any major breakthrough, would not be interested in the awesome prestige, money, and fame that a Nobel Prize confers, stretches the bounds of credibility. In this, Pauling is no different from anyone else, scientist or not. In spite of the frequently idealized view we have of scientists and academics generally, they do pursue fame and prestige.

According to Erwin Chargaff, the brilliant and cantankerous author of *Heraclitean Fire* and another important figure in the DNA saga, "Pauling was at the height of his fame, while Watson was little more than a graduate student. It's logical that Watson would hunger after fame, but why would Pauling need it?" But this sort of argument really does not work—the idea that people don't want more of something just because they already have a lot of it simply contradicts human nature.

Pauling was, in fact, involved in a ferocious battle to conquer the DNA molecule, one which he ultimately lost. As he himself realizes, permission to travel to the protein conference most likely would have enabled him to see Rosalind Franklin's data and X-ray photographs, and perhaps to arrive at the structure of DNA before Watson and Crick.

He still had the alpha-helix however. The support of English scientists was a balm for his battered ego. The Nobel Prize was still very much within his reach. In fact, rumors were already in the air that Pauling might soon head the Nobel committee's list, for the alpha-helix as well as his huge corpus of other work.

# On the Way to His First Nobel Prize

SHORTLY AFTER THE PROTEIN CONFERENCE IN PASA-
dena, Pauling was again in touch with his old friend John Slater
of the Massachusetts Institute of Technology. He was starting
to think about other matters besides DNA and protein chemistry.
Pauling thrived on tension and conflict. His usual way of creating
it was to explore fields other than his own, trying to tantalize
and outthink the experts in their own domain.

He wrote to Slater on November 30. He remembered the
days when Slater was begging him to come to the Massachusetts
Institute of Technology, and genuinely believed that Slater was
still in awe of him. However, twenty years had passed, and much
of Pauling's contact with Slater had consisted of routine discussions about various promising graduate students and clari-
fications of issues the main outlines of which had already taken
shape. But Pauling's letter opened a Pandora's box that left him
indignant, angry, even flabbergasted.

Pauling had recently been working on ferromagnetism, the
type of magnetism found in a bar magnet. He wrote to Slater:
"Finally, I should be grateful to you for your comments on my
paper, 'A Theory of Ferromagnetism.' It seems to me to be a
good theory, and if you have some objections to it, I should like
to know what they are, in order that I might think more about

them."[1] Slater's reply was uncharacteristically cranky. He voiced suspicions about some of the students Pauling had recommended to him when he had no compelling reason for doing so. In all probability, his suspicions were not directed at any of Pauling's students, all of whom were first-class. Pauling would hardly have recommended second-rate students. Rather, the letter was a direct slap at Pauling. Slater wrote to Pauling again on December 16, 1953. After perfunctory thanks for his recommendations, and some innocuous comments on Pauling's latest work on the nitrogen molecule, he launched into the worst attack Pauling had ever suffered from a scientist of comparable caliber:

> You ask for comments on your paper on "A Theory of Ferromagnetism." When you spoke to me about it in Washington last spring, I indicated that I didn't like it very well, and I'm afraid that I still don't. I think my fundamental objection is the way in which you give the impression that an extremely sketchy calculation must be right, because you can get some numbers from it which are in agreement with experiment to three figures. This is the same objection which I have to a great many of your papers. Many of the hypotheses that go into this particular paper aren't even correct in the first figure: for instance, your assumption that six electrons in iron have a free-electron like energy distribution, with a width of 23.3 ev in energy. All evidence which we have from more accurate calculations of energy bands from soft X-ray emission spectra, and from electronic specific heat, indicates that the whole occupied band in iron is only about a third as wide as that. This being the case, I simply cannot treat seriously a theory which starts from such an assumption. I feel that such oversimplified theories do a great deal of harm, in that they tend to make the uncritical reader feel that problems have been worked out completely, when as a matter of fact I think we have hardly made a beginning toward their solution. I am sorry to be critical in this way, but I feel very strongly about the matter, and I believe that a very large proportion of physicists interested in such questions feel the same way about it. Maybe the refinement of the theory which you mention in your letter will tend to remove such objections. I hope so.

Slater was eventually proven right about the defects of Pauling's theory, but he also overlooked or ignored precisely what made Pauling a scientific genius. Pauling's theory failed, and all physicists would agree that modern theory on this subject has moved toward Slater's ideas.

Yet Pauling failed ingeniously. According to accepted scientific theory the magnetic properties of a substance such as iron are a function of its electronic structure—in particular, the spin of the electrons surrounding the nucleus. A single spinning electron acts like a very small magnet. However, electrons within the same orbit around the nucleus have opposing spins, so the magnetic tendencies cancel each other. When there is a significant number of unpaired electrons, conversely, the magnetic qualities increase. The more unpaired electrons there are, the more magnetic is the substance.

The Slater-Pauling dispute, from a strictly scientific perspective, depends on what paths electrons take through magnetic substances—what "orbitals" they occupy. Pauling treated the key electrons as occupying "s" orbitals. Slater, on the other hand, treated the electrons as occupying "d" orbitals. It is known that the energy bands for "d" electrons are considerably narrower than for "s" electrons. Yet a narrow band width is precisely what magnetism requires, since such narrow band widths mean that the electrons tend to remain close to the nucleus of the atom: they are not free to "roam" throughout the metal. By treating the electrons responsible for magnetism as "s" rather than "d" electrons, Pauling had simply given an incorrect account of magnetism.

This type of thinking is typical of Pauling. He had challenged a basic and long-held postulate about electrons and magnetism without regard for the consequences. He moved quickly to a theoretical position, unwilling to wait for more precise calculations. Of course, the theory of ferromagnetism was not nearly as well understood in 1953 as it is today. Even so, more accurate measurements would have indicated to Pauling that the band width was far narrower than he believed.

However, Slater's letter is misleading because it may suggest, on superficial reading, that Pauling's error was just a matter of insufficient computations—just a "mathematical" error. Rather, it was an error in *physical assumptions*. Slater tried to get the best numerical solution he could with the relatively primitive computing equipment available at the time. He computed the Schrodinger equation (although even he had to make some approximations) and it simply turned out that the electrons responsible for ferromagnetism were "d" electrons. Pauling, by contrast, solved no equations; he just made assumptions that the electrons responsible for ferromagnetism were "s" or "p" like, rather than "d" like. In a word, Pauling's "stochastic" method failed him here, though it worked gloriously well for Watson and Crick when they solved the structure of DNA. Pauling's approach failed here for two reasons: there were discrepancies between the X-ray experiments and Slater did detailed calculations and got solutions to the Schrodinger equation, which Pauling did not do.

In fairness to Pauling, however, questions involved here are inordinately complex, perhaps more complex than either scientist realized. It is known, for example, that in the alkali or primitive metals (or "simple" metals) the valence electrons are "s" like (with a small percentage of "p" character). But the transition metals (those showing ferromagnetism, such as iron, nickel, and cobalt) have valence electrons of primarily "d" character. To complicate matters further, the notion of *Fermi levels*, named for the Italian-American physicist Enrico Fermi (who actually did relatively little work in this area, being more concerned with nuclear physics) plays an important role here as well. The Fermi levels, or energies of the highest occupied state, are critically important in determining the physical properties of a substance (mechanical, electrical, magnetic character, etc.). So, in ferro-magnetic substances, the character of the electrons of the highest occupied state, or Fermi levels, is "d" like. (For the sake of comprehensiveness, note that in the rare-earth and the actinides, the Fermi level electrons are "f" like.)

However, Slater's letter was scornful beyond all accepted bounds of propriety. Something was bothering him. Probably

Slater perceived Pauling's error as a rather elementary one—something a solid-state physicist would not have done. Yet Pauling was not a solid-state physicist: he was a structural chemist, accustomed to dealing with huge molecules, far larger than the ones a theoretician like Slater dealt with. Scientists are often territorial about their own fields. Slater almost certainly saw Pauling as an interloper, wandering far afield from his own areas of expertise and experience. This criticism surfaced again when Pauling entered the domain of nuclear physics, daring to theorize about the nucleus of the atom. He has encountered the same territorial resistance more recently from physicians, in response to his speculations about the medical benefits of vitamin C and its relationship to the common cold and cancer.

Slater, more careful, more meticulous and less speculative than Pauling, probably felt that publishing one incompletely verified theory after another was not the proper way to do science. In the case of ferromagnetic theory, the methods that work so well in structural chemistry, especially where biological molecules are under study, simply do not work in solid-state physics. According to physicist Roy Benedek of Argonne National Laboratory:

> Pauling likes to make postulates, and by virtue of his extraordinary insight was able to solve many problems in structural chemistry, unsolvable by direct methods. But a solid-state physicist would say, "Why make assumptions, when you have a detailed analytical framework, namely the Schrodinger equation, with which to work?" Thus, Slater would say, "Well, why don't we go ahead and solve the Schrodinger equation as well as we can and see what the consequences are, rather than make a guess" . . . Pauling, however, put more emphasis on intuition and less on analysis than most physicists would be comfortable with.[2]

Professor Sten Samson of the California Institute of Technology offered another reflection on the contrast between Pauling and Slater:

> One could say that Pauling's "failure" was to plant a lot of seeds, basic ideas, without working them out fully. . . . As soon as Slater

gets an idea he works it out to the end before he gets a new one. But that is also dangerous, of course because you look at the trees and you don't see the forest . . . [Pauling] looks at the forest and lets other people . . . work out the specific individual things in detail; he has a terrifically lively intellect, reading this paper, [taking up a publication of Pauling's] the information here is just tremendous, the ideas flow out of the pen, and there are several lifetimes of work . . . to be done.[3]

Pauling, angry though he was, soon put the fiasco behind him. With the furor over the DNA quest, his troubles with Slater, and the confusion over passports, his tendency to neglect his family emerged; Ava Helen was quick to remind him of his duty. Her temper could be fearsome. As noted earlier, during the Senate battles of the late 1950s, she nearly assaulted reporter Lawrence Spivak on "Meet the Press." At her prodding, Pauling began to curtail his activities considerably. He turned down an invitation from Astbury to attend a symposium on protein structure in Milan, for example. In his reply to Astbury's invitation, he wrote:

I thank you for suggesting that I come to the symposium in Milan next July. I doubt that it will be possible to do so. At the present time my wife and I are thinking of making a trip around the world this winter . . . and the time required for this is such that I believe that I should stay at home next summer, and work—I am trying to get a book done.[4]

The book was *No More War!*, which was published by Dodd, Mead in 1953. The book had developed out of Pauling's escalating passion for political activism. Passport difficulties, once again, were interfering with his work. In December, soon after his difficult correspondence with Slater, he had been planning to go to the Indian Science Congress for six weeks. He was excited. It was the first time he had been offered a chance to see Indian science at work, and though they did not have a lot of top-rate scientists, there were a few whose work Pauling knew.

Yet he got no farther than New York, where, on April 28, he discovered that the State Department had once again refused him a passport. All last-minute efforts to win clearance failed and he and Ava Helen were forced to return to Pasadena. It appeared that appeals were not likely to work until well past the Indian conference. Pauling again forced himself to put the incident behind him.

He immediately wrote Einstein once again, soliciting his help: "I have been talking with the members of a new organization, Everybody's Committee to Outlaw War, and am writing to you now to ask if you could make a brief statement to be used in the publications of this committee."[5] A close friend of the Einstein family, Alice W. Kahler, recalled the exchange well: "Albert thought that Pauling simply had his head in the clouds. Einstein did believe in peace, you know, like we all did. But he knew that sometimes wars just happened."

Einstein's reply was decidedly cool:

> . . . I do not need to assure you that I am wholeheartedly on your side in principle. I think, however, that in the present situation a proposition to outlaw war is quite ineffective. Even if it could be possible to create a mass movement with this slogan it is clear that one cannot prevent competitive armament and the danger of war . . .[6]

Einstein's ideas about war were actually somewhat less pessimistic than it appears here. He had become involved at this time in the World Federalist's Movement; he would often criticize it for not pursuing the idea of world government enthusiastically enough. Realizing the possibly unrealistic character of his own vision, he must have thought Pauling quite out of touch with reality. Pauling's own attitude was more complex as well —he told his young protegé Arthur Robinson many years later, "I'm against war, you know, except wars of liberation." This was a codicil he would append many times to his anti-war stance.

Drawing Pauling's mind in yet another direction was a new battle of conscience. The catalyst this time was his former adversary, J. Robert Oppenheimer. Oppenheimer and Pauling, both great home-grown American scientists, now had something else in common: Oppenheimer had recently been declared a "security risk" by official Washington, specifically, by the Atomic Energy Commission. The scientific community, including Linus Pauling, was infuriated.

On June 7, 1959, he challenged the political establishment again during a commencement address at Reed College in Oregon. He indignantly cited the Security Board's declaration that Oppenheimer was a security risk as evidence of an "inability to think clearly" on the part of Washington politicians: "I fear that in fact the ability to think clearly about great problems is a rare one in our national leaders—that there are not many men in public life who really know and apply the scientific method." Pauling had mixed feelings about Oppenheimer, defending him against disloyalty charges during the McCarthy era, but voicing concern about Oppenheimer's views at other times, as he had done earlier with Millikan. The question of Oppenheimer's loyalty still rages today. He was, nonetheless, given exceptionally harsh treatment by the government and Pauling felt honorbound to fight such treatment.

If Pauling's political initiatives received mixed responses, the greatest tribute to his scientific achievements was imminent. While giving a routine lecture on hemoglobin at Cornell University on November 3, 1954, he was called to the telephone. Within a few minutes he returned to the lecture hall to announce that he had just been awarded the Nobel Prize for chemistry. The applause was deafening. For twenty minutes, the audience of undergraduates and graduate students cheered and stamped their feet, expressing their delight.

After his initial euphoria, Pauling's first worry was, once again, whether he would be able to obtain a passport. He was scheduled to receive the $35,066 Nobel Prize from King Gustav Adolph of Sweden on December 10. He applied for the passport immediately. For some time, he heard nothing. Mail arrived in volumes congratulating him on the Nobel Prize, but Pauling searched only for the passport notice. Though he remained frustrated and anxious, the mail that came consoled and reassured him. His old friend Ernest O. Lawrence, a physicist and member of the President's advisory panel on science during the 1940s, cabled him on November 5: "Molly joins me in congratulations to both you and Helen." Similar missives followed from Astbury, Coryell, Shoemaker, Don Yost (an inorganic chemist who was at Caltech during the 1920s), and even Slater.

Coryell did a little more. On November 2, in a night letter, he cabled Ruth B. Shipley of the passport division of the State Department:

> Would like to thank you for your courtesy to me today and confirm telephone call. I hope that the science advisor and the public relations office of State Department realize the welling up in science circles of appreciation for Nobel Laureate Pauling's great work over three decades and their shock at frequent evanescence of his passport rights. Respectfully, Charles D. Coryell.

There was no immediate response. The Budenz smear of 1952 was probably still in the minds of State Department officials. But the Coryell letter and pressure from other friends and colleagues of the Paulings did have an effect. The sheer prestige of the prize also influenced Washington. To deny Pauling a passport to receive his Nobel Prize would have created a huge international controversy.

Even so, opposing voices were strong, and governmental meetings over the issue were loud and rancorous. Senator Henning protested, saying "Are you in the State Department allowing some group of people in some foreign country to determine which Americans get passports?" But world opinion was too strong and too insistent. On November 27—a scant two weeks before he was supposed to receive the prize—the documents arrived. The Paulings wanted to celebrate, but time was short and they had to begin travel preparations immediately.

Early on December 9, the Paulings were welcomed warmly in Stockholm. At 4:30 P.M. the next day, the ceremonies began in Stockholm's beautiful crystal-lined Royal Concert Hall. Pauling was elegant and beaming; he smiled and chatted with the others on stage, including Ernest Hemingway and three American scientists who were splitting the Prize for medicine: John

Enders, Thomas H. Wellers, and Frederick C. Robbins. Pauling's friends Max Born and Walter Bothe were also present to receive the physics prize.

Professor G. Hagg made a warm if somewhat labored speech to the assemblage. He was considered the most outstanding member of the Nobel Committee for Chemistry, but unused to public speaking. He cited Pauling for having pushed back the boundaries of protein structure:

> It has thus become apparent that one of these structures, the so-called alpha-helix, probably exists in several proteins. How far Pauling is right in detail still remains to be proved, but he has surely found an important principle in the structure of proteins. His method is sure to prove most productive in continued studies.

As his name was called, Pauling smiled at his wife—a trademark on ceremonial occasions—and stepped down from the platform. He was greeted effusively, almost deferentially, by King Gustav himself. The green leather folio was his.

# 12

# On the Trail of a Cure for Mental Illness

AFTER RECEIVING THE NOBEL PRIZE, PAULING GRADU-
ally became more active politically. He also cut back on his
research, as many Nobel laureates do. His finest scientific work
was behind him. He never again, according to old friends and
colleagues, attained the brilliance and productivity of his earlier
years. Where previously he had hammered relentlessly at the
almost intractable problems of chemical bonding and protein
structure, he now began to explore speculative areas of unorthodox medicine. This new research culminated in his work on
vitamin C.

Pauling's first significant step into untapped areas of clinical
medicine was an investigation of the chemical basis of mental
illness. As James Bonner explained in June 1984:

> After he got the prize, Linus got an enormous amount of funding
> for research and at this time he'd become interested in finding
> out about the chemistry of the brain—how the brain works, and
> why people are feeble-minded and what to do about it . . . he
> allocated himself a vast amount of space in Church Labs to work
> on these topics, which were funded by the Office of Naval Research
> and some other organizations.

The chemistry of the brain was a natural follow-up to Pauling's
work on proteins. It presented him with many of the same bio-

chemical problems, but was infinitely more difficult and challenging. While he felt he had essentially solved the fundamental structure of such tissues as hair, bone, and quill, the microarchitecture and behavior of brain cells was uncharted territory. They are composed of proteins which are far more difficult to understand structurally and functionally than quill.

The prestige and freedom of movement that accompanied the Nobel Prize contributed to Pauling's shift in direction. A number of colleagues believe that he had always been curious about such issues as the connection between nutrition and mental illness, but had been reluctant to pursue them. For one thing, he had the structure of proteins to occupy his attention. For another, that sort of research was slightly beyond the boundaries of "conventional" science. Without the Nobel Prize, Pauling could not hope to garner research money, assistants, or even laboratory space for his more progressive interests. Now, however, he had the license to pursue these projects.

He promptly hired Addis, the physician who had cured him of his kidney infection. According to a long-time friend of the Pauling family, Peggy Kiskadden, "Linus was just wonderful. Addis had been having some more political troubles; he'd lost his job. Well, Linus said, 'You just come right down here, and I'll make a place for you.' "[1] This was an error in judgment. According to James Bonner, a fellow chemist at Caltech:

> The supervisor of the work he'd engaged in was a physician who had been his physician when he had Bright's Disease and had been dismissed from his post because he took the Fifth at one of these Un-American Activities [hearings] of which there were a lot in Hollywood. But he was a "laying-on-hands" healer, and no good at basic research, so Pauling ended up running the project himself.[2]

This incident again counters the charge that Pauling cared little about individuals and would run roughshod over them to accomplish his goals. In this case, genuine human concern actually *interfered* with a project that was of the greatest importance to him.

Pauling's work habits were becoming inefficient. He seemed to think of the California Institute of Technology as his own private research laboratory. Bonner notes that Pauling had been grabbing more and more of the limited space in Church laboratories. Caltech Chemist Jack Roberts comments:

> The mid-to-late 1950s and early 1960s were a tough period for us; we had . . . Church lab, and Gates, and we were piling in people. Now Linus was running some projects here and in Gates, but people were saying he really wasn't using space efficiently . . . I had the job of telling him we had to contract. Part of the problem too was that he had set up people to work independently on ideas he had had, which were good ideas, but had not, for one reason or another, worked out the way he thought they would. One of these was in mental health. He thought you could analyze urine, but once he got into it they discovered that there was so much variability in metabolism in normal people, that you really couldn't make a lot of generalizations.[3]

In the end, Roberts and others had to practically push Pauling out, insisting that his space would have to be turned over to other projects and the research curtailed. Pauling was enraged. He felt his work was of the utmost importance and that, with his Nobel Prize to its credit, Caltech should have been glad to provide him with the research opportunities he needed. This was one of the factors that eventually drove him from the California Institute of Technology after over forty years of productive work.

Ironically, Pauling was then doing what is now considered conventional psychiatric work. There has been much talk about the relationships between chemical imbalance, nutrition, and mental illness in recent years. Few psychiatric researchers now believe that all mental illness is purely psychological in origin. But in the 1950s, this hypothesis was highly unorthodox.

The fundamental principle behind Pauling's work was elegant and simple: The brain has an optimum biochemical environment. If the molecular concentrations of these chemicals are disturbed, all sorts of psychological disturbances result. In a few years, Pauling expanded this fundamental principle into the idea that there is a definite link between nutrition and mental illness—arguing that Niacin (vitamin $B_3$) is absolutely critical to sound mental functioning. Researchers now take this claim seriously as well.

This work soon became mired in confusion and controversy. In addition to Pauling's lack of competent help, there was not yet a unified approach to mental illness research. Many psychiatrists still advocated the "talk" therapies propounded in the late nineteenth century by Freud and Breuer, while others gravitated to Jungian, Adlerian, and a variety of other approaches. To add to the complications, behavioral therapy was beginning to gain respect in some psychiatric circles. Also, the contemporary methods of treatment of mental illness, such as the use of electroshock therapy, were generating considerable public horror and fear of psychiatry. Furthermore, Pauling also had little time for the investigations. His protests against atomic bomb research were demanding more of his time. In January of 1954 (as Pauling himself reports in *No More War!*), Atomic Energy Commissioner Willard F. Libby declared that "the fallout dosage rate as of January 1 of this year could be increased 15,000 times without hazard." In 1955, Pauling received moral and scientific support from geneticist and Nobel Laureate Herman J. Muller, who in April proclaimed, "A mutation is bad, no matter whether its presence results from the action of a previous generation in enabling the mutant to breed or is artificially produced by radiation."[4]

Despite Libby's claim, Pauling was furious. He refused to consider the possibility that he might be wrong. There was too much at stake. On March 30, he wrote to Libby, who was still at the University of Chicago, though the government called upon his scientific expertise more and more frequently. The catalyst for Pauling's indignation was a piece Libby had prepared for *US News and World Report* in which he urged, "The world is radioactive. It always has been and always will be. Its natural radioactivities evidently are not dangerous and we can conclude from this fact that contamination from atomic bombs, small in magnitude . . . is not likely to be at all dangerous."[5]

Pauling felt that such a statement was irresponsible, as if

to suggest that since a glass of water isn't dangerous, we would be safe at the bottom of an ocean. Yet his March 30 letter to Libby was polite:

> Some biologists, at any rate, think that at least some kinds of cancer are produced by somatic mutations induced by naturally radioactive potassium, carbon, and perhaps other elements . . . If this is so, there is little doubt that artificial radioactive substances introduced into the body would also produce these malignancies.

The cordial tone of the exchanges between Pauling and Libby soon deteriorated. On April 18, Libby wrote Dr. John Burger, then Director of the Division of Biology and Medicine of the government, asking for Burger's views on radiation as well as on Pauling. Burger was normally a calm and undramatic man, but this time Pauling had gotten to him. To Libby he responded that:

> It is difficult to answer Dr. Pauling's letter because it is obvious that he wants an argument. However, I would suggest that you might wish to consider an answer to him somewhat along these lines: "Your letter itself exhibits some of the reasons why there may be so much confusion with respect to these matters. Most of the things you mention are of the most speculative character about which there is great scientific uncertainty. Yet I notice you using phrases such as 'little doubt' in regard to matters . . . You quote Professor Sturdevant on the basis of his being an experienced geneticist and of substantial authority . . . but you quote him with regard to the field of neoplastic diseases of man in which Dr. Sturdevant has no special competence . . . With such discontinuity in thought, it is hardly profitable to undertake an argument. . . . There are plenty of geneticists who work thoughtfully and critically and who weigh carefully the evidence before making sweeping generalizations for public consumption."[6]

That would sting.

Pauling was about to be forcefully reminded of Slater's all-out attack on his methods in 1953. The tone and general arguments were the same: Pauling had spoken before doing all his homework; he was careless and methodologically sloppy. But there can be too much calculation and too much data accumulation. There are times when the theoretical soundness of one view over another is not as important as minimizing a risk to life and health. In that way, much of Pauling's work is consistent with itself.

In the 1970s he argued that it is surely worthwhile to tout the virtues of vitamin C, even if the data has not all been collected. It is, after all, a relatively harmless substance. If one is stricken with terminal cancer, the consumption of vitamin C becomes a kind of Pascal's wager. Like belief in God, it won't hurt and might do good.

This is also the basis of his battle against nuclear arms testing. Even if he were wrong, what harm would be done? Outside of some jobs and government grants for academics, what would it have cost the world to rid itself of the dangers of fallout?

Libby and Burger had little interest in such reasoning. Following Burger's advice, Libby passed the message on to Pauling. His tone was a little milder than Burger's: "All in all, I believe we are justified in saying that although genetic effects are unknown, the test fallout is so small as compared to the natural background . . . that we really cannot say that testing is in any way likely to be dangerous."[7]

Pauling was just beginning his fight. A controversy soon erupted over lectures he planned to give at the University of Illinois in 1956, on the nature of proteins and hemoglobin. He intended to say nothing about fallout or its politics. Pauling had many friends at the University of Illinois and he felt that allowing politics to intrude on the distinguished George A. Miller lecture in chemistry would be a kind of insult.

However, in late February, Walter Miles, an attorney for the American Legion in Illinois, told the university that the Legion seriously objected to Linus Pauling's appearance there. Miles pointed to Pauling's anti-nuclear activities, his leftist politics, and the fiascos with the California State Senate. The American Legion also insisted that, although Pauling had signed the Broyles Bill loyalty oath (a standard declaration of nonaffiliation with the Communist Party, required of all University of Illinois employees at the time), his political activities invalidated the oath.

In short, the Legion suggested that the university had not done its homework in inviting Pauling to speak, although there is some confusion over whether Miles was really speaking for the Legion. Soon the Illinois papers were filled with comments about Pauling and his impending visit. Dean Frederick T. Wall had been silent, but was under increasing pressure to speak out. Eventually he released a statement: "Dr. Pauling was invited to give lectures at the University because he is an outstanding scientist and a brilliant lecturer, who would have something worthwhile to say scientifically."[8] Pauling, by contrast, refused to dignify the protests by a comment.

Henning Larsen, provost of the University of Illinois, finally wrote a forceful letter to the Board of Trustees in March: "[Pauling] is . . . loyal to America, a fact that is thoroughly substantiated by the issuance of his passport, by his own sworn statement as a voluntary witness before a committee of the United States Senate, and by his execution of the oath required under the Illinois statute."

Finally, after extensive discussions between the Legion, the Provost, and the President of the university, tempers eased and the lectures took place. On April 4, Pauling spoke to a capacity crowd on the structure of proteins and later gave several more lectures on metallic bonding, hemoglobin, antibodies, and several other topics.

Despite criticism, Pauling was not about to stop protesting. At the beginning of 1957, the Eisenhower administration clarified its policies on nuclear weapons. Conference after conference took place within the administration, resulting in a five-point disarmament program presented to the General Assembly of the United Nations by Henry Cabot Lodge. At its core, the program called for the end of all nuclear weapons manufacture and some reductions in conventional weapons.

Nobody was impressed. The Soviets wanted the clause about "international inspectors" struck. The United States would not agree and thereby guaranteed the death of the proposal. Nor did official Washington have much of world opinion on its side. Many nations saw the suggestion of a United States test ban as a phony reward for total Soviet nuclear disarmament; in effect, a kind of nuclear blackmail, in which the United States would keep a secret stockpile, while the Soviet Union would have to dismantle its own. However, the Soviets were criticized as well. Norway, among other nations, had been exposed to crippling and horribly disfiguring nuclear fallout from Soviet tests. World hysteria continued and the arms race kept escalating.

Within months Britain entered the game, planning to test its first H-bomb in May. Prime Minister Harold Macmillan wanted desperately to meet with Eisenhower to make sure that American nuclear policy would remain stable. He wanted the United States to maintain that weapons testing was a "necessity." Consequently, Eisenhower and Macmillan met in Bermuda in March of 1957 and issued a joint communique. Nuclear testing would continue, but care would be taken to minimize the dangers of radiation and fallout.

Pauling was not impressed by these developments. But he was busy trying to prove to his colleagues that his political activism was not interfering with his scientific professionalism. He kept in touch with old scientific colleagues, discussing biological and medical issues with Leo Szilard and analyzing routine technical matters in structural chemistry. John and Laree Caughey, who were with the American Civil Liberties Union for over twenty years, reminisced:

> It was the McCarthy era; so many lives and careers were lost. We knew of many who committed suicide in those days. But Linus was so courageous, willing to have his name used in all sorts of causes. He was worried about bomb-testing. He was one of the plaintiffs in a lawsuit to stop nuclear testing . . .

It only took one critical university appearance to transform Pauling into a fully committed political activist. In May of 1957 he spoke at Washington University in St. Louis. The original title of the talk was "Science in the Modern World," though it really ended up as a lecture on the evils of nuclear warfare. Before an audience of over one thousand graduate students, undergraduates, and faculty, Pauling grimaced, flailed his arms, joked, and mocked the administration. When told that "bombs will destroy the world," the audience cheered him and applauded wildly.

Barry Commoner described the aftermath of this talk in a 1984 interview: "Pauling, Condon, and I worked most of that night drawing up a petition; he was as excited about the project as anyone had ever seen him." The lecture had moved Pauling so much that he lost some of his famous scientific efficiency and aplomb. According to Professor Edward Hughes: "Pauling hired my wife to do the secretarial work for the petition . . . to negotiate a treaty. . . . Linus later lost a lot of signatures and my wife finally found them in Pauling's breadbasket."

So, thanks to Bernice Hughes, Pauling, Commoner, and Condon finally completed the appeal. The text was straightforward:

> Each nuclear bomb test spreads an added burden of radioactive elements over every part of the world. Each added amount of radiation causes damage to the health of human beings all over the world and causes damage to the pool of human germ plasm such as to lead to an increase in the number of seriously defective children that will be born in future generations.

The appeal is interesting in that there is little to justify the long-held charge that Pauling was a "unilateralist." The appeal, in fact, goes on to speak of "international agreements," as well as a "general disarmament agreement." Later, Pauling did make statements that could be interpreted as supporting unilateral initiatives, but here his perspective was not unilateral; and he was usually careful to specify that agreements between nations should be mutually verifiable.

By June 3 of that year, less than a month after the Washington University speech, over 2500 American scientists had signed the petition. It was impressive. Nobelist H.J. Muller, whose relations with Pauling were still cordial, had signed. Over forty members of the National Academy of Sciences added their voices also. Ralph Lapp, who had devoted many years and much hard work to warning scientists and the general public about the perils of nuclear weaponry, signed as well.

Pauling was exhausted. He had kept up a killing pace, even with the benefit of considerable help from friends and sympathizers. Once over 1500 signatures reached him in two days. His great charisma and charm were of decisive importance in garnering so much support.

For all that, he did not convince everyone. His success in attracting the big names in physics was relatively meager, possibly because they realized that they knew nothing about the effects of radiation on biological substances. The editor of *The Bulletin of the Atomic Scientists*, Eugene Rabinowitch, certainly didn't like the idea. Rabinowitch wrote Pauling on May 18:

> I am afraid you'll be disappointed with my answer to your appeal . . . I am not convinced that a strong quantitative case for the cessation of testing can be made simply on the basis of the threat to health or genetic endowment of mankind. I have no reason to believe that Dr. Libby's figures are not approximately correct . . . Switching the argument entirely from the (probably small) *relative* increase in radioactivity caused by tests, to the high *absolute* number of deaths and injuries even this relatively small increment . . . will not make it convincing for those—and this includes the political leaders of all countries—who believe that such casualties must be weighed against the importance weapon-testing has— they believe—for national defense. Another point in which I am personally skeptical is the rather widely accepted assumption that the cessation of tests is likely to become a first step towards controlled nuclear disarmament . . . This, to me, is the expression of an unfounded belief in the possibility of reversing the advancement of military technology which has occurred since 1945.

The Rabinowitch testimony is important for a rather ironic reason. Rabinowitch had a long history of opposition to the spread of nuclear weapons. He had been the principal author of the controversial *Franck Report*, which warned against the use of the atomic bomb in Japan and argued for immediate freezing of nuclear technology. Oddly, Rabinowitch had by now become complacent, on the assumption that, as he stated it in his letter to Pauling, "the conversion of armed forces of all major nations to atomic weapons is as irreversible as has been the introduction of firearms after the discovery of black powder." In a word, Rabinowitch believed that the existence of world-wide nuclear armaments was now a *fait accompli*. Rather than try and squash the nuclear threat, mankind had to come to terms with it.

Joel H. Hildebrand also refused to sign Pauling's petition. That hurt, since he was a past president of the American Chemical Society and Professor Emeritus at the University of California, a man whose support Pauling certainly wanted. Like Rabinowitch, he claimed ". . . great confidence in the information on fall-out that has been made public by Dr. W.F. Libby." He went even further than Rabinowitch in assailing what he clearly thought were emotional and unsupported appeals by Pauling. He made some points which are, in themselves, telling and objectively stated: "My scientific experience has not been such as to justify me in asserting that 'I have knowledge of the dangers involved and therefore a special responsibility to make these dangers known."

Hildebrand's statement is the most devastating argument against Pauling's crusade. Even in 1957, science was already so compartmentalized that the smallest excursion outside one's own field put a scientist in a position of weakness. The greatest nuclear physicist was a layman in classical botany, as was the solid-state physicist in structural chemistry, and the microbiologist in genetics. Even within one general field, the same principle held: for instance, for a classical botanist and a plant molecular biologist.

Hildebrand had uncovered the great fallacy of Pauling's crusade. Pauling was disturbed but could do nothing, considering the scope of Hildebrand's influence. Hildebrand went on to blast Pauling's fundamental assumptions, asserting that ". . . you do not know whether fall-out may not be substantially reduced as a result of future tests. Scientists should be sure of their ground before claiming scientific authority for alarmist assertions."

That was not Pauling's way. He had learned very early in life to take risks, often to act first and gather data afterwards, a method which sometimes paid off and sometimes did not. He had risked financial difficulties as well as parental disapproval; and he had risked his professional credibility by publishing his own controversial version of the DNA structure. The crusade against nuclear testing was one more such risk.

Hildebrand, by contrast, was a careful and methodical researcher, in the style of John Slater. He went on to say:

> Your statement goes far beyond "making the dangers known"; it enters the realm of international diplomacy, where a scientist possesses no peculiar knowledge or wisdom. I stated my position in such matters several years ago as follows: "I am not criticizing the advocacy of opinions upon any subject of public interest, but only insisting that in such cases the scholar should descend from the professorial rostrum, and not talk as if his knowledge made him a better judge of candidates." Or, I may say, of international diplomacy.

Hildebrand was right in saying that Pauling was doing more than "making the dangers known"—he was in fact advocating policy decisions. However, Hildebrand's viewpoint may also have been influenced by his friendship with Libby.

Above all, it must be noted that the body of scientific knowledge with regard to the biological effects of radiation was at that time uncertain and contradictory. When Pauling called attention to the dangers of carbon-14 (which was produced by hydrogen bombs), he was roundly attacked by geneticists for making "erroneous" and "exaggerated" statements. Yet, according to Pauling's calculations, in a six-year period radiation exposure could result in about one million serious birth defects and nearly two million stillbirths. And, as Pauling put it, such radiation ". . . will cause many millions of people to suffer from minor hereditary defects." Furthermore, and perhaps most importantly, the data on which Pauling's calculations were based had been provided by Libby himself!

Pauling's opponents occasionally resorted to sarcasm. On May 29, he received a letter from his old friend Joe Mayer of the University of Chicago:

. . . It seems to me, however, that the danger from testing is simply trivial. Clearly, the real danger is in a war where such weapons are used. In any case the decision on this subject of which I am not firmly convinced one way or another, is not one for which my training as a scientist makes me peculiarly expert. Our son Peter is accepted at Cal. Tech., which makes us happy. However, I suspect the chest X-ray required for admission will harm him more than fallout from testing.

The critical question at this point is what exactly did Pauling know about radiation and the effects of fallout? We cannot be certain. Evidently, Pauling had been busily looking into the facts. On March 5, 1958, for example, he wrote Dr. M. Demerec at Cold Spring Harbor, asking if he ". . . would be good enough to tell me what your own independent estimate of the increase in mutation rate is." Pauling himself had calculated earlier that bomb testing at the present rate represented, most likely, a one percent increase in the mutation rate in humans.

Most other scientists, however (as indicated in the above letter from Mayer) at this time believed that the effects of radiation on human health were insignificant.

# *13*

# Peace Crusading
# in High Gear

PAULING PERSEVERED IN SPITE OF THE DISAPPOINT-
ment of Mayer's opposition, and soon completed work on the
petition. He wrote Eisenhower on June 4, 1957 from his stately
home on 3500 Fairpoint Street in Pasadena. This was puzzling,
since he usually wrote from his office at Caltech. According to
Professor J. B. Koepfli, now at the University of California, he
began using his home address because he was coming under
increasing pressure to dissociate his political activities from the
Institute. But that was almost impossible; Linus Pauling was
virtually synonymous with Caltech. The administration and the
board of trustees grew more frustrated with each new peace
iniative and with each passing week.

Pauling's letter to Eisenhower was a consummate achievement.

> I am sure that your concern about the biological effects of nuclear
> weapons will cause you to be interested in the appeal to stop the
> testing of these weapons that was prepared by about 2000 Amer-
> ican scientists, including many of the most distinguished biolo-
> gists in the country.

He concluded: "If you should feel that I could be of service to
you in your consideration of this great problem, I shall make

every effort to come to Washington at your invitation, to answer whatever questions you wish to ask me."

Before Eisenhower could consider Pauling's proposal, the press got word of the matter. On June 19, Fulton Lewis Jr. wrote in *The New York Mirror* that:

> A substantial majority of Dr. Pauling's scientist-pals being heard by Holifield's subcommittee are the naive, unworldly, politically immature type who refuse to recognize the Machiavellian nature and machinations of the Communist conspiracy—the type who rushed to public defense of J. Robert Oppenheimer in the face of damning evidence.[1]

Eisenhower was in a quandary. Pauling was widely known among the general public, and a respected and vocal member of the scientific elite. Failure to send him a personal reply might compromise chances of future scientific support, while replying would antagonize the president's conservative supporters, such as Teller, Nixon, and William F. Buckley Jr. The White House finally found a strategy and, on June 29, Sherman Adams wrote Pauling a masterfully vacuous letter:

> The president has asked me to reply to your recent letter to him and to thank you for bringing to his attention some of the names of the signers of a statement which you have prepared. Since the receipt of your letter, extensive hearings on the subject before a committee of the Congress, [with testimony] by scientists who appeared as witnesses, are reported to have shown little or no uniformity of opinion. The testimony is presently being studied. Your interest is appreciated.

In other words, since a group of scientists as prestigious as Pauling were unable to come to a firm conclusion, Pauling's presence in Washington was quite unnecessary. This polite brush-off from the president was keenly disappointing, as the petition had been Pauling's high card. And he had played it.

Pauling always dealt with disappointment in one area by simply turning his energies to another. On August 24, he participated in a symposium on the origins of life held in Moscow. He was quoted in the *Daily News* as saying "It's amazing how closely scientists in their work all over the world parallel each other."[2] One supposes that Pauling had forgotten that Soviet scientists had rebuffed his resonance theory some years earlier.

Yet the visit to Moscow did contain surprises. He met and talked with the Soviet people, and sensed the same hopes and fears that the American people harbored—especially the great fear of nuclear annihilation. This was enough to keep his peace efforts going, despite the disappointing result of the American petition. This time he wanted to gather signatures from scientists all over the world. As he wrote to Niels Bohr on October 20:

> The problem of averting the impending catastrophe of a great nuclear war still exists. The scientists of the world must continue to do their part in the search for a solution to this problem . . . The list of the signers of the appeal should be sent to me, at the address given at the top of this letter, before 1 December 1957. At some time after that date I propose to make a statement about the appeal to the United Nations and to the nations that are testing nuclear weapons.

This appeal was subtly different from the American petition. Here, Pauling was talking about the dangers of nuclear war, rather than simple fallout. He doubtless backed down from his earlier position because of the numbers of high-powered scientists who had told him that worrying about fallout was silly. Mayer was among them, and Pauling respected Mayer's judgment.

There were other, more immediate personal dangers for Pauling. The new peace petition had to be put aside—if only momentarily. The pressure on him at Caltech was intensifying. The university had forced him to curtail his use of research and lab space. Finally, on January 1, 1958, he had had enough. He resigned as chairman of the Division of Chemistry and Chemical

Engineering, although he remained on the faculty. As Jack Roberts told me:

> Linus was not popular in those days with conservative chemists, though [he and I] got along well. I recall one day he stopped me right in the parking lot outside the window and asked what I would think if he got out of being the division chair; now this was a period when he'd been through some investigations and the trustees were ready to throw him overboard. Du Bridge and Bacher [chair of the trustees] recognized the importance of holding the line, and they did, but they lost some of the trustees. Herbert Hoover Jr. resigned because they were holding onto Linus.

By the beginning of 1958, Pauling had also recognized that petitions alone would not eliminate war. He used the time he had been devoting to his chairmanship to widen his assault on the problem of nuclear destruction. He was already deeply involved in writing *No More War!* Concurrently, he engineered a public debate between himself and Edward Teller, the well-known conservative scientist and academician.

Teller had become closely identified throughout the world with conservative and fiercely anti-communist views. Short, with thick eyebrows and a squat build, Teller is an honest, straight forward man. Like Pauling, he was a scientific genius who had, in later years, turned his attention to political causes. Many labeled him a right-wing extremist. (It has often been alleged that this attitude was due to his family having suffered at the hands of the Soviets. In fact, Teller had fled Hungary to escape the Nazis. In 1919, Hungary had been a communist state, though of the "home-grown" variety rather than a Soviet state. A right-wing government eventually took over, and it was not until 1948 that the Soviets took power.) However, Teller is a rigorous, respected scientist, and an intensely private man, who has always required considerable coaxing to speak out on anything, especially anything connected with Pauling. He wrote me in the Fall of 1984, "Dr. Pauling and I disagree in a most thoroughgoing manner on many issues, though much of his scientific work is excellent."

In 1953, Teller left the University of Chicago to join Ernest Lawrence at the University of California at Berkeley and, for a number of years, worked at developing new types of nuclear power—always believing in nuclear power and superiority as the only real road to peace in the world. Obviously, he was light-years apart from Pauling on the issue of nuclear testing. On June 20, Teller appeared before the military applications subcommittee of the Joint Committee on Atomic Energy, where he startled the world with the claim that it would be a "crime against humanity" for the United States to stop testing nuclear weapons before an allegedly "clean" bomb could be built.

Of course the academic community was furious with Teller, given his almost complete lack of support for their views, which tended to be anti-nuclear. He faced even more opposition after the publication of Nevil Shute's novel *On the Beach*, which described the final days of humanity after a nuclear holocaust. Scores of Americans shuddered and prayed as weekly installments of Shute's novel appeared.

Pauling and Teller rapidly emerged as the leaders and spokesmen for opposing sides of the nuclear debate. On January 13, Pauling brought everything to a head when he personally presented his second petition to Dag Hammarskjold, then Secretary-General of the United Nations.

On February 21, Pauling and Teller met in a debate on KQED-TV in San Francisco on the topic "Is Fallout Overrated?" moderated by the calm and unflappable James Day. Pauling began by rebutting a recent article Teller had written for *Life* about him and his petition; characteristically, he asserted that the magazine had "misquoted" him. The first sentence of the *Life* piece read, "The petition said that the tests were endangering both the present population of the world and generations yet unborn."[3] The article then goes on to label that claim false. But Pauling denied that his petition said that, and gave the "correct" version of the petition. Pauling was engaging in hairline distinctions, since the *Life* article really did state the essence of the petition. Teller began more cordially, heaping praise on Pauling's early work on crystal structures:

> It is a very great pleasure to appear on this broadcast together with Dr. Linus Pauling. I have admired many phases of his work. Without any particular reason for selecting it, I would like to mention one: his research on the structure of silicates in the rocks, giant molecules and his later related work on the giant molecules of the protein in our bodies.

He then issued his familiar warning about the great dangers of allowing Soviet aggressions to go unchecked, and soon came to the key question—genetic damage to unborn generations:

> I would like to say this: there is no doubt that some radioactivity is spread throughout the world by nuclear explosions. Dr. Pauling says this causes damage. He expresses his concern that this damage will be quite serious . . . Now let me tell you right here, this alleged damage which the small radioactivity is causing—supposedly cancer and leukemia—has not been proved, to the best of my knowledge, by any kind of decent and clear statistics. . . . there is the possibility, furthermore, that very small amounts of radioactivity are helpful . . . We know enough about the mechanism of heredity to be sure that changes will be made in the germ plasm, just as Dr. Pauling has said, and many, very many, probably the great majority of these changes will be damaging. Yet without some changes, evolution would be impossible.

Pauling and Teller both held their own in the debate, despite Pauling's superlative skills in that format. At one point, however, Pauling scored neatly, referring to a comment Teller had made:

> Here is a statement, a paragraph about the people in Tibet who were exposed to large amounts of cosmic radiation, and it says, "Yet the genetic differences have not been noticed in the humans of Tibet." Surely the authors of the article, before they wrote it,

made the calculation and found out that the geneticists of the world agree that there should be a fifteen percent increase in the number of defective children born. . . . Who believes, who *is* there who believes, that medical statistics are good enough in Tibet to detect this fifteen percent increase in the number of defective children, as compared with other countries of the world? This is a red herring.

Ed Hughes remembered this remark, as did many others:

> Well, Teller was a Hungarian . . . and a bitter anti-Soviet and most people feel he's allowed this to override his good judgment; I remember one thing in this debate where he said if Pauling was right, the people of Tibet should have a higher incidence of cancer because of the high altitude, because they were not protected by layers of atmosphere; Pauling pointed out that of all the countries in the world, this one has the poorest statistics.[4]

According to Jack Roberts:

> Everybody was playing the game the way they saw it; the thing that distressed some of us was, you know . . . they were talking about the same numbers but looking at them in different kinds of ways, twisting the data to favor their politics and that's nothing new in science or anything else.[5]

Some of the other participants in the nuclear dramas and policy battles of the 1950s were much worse than either Pauling or Teller in this regard. According to William Friedlander, the eminent historian of science and public policy at Washington University, the investigation of the Atomic Energy Commission had revealed evidence of corruption, and the climate of the times just added to the confusion:

> Stevenson had raised the issue of fallout as a hazard and Ike, with Atomic Energy Commission information, responded that it was no hazard. It later transpired that earlier, in 1954, the Atomic Energy Commission had funded a secret project under Willard Libby on the West Coast called Project Sunshine; the purpose of

the project was to precisely measure the effects of fallout as a hazard. Now that was known to the Atomic Energy Commission at the time they were reassuring Ike that there *was* no hazard, but it wasn't the first time the Atomic Energy Commission lied publicly.[6]

In a word, the country was in chaos over the issue. Contradictory statistics and charges and countercharges abounded. The debates only sharpened the sense of mission both Pauling and Teller shared. Teller went on to write and publish a book called *Our Nuclear Future*, an impassioned argument for more testing. Pauling began a series of lawsuits that would last, more or less continuously, from 1958 up to the present day. On February 24, he wrote to the geneticist Millislav Demerec about this ambitious idea:

> As one of the means of attempting to bring about cessation of further bomb tests . . . some concerned citizens are proposing . . . suits to seek to enjoin responsible officials in the USSR, Great Britain and the United States from further detonation of these weapons. . . . The sponsors of this action would like to have some prominent scientists join as plaintiffs in this suit. . . . Is this something you might consider? . . .

At the same time, he continued work on *No More War!*, trying to enlist the support of Millislav Demerec again, as well as H. J. Muller and numerous other scientists. The results were mixed. Demerec wanted to help with the genetic information, but would have no part of a lawsuit. On March 6, he wrote a terse letter to Pauling: "Despite my strong opposition to the continuation of atomic bomb tests, I feel that a court action as an attempt to stop these tests is not justified." Naturally, all of this activity fueled new assaults on Pauling's allegiance to the United States. One of the silliest occurred in the right-wing journal *Counterattack*, which concluded with Budenz's famous accusation that Pauling was a party member "under discipline," a charge now known to have been groundless.

Pauling was proving to be a continued irritant to the Eisenhower administration. A hurriedly scrawled memo gives a revealing and insightful picture of day-to-day workings at the nation's highest office. Addressed simply to "Mary" (probably Mary Rawlings, who regularly acted as a liaison of sorts between various offices at the White House, particularly Admiral Strauss'), it reads, "Would you please check Strauss' office & see what's the story on this. It's getting old and this Pauling is a rather important person, I think. Helen."[7] Most likely, this memo was occasioned by Pauling's impatience at the lack of any reply to a letter he had sent to Eisenhower on June 4, 1957.

Despite lack of assurances from the President or Admiral Strauss, Pauling went ahead with his suit. On April 4, along with Norman Thomas, Bertrand Russell, and many others, he announced the action while filing it in District Court in Washington. They named as defendants Defense Secretary Neil McElroy and the members of the Atomic Energy Commission, claiming that "past and future explosions did and will cause [the public] . . . to be damaged genetically."

The wire services lapped up every morsel. In the April 10 issue of the *Washington News*, John Troan, a science writer for Scripps-Howard, wrote that: "Ghost statistics are being resurrected here by atom-bomb foes seeking a court injunction to stop nuclear tests . . . about to begin in the Pacific." As did so many others, Troan expressed his faith in Libby's data. Referring to Pauling's claim that the incidence of leukemia increases directly with an increase in radiation, he claimed that ". . . Dr. Willard F. Libby . . . has quoted figures showing the exact opposite is true."

Still, nothing much happened. The Supreme Court ultimately refused to hear the case, but a great deal of publicity had been generated. Pauling kept up the pressure from other flanks as well. On Sunday, May 11, he engaged in a famous debate with Lawrence Spivak on "Meet the Press." The interrogators did not mince words with Pauling. One reporter asked:

Wouldn't the American public, which as I say is anxious to get to the truth of these matters . . .—doesn't the fact that you in the past have always rather mouthed the communist point of view

. . . influence [the American public] to put more credence in Dr. Libby and Dr. Teller?[8]

Pauling responded: "I deny that I have mouthed the communist point of view. I challenge you to prove that I have." Spivak then referred to Pauling's defense of the Rosenbergs, a fact that many used against Pauling in later years, but that argument is specious: that Pauling defended communists does not warrant the conclusion that he himself is a communist. (Whatever the case, one cannot fail to note a poignant historical irony here: at about this time, although Pauling's peace initiatives were welcomed by the Soviets, criticism was building in the Soviet Union towards Pauling's "resonance" theory of chemical structure, the idea that certain kinds of chemical bonds are hybrids or "mixtures" of two or more different structures. Because Pauling's principles here appeared to be in conflict with Marxist ideology and metaphysics, the Russian scientific community [although Pauling had friends within it] denounced him as "an idealistic representative of the capitalist West.")

The program became increasingly tense. Pauling was bristling in response to further allegations of communist leanings, coupled with assertions by Frank Conniff:

. . . here we have just witnessed you downgrading the whole community of scientists who have disagreed with your point of view. Wouldn't the American people be more inclined to believe scientists of the calibre of Dr. Teller, Dr. Libby, who are not tainted . . . with a rather prolonged record of association with communist fronts?

Conniff's objectivity had essentially abandoned him at this point. It was wild of him to suggest that Pauling's associations with "communist" front organizations (a shaky claim at best) made his views any less objective than Teller's. Teller, as a bitter anti-Soviet, had a very specific axe to grind. Pauling now erupted:

Mr. Conniff, I would like to see what the scientific community feels about my standing relative to Dr. Teller's. You have Dr.

Teller, Dr. Libby. There you are. You have two or three scientists as spokesman for the AEC on the one hand and they make dishonest, untrue, misleading statements. They mislead the American public.

Pauling was clearly wrong in saying that Teller was being dishonest. Teller clearly believed his own claims, though they may have been untrue. The question of Libby's veracity is something else again. There is strong testimonial evidence, as noted earlier, that the AEC has lied to the public more than once, and Libby may well have felt considerable pressure to make statements that were not supported by the facts. There is, of course, no evidence of any personal dishonesty on Libby's part.

In the end, Pauling and Teller parted company cordially. Neither ever succeeded in changing the other's mind. But they had each presented most persuasive arguments for their respective points of view, and these were highly publicized. Newspapers made quite a bit of the communist allegations which emerged in the course of the controversy, while giving relatively little attention to the technical details. They all but ignored Pauling's claims about the dangers posed by carbon-14, for example. On May 22, the *Washington Post* quoted Spivak as asking Pauling why "you seem to be interested in Communist human beings." Pauling responded by recounting a little-known episode in which he had signed a petition requesting that a general named Smith be granted the use of a hall in Los Angeles. Smith, a rabid ultra-conservative and fierce anti-communist, had been denied the hall because some feared that he planned to launch a fascist attack on United States policies. While it is true that over the long haul Pauling associated with and sympathized with left-leaning people, he would, on occasion, defend anyone whose rights were being trampled, even someone like Smith.

The *Post* also quoted Pauling's replies to questions about how much money it required to finance the round of petitions: "I paid for it myself: I got the money. It cost about $600. We got those signatures for three cents apiece . . ." As Professor Barry Commoner recalled: ". . . it was just pennies out of a basement; I really don't know how people got the idea that it cost a fortune.

Just a mimeo machine and some postage did it." Reason had obviously taken a back seat to anti-communist hysteria.

Pauling's book *No More War!*, which was published in 1958, created considerable controversy in the United States and abroad. Peter Collins, the sharp-tongued reviewer from the British journal, *The Sunday Times*, went straight to the point:

> The first part of this book provides an irrefutable argument for the prevention at all costs of nuclear war. . . . While giving consideration to the opinions of the scientists who disagree with him, [Pauling] is most outspoken in his criticism of others such as Edward Teller who, as spokesman for the U.S. Atomic Energy Commission has, he maintains, deliberately concealed or distorted the real facts.

The book itself is a daring work and a surprisingly good effort at defending what is, in the ultimate analysis, an untenable thesis. As William F. Buckley, Jr. has remarked, "There are wars because there are things worse than wars, such as the loss of our national sovereignty." The book tried to argue for the elimination of war (except for wars of liberation, which Pauling always defended). It suggests that a "Secretary of Peace" be added to the president's cabinet. It also recommends a world peace research organization under the auspices of the United Nations which "should include many scientists, and . . . other specialists—economists, geographers, specialists in all fields of knowledge."[9] The writing style is tedious, since writing is not Pauling's forte, but it is a solid achievement. Unfortunately, some of Pauling's ideas were too idealistic, such as his vision of a World Peace Organization (the expense of which would have been formidable).

On August 21, he wrote to Eisenhower yet again:

> I send herewith to you a copy of my new book, *No More War!* I am sure that you are sympathetic to the thesis of the book, as expressed in the following words on page 194: "May our great nation, the United States of America, be the leader in bringing *morality* into its proper place of primary importance in the conduct of world affairs."

It is just this sort of claim, however, that has, possibly unfairly, brought upon Pauling the charge that he is a starry-eyed visionary, out of touch with reality and the politics of the real universe. The proposals set out in *No More War!* were stillborn. They were too vague and impractical. Pauling did try and stir up more interest among other scientists, writing to Harold Urey and others:

> I am thinking seriously of asking a number of leading scientists throughout the world to join with me in setting up a World Academy of Sciences . . . I have in mind that the World Academy of Sciences would be interested in promoting useful knowledge and fostering the progress of science in ways similar to those in which national academies of science now function, except, of course, that there would be no national obligations.

Neither Urey nor anyone else was interested in this idea. It sounded a bit too much like the World Peace Organization in a new guise. Pauling, of course, was frustrated. Rebuffed by Eisenhower, rebuked by many of his scientific friends, and accomplishing relatively little of great import in science, he returned to the lecture platform with a vengeance. Speaking at the commencement exercises at Reed College in Oregon, he gave his most provocative speech to date. Without hesitation he told the graduating class, "Admiral Strauss has shown that he doesn't have the personal integrity that we would like to see in people in government service."[10] How did Pauling come to that position? Senator Clinton Anderson of New Mexico (then chairman of the Atomic Energy Commission) had charged that the United States was stockpiling "dirty" bombs, but had announced that the Atomic Energy Commission was trying to develop "clean" bombs. Strauss had replied that the United States was not adding anything to the bombs that would increase the total amount of radioactive materials they produced.

The debate was a bit fuzzy. Who knew what a "clean" bomb was? As we have seen, the Atomic Energy Commission had stretched the truth to the American public on other occasions.

Pauling's charge against Strauss did get some press, but he still wasn't generating the attention he wanted.

Thus the Paulings decided to try and enlist the aid of peace activist Albert Schweitzer, believing that an endorsement by Schweitzer would add fuel to the peace initiatives. They thought this possible because Schweitzer's views on peace were so close to theirs. Pauling and his wife set out still one more time on a world tour. Arriving in Africa, they were met by Dr. John Catchpool, the chief resident at Schweitzer's hospital in the Gabon, by the banks of the Ogowe' River. Catchpool described the memorable encounter:

> I remember very clearly when I first met Dr. Pauling. It was in 1959, I was chief resident or head physician of Albert Schweitzer's hospital . . . Pauling felt that Schweitzer . . . would speak with more authority than anybody else on moral issues. Of all the Nobel Prize winners, he was the moralist, the man who'd made his whole life his example.[11]

In fact, in 1956, Norman Cousins, the editor of *Saturday Review*, had asked Schweitzer to add his voice to those opposing nuclear testing. Schweitzer had been watching the anti-test efforts of Pauling and others very closely. As Schweitzer explained at the time: "All peoples are involved; therefore the matter transcends the military interest that the test be stopped."

The visit with Schweitzer was the high point of Pauling's overseas voyage, as he himself told the *Oregon Journal* just after his return. Pauling explained that Schweitzer had told him people had to start thinking for themselves about world problems, rather than depending on political or religious leaders for solutions. It was a splendid visit in many ways. Ava Helen was thoroughly charmed by Schweitzer and spent many happy and productive hours with him, admiring his work, the energy of the natives, and the efficiency of the hospital. Above all, both Paulings marveled at Schweitzer's single-minded dedication. Not surprisingly, Schweitzer later helped sponsor Pauling's Oslo Peace Conference Against the Spread of Nuclear Weapons, held in

1961. Pauling, in turn, quoted Schweitzer in his "Humanism and Peace" lecture before the American Humanist Association in Cleveland: "Dr. Albert Schweitzer believes that not only man but also other forms of life should be included in the field of our concern. He has expressed this belief in his principle of Reverence for Life . . ."[12]

PROFESSOR F.A. LONG congratulates Linus Pauling for his Nobel Prize, 1954. News of Pauling's first Nobel was well-received by the scientific community. Reactions would be much more ambivalent when Pauling was awarded the Nobel Peace Prize in 1962. *Photo courtesy of the Oregon Historical Society.*

J. ROBERT OPPENHEIMER. Pauling's relationship with Oppenheimer was a complex one. They were often on good terms, but periodically, tensions existed between them. Pauling declined Oppenheimer's offer to participate in the Manhattan Project. He may also have been skeptical of Oppenheimer's eclectic interests (Eastern philosophy, for example). However, when the Atomic Energy Commission declared Oppenheimer a "security risk," Pauling angrily rushed to his defense. *Photo courtesy of the Physics Today Collection, the Niels Bohr Library, the American Institute of Physics.*

LINUS PAULING at a Senate Internal Security Committee hearing, 1960. Several days before the hearing, after Pauling spoke to the Women's International League for Peace and Freedom, he was surrounded by well-wishers, and a member of the crowd slipped him a note. The "note" was a subpoena. *Photo courtesy of the Oregon Historical Society.*

LINUS PAULING in 1962, just days after he and Ava Helen demonstrated in front of the White House—and crossed their own picket line to join President and Mrs. Kennedy for dinner. *Photo courtesy of the Oregon Historical Society.*

EDWARD TELLER *(seated, far right)* during the making of the documentary, "The World of Jimmy Doolittle," and NBC Special Project, 1962. Teller and Pauling were diametrically opposed in their political views, particularly on the issue of nuclear weapons. In fact, they debated the likelihood and relative dangers of nuclear fallout on KQED-TV in San Francisco in 1958. *Photo courtesy of the Niels Bohr Library, the American Institute of Physics.*

LINUS PAULING is led off a cliff by a rescue party, Big Sur, California, 1960. On a Saturday morning in February, Pauling set out on a routine survey of his Big Sur ranch. As he made his way along the cliff's edge, he slipped on loose gravel and froze in terror. As he told reporters, "I got the jitters and decided to stay there until I was found." *Photo courtesy of Wide World Photos.*

LINUS PAULING with his first science teacher, Pauline Geballe, at the sixtieth reunion of his graduating class at Washington High School, 1966. Pauling did not actually graduate from high school because he refused to take a course in civics, arguing that he could learn all he needed to know from his own reading. He proved to be right. After he was awarded the Nobel Peace Prize in 1962, Washington High School granted him a diploma. *Photo courtesy of the Oregon Historical Society.*

LINUS PAULING with one of his Nobel certificates, c. 1970. The negative responses of some California Institute of Technology faculty to news of his Nobel Peace Prize may have been one factor in Pauling's decision to leave Caltech after nearly forty years on the faculty. *Photo courtesy of the Department of Information, Oregon State University.*

LINUS PAULING with friends and family members. Seated, from left to right, Thomas Vaughn of the Oregon Historical Society, sister Pauline Emmett, Ruth Jacobson, sister Lucille Jenkins. Standing, from left to right, P.M. Stephenson, Linus Pauling, Michael Ney, and Lou Flannery of the Oregon Historical Society. *Photo courtesy of the Oregon Historical Society.*

AVA HELEN PAULING *(left)* with Mrs. Raymond Graap, president of the Women's Alliance of the First Unitarian Church, 1963. One reporter described Mrs. Pauling in the *Oregonian* as being dressed in all the "tiny details that are so womanly . . . [U]nder her gentle exterior, she stands so firm in her fight for disarmament and peace." Ava Helen discussed the role of women in the struggle for peace. *Photo courtesy of the Oregon Historical Society.*

LINUS PAULING at the opening of the Pauling Room for Special Collections, Kerr Library, Oregon State University, 1986. Since the early 1970s, Pauling has dedicated himself to the study of Vitamin C. His views on the medical benefits of this vitamin have caused great controversy among the medical establishment. After years of refusing to consider the issue, the scientific community, represented by Charles Moertel of the Mayo Clinic, finally decided to test the benefits of high-dosage Vitamin C treatments. The results were inconclusive. *Photo courtesy of the Department of Information, Oregon State University.*

LINUS PAULING and his daughter, Linda Kamm, greet well-wishers at a reception at Oregon State University, 1986. Pauling's most recent scientific work has been in the area of high-temperature superconductivity. As always, his approach is original and controversial. *Photo courtesy of the Department of Information, Oregon State University.*

LINUS PAULING meets with 1986 members of his fraternity at Oregon State University. Pauling was chided by classmate Tony Schille for failing to be more involved in campus activities. However, Pauling's college days were a combination of academic achievement and financial hardship, until the college offered him a teaching position. *Photo courtesy of the Department of Information, Oregon State University.*

LINUS PAULING with Helen Caldicott, scientist and well-known peace activist, who delivered the 1984 Ava Helen Pauling Lecture for World Peace at Oregon State University. After he won the Nobel Peace Prize, Pauling gradually became more politically active. Ironically, although Pauling was criticized for his leftist sympathies, he reportedly voted for Republican Herbert Hoover in 1928. Later he often referred to himself as a "Rooseveltian Democrat." *Photo courtesy of the Department of Information, Oregon State University.*

LINUS PAULING with Adolfo Perez Esquivel, Nobel Peace Prize laureate. Esquivel delivered the 1987 Ava Helen Pauling Lecture for World Peace at Oregon State University. *Photo courtesy of Mark Floyd.*

LINUS AND AVA HELEN PAULING visiting the Oregon State University Archives, 1980. Seven months after this visit, Ava Helen died of stomach cancer. *Photo courtesy of the Oregon State University Archives.*

# *14*

# A Brush With Death

AT THE BEGINNING OF THE 1960S, THE PAULINGS WERE tired from their travels. Ava Helen felt Linus needed a rest, and they began taking more time off at their ranch on the Big Sur, the beautifully wooded area overlooking the Pacific on the coast of California.

He had no reason to be apprehensive when, in early February of 1960, he set out on a Saturday morning to begin a routine survey of his land and inspect fences. The footing was unexpectedly treacherous. As he made his way along the cliff's edge, he slipped on loose gravel and froze in terror. One more slip and he might fall 500 feet from the cliff down to the Pacific. When he did not return by midnight, Ava Helen reported him missing. Rumors flew. Some reports had him dead. A battery of forest rangers, sheriff's deputies, and bloodhounds as well as two H-189 Army helicopters from Fort Ord set out. They soon found him. Pauling later spoke of his state of mind in a newspaper interview: "I got the jitters and decided to stay there until I was found."[1] He told reporters: "Being a scientist, I took a stick and tried to keep time by movement of the constellations . . . I kept moving my arms and legs to keep warm. Then I lay down under a large map I had in my pocket. That helped conserve body heat."

The incident took some of the pleasure out of their trip to

Big Sur, and the Paulings soon returned to Pasadena. It was at least a month before Pauling had sufficiently recovered from exposure and fright to do much of anything. In fact, even when he was able to work, he had to cancel some minor projects. He had been in touch with Charles Humbold, the editor of *Mainstream* magazine regarding some planned articles, and wrote Humbold on March 8, 1960, more than a month after his brush with death: "I have had some trouble in taking care of my correspondence during the last month, and have only now been able to answer your letter of 4 February . . . I wonder if you would be interested in a little article by me . . ." On April 6, he wrote Humbold again:

> I have been kept so busy during recent weeks that it has not been possible for me to complete the preparation for publication of my article . . . It now looks to me as though I shall not be able to do the job before leaving . . . for Europe . . . I shall, I think, give up the plan.

According to close friends such as Jerry Donohue and Laree Caughey, Pauling was simply too frazzled and exhausted to keep up with all of his work. It is worth noting that this was one of the very few times in Pauling's career when he did not keep a commitment. One must conclude that the accident at Big Sur had a most profound, though temporary, effect on him. But the rest of the year was hardly wasted: he published a minor but nonetheless important paper with Jones and Zuckerkandl, comparing various animal hemoglobins and investigating questions of genetics and evolution.

Pauling had scarcely begun to take up his scientific work again when the charges of communist sympathizing and questionable loyalties began again in earnest. Ava Helen became increasingly involved at this time with the Women's International League for Peace and Freedom, a left-leaning group that covertly aimed at the realization of world socialism.

In late June of 1960, Pauling was giving a speech at a Washington meeting of the League at the Willard Hotel. The speech

ended routinely, as well-wishers and autograph-seekers surrounded him. One of the pack slipped Pauling a note. When the
Paulings arrived home Linus realized that the "note" was a subpoena to appear in Washington before the Senate Internal Security Committee. As Pauling described the event:

> Someone handed me a poem . . . someone else a newspaper clip-
> ping . . . someone else some mimeographed material. There were
> a few notes, different pieces of paper. I just put it all in my pocket,
> without looking at them. . . . suddenly I stopped in my tracks.
> There was a subpoena signed by Senator Eastland. I have no idea
> who gave it to me.[2]

Ava Helen was furious—more so than Pauling. She admitted
surprise, "mostly at the waste of time . . . [I am] also very un-
happy that the government should be misusing its proper function and power."

The hearing was held at 8 A.M. on June 21. James Eastland
was there as chairman. Sam Ervin of North Carolina was present, as was Roman Hruska of Nebraska, Everett Dirksen of Illinois, and Kenneth Keating of New York, with Estes Kefauver
of Tennessee sitting in as a member of the Judiciary Committee
(parent to the subcommittee). Most disturbing to Pauling, however, was the presence of Thomas J. Dodd of Connecticut, a
vehement right-winger who especially disliked Pauling.

In the introduction to its "Report on the Hearings of Dr.
Linus Pauling," the committee gave its reasons for summoning
Pauling:

> On January 15, 1958, Dr. Linus Pauling filed with the United
> Nations the text of a petition which called for an immediate ban
> on nuclear testing. . . . According to his final claim, his petition
> bore the signatures of 11,021 scientists in 49 countries. The Senate
> Subcommittee on Internal Security had for some time felt that
> Dr. Pauling's petition warranted investigation. The decision to
> request Dr. Pauling's testimony was reached as a result of newly
> available information, including evidence of serious Communist
> infiltration in the various movements urging a nuclear test ban.[3]

If Pauling had been annoyed before, he was furious and immovable now. The committee was asking for two things: the actual signatures of all those names which were listed on the petition, and the names of those who had helped gather the signatures. As they saw it, these requests were nothing if not "simple and reasonable."

Pauling had learned the strategy and tactics of committee-fighting during the California hearings of 1952. He used every conceivable public relations weapons against them—interviews, public hearings, and name-calling. In an Associated Press dispatch of June 22, for example, he described Senator Dodd, Edward Teller, and a few others as "militarist, H-bomb scientists and military contractors . . . the greatest of all enemies of the United States." While Pauling dazzled the press with his theatrics, the front pages were also filled with complaints from the committee about Pauling's behavior. As they said, "Dr. Pauling's response to the subcommittee and his general conduct in relationship to it has from the beginning been discourteous and defiant."[4] But Pauling had been *subpoenaed*. Under the circumstances, it is difficult to imagine how terms like "discourteous" can be appropriate.

Pauling went further than ever: he filed suit on August 22 to force the committee to stop interrogating him. He felt that he had no alternative, since he believed disclosing the names of those who had helped him would place many well-meaning people in jeopardy. On August 26, Federal Judge Joseph C. McGarraghy dismissed Pauling's suit, thereby upholding the government's argument that the courts could not interfere with a subcommittee; he held that these legislative functions were normally outside the jurisdiction of courts. However, the suit did generate publicity. Pauling declared, "I'm not surprised by the decisions, and I don't think my trip here has been a waste of time. I think it has helped build up public opinion against actions . . . like the subcommittee's."[5]

Pauling wasted no time in appealing to the Supreme Court. With the help of his attorney, A.L. Wirin, he managed to irritate just about everyone not on his side with his publicity maneuvers and requests for postponements. Pauling always loved to irritate and torment his political opponents. In its report, the subcommittee wrote:

> Dr. Pauling carried on an unremitting campaign against the subcommittee in the press. In early October he printed an advertisement over his own name in the *Washington Post* and other papers [which read]: "I ask that you join with me in getting rid of Congressional committees that exceed their authority and subvert the Constitution and the Bill of Rights . . ."[6]

Pauling's confidence ebbed when, on the morning of October 10, the Supreme Court denied his request for a stay, pointing out that it would constitute unwarranted interference with the legislative process. Later, at 2:30 P.M., the subcommittee received a telegram from Pauling's lawyer saying Pauling would not appear before the subcommittee and bring documents ordered, and asking for a postponement. That same afternoon, Pauling held a press conference saying he had no intention of showing up at the October 11 subcommittee meeting. Unwilling to be rattled, the vice-chairman of the subcommittee wired Wirin at Los Angeles, denying the postponement request. He even issued a new supoena, again ordering him to appear at 10:30 A.M. the next morning.

With a postponement denied, Pauling had to appear. He strode confidently into the subcommittee hearing room, bearing three volumes of names he had collected. He was forced to bend this time, though only very slightly. He named Edward Condon and Barry Commoner as the initiators of the petitions, but balked at revealing any other names.

Dodd was furious and Pauling was the very soul of self-confidence. Dodd denounced Pauling as "deliberately contemptuous." Pauling responded in kind during a tea in his honor given by the Women's International League for Peace and Freedom. The subcommittee was a "discredit to the Senate and our country. This evil committee perhaps isn't evil because of the senators who are on it—except for their negligence—but perhaps because of the people who run it."[7] He also made reference to the strain of the proceedings on Ava Helen, saying that he was "looking for the time when my wife can bake bread for me instead of spending all her time writing letters for me." The question naturally arises as to whether the type of sexism revealed in this remark is characteristic of Pauling himself, or simply of the 1960s. As always with such questions, it is difficult to separate the person from the *Zeitgeist*. The consciousness-raising of the feminist movement was still far in the future and the association of women with domesticity was customary at that time. It is almost certain that Pauling would not talk that way today. For one, he has a long and venerable history of tolerant and non-patronizing attitudes towards all so-called minority groups. Furthermore, there is overwhelming evidence that he always had the very highest regard for both his wife and for women in general. Indeed, as noted earlier, he worked very hard, according to Professor Jack Roberts, to have a woman admitted to the graduate program at the California Institute of Technology, despite almost unanimous opposition. Therefore, the above remark is best attributable to the tenor of the times.

The final meeting of the subcommittee on October 11 disintegrated as quickly as it had started. Pauling's sharp repartees and outflanking of the senators brought spectators to their feet, applauding wildly more often than not. By mid-afternoon, the crowds had dwindled, the students packing the halls were gone, and even Pauling's attorney was yawning visibly. Soon, the committee simply stopped calling him back. No charges were filed and no penalties were imposed.

The nuisance of the committee hearings now behind him, Pauling began work on another petition. Unlike the 1958 petition which was intended to stop the testing and manufacture of nuclear weapons, this one was designed to stop the spread of already existing weapons. Pauling had, over the intervening years, realized that he could only make progress with more modest petitions. He worked quickly, and it was ready in March of 1961. The text declared, "It is our hope that the spread of nuclear weapons can be prevented in order that an effective attack may be made on the problem of achieving peace and disarmament through international agreements and international law."

The petition was timely: France had already begun carrying

out nuclear explosions and there was every expectation that other nations would soon follow. Some nations were even suggesting that nuclear weapons should be turned over to NATO. If there was any further doubt of the petition's relevance, the timeliness of Pauling's move is confirmed by the fact that the world was soon to approach the brink of disaster during the Cuban Missile Crisis.

However, the petition received comparatively little press coverage. Public interest in and sympathy for such moves no longer generated the controversy it once had. Why, exactly, this is so is difficult to answer; however, some discussion of the political atmosphere before, during and after the most intense period of Pauling's peace campaigning may be helpful. Additionally, it may be helpful to compare Pauling's situation with Einstein's. The two were in many ways similar. Both were great scientists; both leaned strongly to the left, and both were active politically and in similar causes. Some excellent ideas emerge from Jamie Sayen's book, *Einstein in America*. According to Sayen, a firm United States policy towards nuclear weapons and Russia was already being formulated soon after World War II, No doubt, many high level government officials did perceive that the Soviets were, in fact, a real threat. This perception led the government to begin playing down the dangers of atomic and hydrogen bombs. Indeed, sometimes families of Americans killed by bombs in Japan were told that the deaths had been caused by other means. Later the government created the illusion that the United States had lost its exclusivity in bomb-building because of subversives who were intent on destroying the American way of life.

During the Pauling/Einstein period, the government regularly consulted with experts like Libby and Teller, who sympathized with the policies of the Cold War. Mavericks like Einstein and Pauling who battled the philosophical assumptions undergirding foreign policy were rashly labeled communists or naive traitors.

The situation was exacerbated by the social and economic conditions during the depression. The economic measures of the New Deal served to consolidate governmental power, and because many of the hired government experts were part of an intellectual elite, often trained at fashionable Ivy League universities, a gap in trust and credibility between the government and the public developed almost immediately.

Whatever the cause, after the war the rhetoric of the Truman administration fueled the anti-Communists' hysteria, and the hysteria deepened during the Eisenhower administration. According to Richard Nixon, Louis Budenz, and others, the United States was riddled with "communist" intellectuals determined to obliterate the American system of government. Among American conservatives, only William F. Buckley sounded an occasional note of reason and restraint. Critics of the anti-Communist stance were branded "irrational" or "disloyal." Pauling's considerable personal charm and charisma had provided a buffer against these attitudes. The buffer was now collapsing.

While the government fought to make a confused and frightened American public believe in the purity of their anti-Communist campaign, few realized, as Sayen points out, that the Communist infiltration into Eastern Europe and Asia was the result of the war with Germany and Japan and not the result of a mythical communist "conspiracy." Instead of admitting that errors had been caused by governmental blunders and a misreading of economic and historical circumstances, failures were blamed on conspirators within the United States. Thus the smear campaigns on men like Pauling, Einstein, and Oppenheimer. Reactionary elements in power were seeking to discredit their frequent criticisms of American Cold War Policy.

By the time of Pauling's petition, the height of the anti-Communist campaign had passed, hence, the relative lack of media coverage. Still, Pauling's efforts may have had some long-term effects. Many believe, for example, that he played a role in persuading the nuclear powers to institute at least a partial nuclear test-ban treaty in 1963. That, in turn, led to the Nobel Peace Prize for Pauling.

Pauling had learned from his earliest scientific work that one must always re-evaluate techniques. When classic X-ray diffraction techniques were not powerful enough to decipher the structures of substances which were not found as solid crystals, he turned to electron diffraction. Similarly, he now realized that petitions alone were not powerful enough to accomplish one's goals—especially where governments were concerned. He was still considering lawsuits as a means of stopping nuclear tests and generating publicity. Despite its failure, his suit to stop the subcommittee had generated much publicity, as had his earlier suit to stop the testing of nuclear weapons. With the public interest in his peace initiative waning, he turned his attention to another goal, and used lawsuits as his tool.

Tired of being vilified and called "anti-American," he sued a newspaper in March of 1961 for libel, as he had wanted to do for a long time. In the suit he charged that the Bellingham Publishing Company (publisher of the *Bellingham Herald*) as well as four people whose letters the paper had published, had tended to discredit him and hold him up to public contempt and ridicule. The occasion for the letters was one of Pauling's provocative speeches given at Haggard Hall on the Western Washington College campus. This time Pauling won a small victory. Though the defendants filed for motions of dismissal of the $400,000 libel action, the paper did settle out of court for a reduced sum. Inspired by this victory, Pauling would go on to file a string of libel actions.

Groping for other alternatives to his peace petitions, Pauling next tried his largest, most radical and innovative offensive yet. With the help of his wife and friends from all over the world, he began organizing a peace conference which was to be held on May 2, 1961 in Oslo, Norway. Pauling publicly announced that it was intended to prevent the arming of NATO nations with nuclear weapons, a point he had addressed in a press conference in the Carnegie Endowment Building on United Nations Plaza a few weeks earlier.

The conference was a gathering of over sixty academicians (mostly scientists) from Poland, Sweden, Denmark, Japan, the Soviet Union, and other nations. Officially titled the "Conference Against the Spread of Nuclear Weapons," it began with sparse ceremony in room 344 of the Oslo Grand Hotel. Pauling's opening remarks reflected the brash confidence that by now had become his trademark:

Our experience in attending some of the Pugwash Conferences had revealed to us the value of conferences of this sort, in which scientists and other informed people from many countries meet to study and analyze some aspects of the present great world situation. . . . The argument that in order to achieve peace and disarmament the great nations must first increase their military might is grossly fallacious. The transfer of nuclear weapons to the NATO nations and the nations of the Warsaw Pact would surely increase the danger of war . . .[8]

He seemed to be preaching to the already converted. But the Paulings were dedicated. Ava Helen spoke also:

It's a bit strange that it is my job to welcome you, but I feel good too, because I feel so at home in Oslo. . . . General Omar Bradley said that wars could be prevented as easily as they can be provoked, and those who fail to prevent them must share the guilt for the dead. We tonight feel that we are working to save humanity itself.

The conference provided one of the rare occasions when Pauling publicly admitted to not knowing something. In a discussion of the destructive effects of nuclear weapons, he said, "Then for the 20 megaton bomb, . . . the second stage involves lithium deuterite, the third stage involves ordinary uranium. You see, I know so little in this field that all I can do is to make a calculation."

The scientists concluded by making four recommendations, all involving the idea that the nuclear weapons of the world should be held in check. None should be sent to NATO or transferred to other countries. They also suggested that no more testing should be carried out by other countries; that demilitarization of central Europe would help the cause of peace; and that disarmament would raise the standard of living in the world.

Inspired by the conference, Pauling blasted the neutron bomb at lectures all over the country, calling it a "political weapon, not a military weapon" and a greater fraud than the so-called "clean" H-bomb. He also attacked the concept of fallout shelters; he felt they were ineffective and thought they might give people false hope. As he described his views:

> The palliative effects of shelter construction and training the populace can be completely neutralized by increasing the scale of the attack by a factor of 4 . . . The statement by *Life* magazine that all but five million Americans could be saved in a nuclear war is ludicrous.[9]

# 15

# At War With Herman J. Muller

THE EFFECT OF ALL THIS FRENETIC WORK WAS BEGIN-
ning to show. By early 1962, the lack of progress toward peace
and the sheer strain of the drives, petitions, hearings, lawsuits,
and conferences had made the Paulings despondent. In February, Ava Helen wrote their old friend and fellow peace activist,
the Reverend A.J. Muste:

> Your letters of the 25th and 30th of January came just after we
> returned from Chile . . . I hope your project in Washington went
> well. I have not seen anything about it in the papers, but I haven't
> had much opportunity to see the papers. We feel rather depressed.
> Each day brings more backward steps. I try to think of a new
> approach or new words and it seems we have used them all and
> still events bring us closer and closer to the final agony.

The resistance to the Paulings' efforts was relentless. As they
prepared for a lecture tour under the auspices of the American
Friends Service Committee, which was to begin in March, they
worried that, in the end, they would generate only more vilification in the press.

Yet before Pauling could plan peacefully for that tour, he
first had to solve another problem. He came under attack in

regard to a speaking engagement at the University of California. Not wanting to focus on Pauling's long history of left-leaning associations, Chancellor Herman T. Spieth invoked the "criteria of expertise" of the Board of Regents, which meant that speakers on campus had to limit themselves to their field of competence. Hence Pauling, as a chemist, should not be permitted to speak on a political issue like disarmament. As Spieth put it, "Dr. Pauling lacks competence in the subject of disarmament, since it is basically a political question and he is a chemist."[1]

Yet many wanted to hear Pauling talk about disarmament at the University of California. Suddenly, Spieth was besieged by letters and editorials. On February 13 Ralph Schleming, the Executive Secretary of the California State Federation of Teachers, wrote Spieth as follows:

> . . . I was shocked at the news of your action regarding Dr. Linus Pauling. Are you saying that a degree in a field is the only valid criterion of competence in a field of knowledge? . . . I am afraid that the next approved speaker will be looked up on very carefully to see if you plan to apply your policy at all points. . . . I have noted that the legislature has not been called upon to correct abuses and weaknesses at the University level to the same extent as the other levels of education. If educational leadership at the University does not give cause, such remedies will not be called for. However, the opposite can be true.

Spieth finally bowed to the pressure from the State Federation of Teachers. By February 23, Pauling was able to write Clark Kerr, then President of the Berkeley campus, to say he had spoken at the Riverside campus the previous evening. The subject was disarmament.

Only several months after this victory, Pauling was drawn into another battle. This time he was not fighting a subcommittee or a right-wing group, but a friend, a respected scientist and fellow Nobel-Prize winner—Herman J. Muller, one of the great geneticists of the century. The conflict developed slowly but inevitably. On October 21, 1961, Pauling wrote Muller as follows:

A rumor has reached me that you are angry with me. No information as to why you are angry was contained in the rumor, or at any rate has been told to me. I do not know whether to take this rumor seriously, but it has troubled me, and I have decided to write to you . . . Perhaps the rumor is true, but your feeling might be based upon some misunderstanding. I hope, if this is the case (that the rumor is true), that you will write to me about your dissatisfaction with me, and give me an opportunity to attempt to clear up the matter. I do not remember having taken any action to cause trouble between us, but I know that misunderstandings sometimes arise between people.

Muller failed to reply immediately and his apparent disaffection only deepened Pauling's sense of frustration, for Muller had been a good friend and a valuable scientific supporter as well as a faithful political ally. Pauling's simple, almost childlike concern was moving; Muller seemed an unlikely opponent. Besides being a fellow Nobelist, he shared many of Pauling's attitudes towards politics: both men leaned to the left. In fact, Muller's name found its way onto an official, 1957 FBI document called "Communist Exploitation of Radiation 'Fall-Out' Controversy," in which he was described as an American who ". . . while employed at the University of Texas . . . had procommunist sympathies." Both men were also wary of totalitarianism.

Yet their views were only roughly similar. In contrast to Pauling, Muller was prepared to risk nuclear war to avoid totalitarianism. Though he leaned to the left, moreover he feared the consequences of totalitarian dictatorship of *any* sort, right or left, even more than did Pauling. Muller had also become increasingly irritated with Pauling's theatricality and hastiness in politics, a quality which Muller perceived as the essence of naivete. Muller finally answered on April 3, 1962:

> Some time ago you wrote me a nice little note asking me if I were mad at you. I have been afraid that my dilatoriness in replying may have made you feel that I really was, especially since, as you doubtless realize, we do not see eye-to-eye about matters of international and resultant national policy. Frankly, I feel that to-

talitarianism, of whatever stripe and color, would be just as great a tragedy for mankind as nuclear war, even if nuclear war is avoided. I think that if all the emphasis is placed on nuclear war the way for the coming of totalitarianism of one kind or another will be made easier . . .

Pauling was not buoyed by Muller's reply and certainly not convinced by his argument. By this time, the Paulings were desperate to find some new means of drawing world attention to the frightening possibility of nuclear annihilation. This time Pauling went beyond petitions and lawsuits to a direct confrontation with the Kennedy White House. He began by sending a provocative telegram in response to Kennedy's decision to proceed with atmospheric nuclear testing: "Are you to give the orders that will cause you to go down in history as one of the most immoral men of all times and one of the greatest enemies of the human race?"[2] Barry Goldwater reacted strongly to the message in May:

I suggest that this is not only strong language to direct to the president of the United States, but it is also insulting and arrogant. In fact it is so unfair to the President and so unworthy of a renowned scientist that I believe the White House would have been justified in dropping Dr. Pauling from the list of Nobel Prize winners in the Western Hemisphere invited to dinner with President and Mrs. Kennedy.[3]

However, on April 29, the Paulings did accept the president's invitation—but not before joining a pacifist picket line and demonstrating in front of the White House on the afternoon of the dinner. At exactly 6 P.M., Pauling crossed his own picket line. Pauling's sister-in-law, Gorgo Miller, commented:

That same night they went into the White House and he danced with Mrs. Kennedy in the rotunda of the White House! That takes some guts; but that was Linus; if he felt like doing something he went ahead and did it. He had a mind of his own. Well, I thought it was beneath his dignity.

Perhaps his sense of mischief was at work. Aside from a few words from Caroline ("what has Daddy done wrong now?"), the incident of the demonstration was ignored.

After the dinner at the White House, Pauling continued to file lawsuits and vilify politicians. But he was still worried about Herman J. Muller. In Jack Harrison Pollack's profile of Muller for *Saga* magazine, Muller castigated the proponents of disarmament: saying, "These people grossly underestimate the danger that the Russians *would* take over if we unilaterally disarmed." Pauling immediately fired off a countersalvo to *Saga* on May 10, 1962:

> In an otherwise apparently reliable article about Dr. Herman J. Muller by Jack Harrison Pollack . . . there is a serious error that is damaging to me and to the National Committee for a Sane Nuclear Policy and other organizations working to end all tests of nuclear weapons. I am writing in order that this error may be corrected. . . . Dr. Muller here essentially states that those people, of whom I am one, who are working to end all nuclear weapons tests also advocate unilateral disarmament by the United States. This broad statement is untrue. I have never advocated unilateral disarmament and I know that the National Committee for a Sane Nuclear Policy has never advocated unilateral disarmament . . . I have been damaged by your publication of an untrue statement.

Interestingly, the *Saga* article didn't even mention Pauling by name, though he was a natural target of Muller's criticisms. His hypersensitivity to criticism revealed the stress he had been under in recent months.

Under pressure from both *Saga* and Pauling, Muller did publish a retraction. It was feeble at best:

> The letter from Dr. Linus Pauling is to be welcomed for its direct statement that he and organizations with which he is connected are not advocates of unilateral disarmament. In view of this, I regret that the statement of mine . . . may have led readers to infer the contrary.

Further on in the letter he asked: "Nevertheless, . . . is not Dr. Pauling's recent demand that the U.S.A discontinue nuclear testing, despite this prior resumption of tests by the U.S.S.R., a form of advocacy of some degree of unilateral disarmament?"

It was difficult for Pauling to claim that he wasn't a "unilateralist." Many of his public statements and actions did leave that impression. However, all he could think about was how to force Muller to back down. Criticism from politicians and nonscientists was a matter of course, but public criticism by a scientist of equal rank and credibility could be very damaging to him.

He wrote Muller on May 29, pressuring him for even stronger concessions: "You are, I think, wrong in suggesting that the Soviet tests caused us to fall behind, in respect to nuclear testing . . . in my opinion you are not justified in describing a failure to take an action in the direction of increased armament as unilateral disarmament. . . ." The battle continued for sometime. Muller published more attacks on the peace movement, SANE, and Pauling; Pauling fired back. Finally, Pauling, at the very end of his patience, wrote Muller on June 18:

> I regret very much that I am forced to write this letter to you. I have complained to you before about the false and seriously misleading statements that you have been making about me. . . . Perhaps the worst example is the most recent one, in the article by you in *This Week* magazine for June 10, 1962. . . . Now, I have to tell you that if you continue to make libelous statements about me, I may be forced to institute suit against you.

Pauling's statement was extreme, for nothing Muller had said even came close to being "libelous." Never in his life had Pauling been so furious with a fellow scientist. As he had informed Muller, he wrote to *This Week* as well, demanding not just a retraction, but an apology. A little more correspondence followed between Pauling, Muller, and *This Week*, and the magazine eventually published a vague retraction and apology, though again, as with the *Saga* letter, Muller seemed merely to reaffirm the opinions that had originally angered Pauling, referring to those "who advocate the cessation of nuclear testing by the United States, and the taking of steps toward disarmament, even in the absence of such measures by the Soviet Union. . . ."[4] Happily, the suit against Muller was never brought, but to this day Muller's widow remains bitter toward Pauling and refuses to discuss the case.

Pauling did file other libel suits, including actions against the *Daily News*, the *Bellingham Herald*, and other periodicals. All of these cases were settled out of court, with the exception of one. Pauling's suit against the *National Review* was his biggest legal battle to date. As will be seen in chapter 16, he pursued it for the better part of the decade.

The evidence of Pauling's strong leftist views was incontrovertible, and other major publications besides *National Review* and the *Daily News* remarked on them. But once legal proceedings against the various periodicals had begun, Pauling left the details to his attorney. He was now concerned with other matters. On October 10, the Nobel Committee announced that Pauling had won its Peace Prize. Unlike the academic prizes, the Peace Prize is not an annual award; no Peace Prize had been given the year Pauling had won the chemistry prize. And unlike Pauling's chemistry prize, the Peace Prize was genuinely unexpected. At the time, the Paulings were staying at their Big Sur ranch, with no telephone handy. Their daughter Linda finally reached a forest ranger who answered an old-fashioned crank magnetophone. He knew who Linus Pauling was and, quite obligingly, hiked five miles to the Pauling ranch.

Friends and family were understandably ecstatic. His friend and former student John Catchpool reminisced: ". . . I just let out a whoop of joy. I said, here it is—at last, you know, here's the proof that the world has listened to him."[8]

For a short while, Linus and Ava Helen basked in the well-wishes and publicity of family and close friends. Then, the joy dissipated. Reactions from outside the Pauling circle were negative. Even Pauling's hometown papers were not impressed. On October 16, Oregon's *Salem Statesman* wrote:

Award of the Nobel Peace Prize to Dr. Pauling, whatever the committee's reasons, inevitably associates this semi-sacrosanct honor with extravagant posturings of a placarding peacenik . . . The Linus Paulings of the world have, at the very least . . . made themselves not only nuisances, but dangerous nuisances. The award is bound to play into the hands of those who can't see, or try to obscure, the difference between advocating war and advocating the deterrence of war, and this hardly serves the cause of peace.

The *Christian Science Monitor* was typically modest and restrained, saying only that:

> . . . he has been vilified in some quarters. His patriotism and loyalty have been questioned. Yet, while some of his associations may seem dubious, he has never to our knowledge acted dishonorably. And he has been as quick to condemn Soviet tests as tests held by his own country.[9]

The criticisms were not just from American papers. In an editorial, the Norwegian paper *Morgenbladet* noted that:

> Scientists, politicians, and military experts who are responsible for the security of the West have continued their work to safeguard liberty in spite of Prof. Pauling's assertions and demonstrations . . . then . . . the Nobel committee gives the Nobel Peace Prize to Pauling. It is a slap in the face.

The most publicized editorial came from *Life* magazine. This editorial, entitled "A Weird Insult from Norway," attacked Pauling bitterly and was often mentioned by him in years to come. This vitriolic response from *Life* was due to the fact that the Peace Prize followed so closely on the heels of Pauling's blasts at the Kennedy administration's handling of the Cuban Missile Crisis; Pauling had been, according to *Life*, "critical of President Kennedy's bellicose method of handling the crisis in Cuba."[10] Later, Pauling went even further. In December 1963, he announced that he was sponsoring disaster relief to Cuba. Nominally, the aid was intended for the relief of victims of a recent hurricane there, but at the time many felt that this action, coming so soon after Pauling's other Latin-American moves, was intended to further embarrass the administration in the eyes of Cuba and the world.

Yet even before the December announcement, *Life* had seen enough. The editorial stated:

> Last fortnight, in an extraordinary insult to America, the Nobel Peace Prize Committee conferred its prize for 1962 on none other than Linus Pauling . . . However distinguished as a chemist, the eccentric Dr. Pauling and his weird politics have never been taken seriously by American opinion.

It went on to insinuate that Pauling's agitation for peace had *not* led to the partial test-ban treaty: "The peace award, delayed by one year, seemed to honor Pauling's years of agitation for a total ban on all kinds of nuclear testing, with or without any policing, and to imply that this agitation led somehow to the Kennedy-Macmillan-Khrushchev treaty for a limited test ban."

The *Life* editorial makes a good point. Although many felt that Pauling's activities played a major role in bringing about the test ban, other factors were probably more important. Kennedy's strong stand on the Cuban missiles (a stance Pauling decried) showed that the United States was not a "paper tiger." The government would, if pressed, back up its public rhetoric on nuclear power and international diplomacy. That strong position forced Khruschev to the bargaining table.

Furthermore, during the latter part of the 1950s, the public concerns over fallout and the dangers of radiation were already ebbing. Government agencies had begun, in the mid-1950s, to issue intermittent releases showing that strontium-90 levels were declining. In September of 1959 for example, the Public Health Service reported that the strontium content of the nation's milk supply was completely normal, a datum later confirmed by the Atomic Energy Commission. The latter pointed out, for example, that the strontium levels in St. Louis fell from 37.3 in April of 1959 to 11.2 by June. (Professor Olby and others believe, however, that abnormal levels continued for years afterward.)

Eisenhower also contributed to the campaign of public reassurance. First, he issued an order on August 14 of 1959, which took responsibility for radiation safety away from the Atomic Energy Commission. Next, he created a new Federal Radiation Council, headed by Arthur Flemming, to set safety standards and oversee the implementation of protective guidelines by such organizations as the Food and Drug Administration. However, Pauling's efforts certainly did have an effect, despite his critics' protests, and even though other factors were at work.

The criticism continued. Pauling was especially embittered by the letters of protest written by his fellow members in the American Chemical Society. As a result, Pauling resigned from the Society, although he had been a member for many years. As he explained in a letter to Professor Aaron Ihde of the Chemistry department of the University of Wisconsin on April 19, 1965:

> In answer to your letter, I have to say that I did resign from the American Chemical Society, in 1963, because of my dissatisfaction with the attitude of the Society toward me. I remember that some members of the Society sent in letters of complaint about the handling in *Chemical and Engineering News* of the news that I had been awarded the Nobel Peace Prize.
>
> I resigned when the Board of Directors rejected my request that *Chemical and Engineering News* publish an explanation of or apology for their misrepresentation of the bomb-test suits, as . . . my letter was published, but without any explanation or apology of C&EN. When my appeal to the Board of Directors was rejected I decided that the Society was one that I did not want to be connected with any longer.

Pauling received little more appreciation back at Caltech. While there were individual warm wishes over the Peace Prize, the administration, the trustees, and even fellow chemistry department faculty responded negatively. As Pauling himself recalled, Lee DuBridge, then President of the California Institute of Technology, remarked that "It's really a remarkable thing that someone should get a second prize, Professor Pauling; but there is of course a difference of opinion about the value of the work you have been doing." And James Bonner told me, when I visited him at the California Institute of Technology:

> When Linus got the peace prize, this was celebrated and there was an official reception for Linus in the biology division, but nothing was done in the chemistry division: Linus felt very badly about that. The idea among senior profs in chemistry and chemical engineering was that Linus's activities were no part of chemistry; they were just giving Caltech chemistry a bad name, and let's get down to serious chemistry.

Some reacted particularly bitterly:

> Now there were people in the chemistry division that were extremely annoyed, senior members like Don Yost; he thought Linus was being a real charlatan, and Professor Swift thought so too; and these people were senior to Linus in their tenure at Caltech . . . Don Yost owed his life to Linus who . . . when Yost got a life-threatening disease in 1944 . . . arranged for him to get penicillin, which was generally unavailable . . . and he survived to 97!

The end was near. After forty years, Pauling was wavering in his loyalty to the Institute. One week after being awarded the Peace Prize, he decided to leave. Jack Roberts recalled that difficult time:

> I had the job of going to tell him that we wanted him to contract; part of the problem was that he had set up people to work independently on ideas he had had which were good ideas, but for one reason or another, had not worked out . . . Well, we suggested that those programs be curtailed and the space be turned over . . . He said OK but was not happy . . . I remember that when he came in and told me he was resigning, I conveyed the news to DuBridge and Bacher who were in some sense relieved.

The use of space was a consideration, but it was somewhat less important than the disappointing reactions to his Peace Prize, which really were the decisive factor. James Bonner told me of a letter he'd received from Pauling at the end of 1963—three pages of Pauling's dissatisfactions and feelings: "He said Caltech was a horrible place and it would not be any better until it got rid of Bob Bacher and Lee DuBridge. We used to say we had two administrative officers, Bob Bacher who was for talking to you, and Lee DuBridge who was for listening to you."

Pauling did try to carry on his political activities without involving Caltech, but it was impossible. According to Professor Koepfli:

> Linus tried to dissociate himself from Caltech, even to the point of using his own personal stationery, but it was just impossible; you could disavow your speaking for the institution, but the fact is that he was sufficiently well-known that he was too much a part of Caltech. Bacher even talked to Pauling to smooth things out.

Once Pauling had made the decision to leave, his feelings about the California Institute of Technology ebbed in their fury. He had, after all, spent many happy and productive years there and many remained friendly to him. Jack Roberts recalled:

> ... despite the fact that the administration felt they had their share of irritations, we asked him if he'd like to be what we call 'research associate,' which actually is the title Eddie Hughes has and to my surprise, he accepted immediately! Well, if he was really so burned up with the Institute, he would have said, "the heck with you guys."

He refused to dawdle. Nor was he about to be put to pasture to meditate about the good old days. He had, some time earlier, begun tentatively searching for a new academic home. Within months, he settled on the Center for the Study of Democratic Institutions in Santa Barbara, where he remained for three years. His resignation from the California Institute of Technology became effective on June 30, 1964, but his appointment at the Center had begun in late 1963. Having ended his career at Caltech, he gave a press conference on October 18: "The award of the Nobel Peace Prize will have, I believe, the consequence that I shall devote the major part of my time in the field of international affairs, and I shall be able to carry out this work more effectively in the Center than in the In stitute."

# *16*

# Squaring Off With
# William F. Buckley, Jr.

SO BEGAN PAULING'S ASSOCIATION WITH THE CENTER
for Democratic Institutions. It is difficult to imagine a scholarly
institute less amenable to Pauling's scientific curiosity. Mainstream science, however, had not been Pauling's primary intellectual concern for some time now, and the Center did have
certain advantages. For one, it was a beautiful place with a
wooded campus and a collegiate feel. For another, the Center
had always prided itself on welcoming the unusual and the
unorthodox.

It was a "think-tank" for political influence. According to its
founder, the renowned educator Robert M. Hutchins, the Center

> . . . does not engage in political activity. It does not take positions
> about what ought to be done. It asserts only that the issues it is
> discussing deserve the attention of citizens. It attempts to show
> what the positions are that may be taken and what the conse-
> quences of taking one or another are likely to be. The Center tries
> to think about the things it thinks its fellow-citizens ought to be
> thinking. It tries to bring the issues into focus so that they may
> be clearly seen and intelligently debated.[1]

The value of such an appointment to Pauling is hardly obvious.
His entire life had been bound up with science. While it was not

hard to imagine him leaving his field for a few months or so, in the past he had always been able to return to the facilities of The California Institute of Technology. At the Center, there were no real laboratory facilities, no institutionalized scientific research, no scientific atmosphere to speak of. The inspiration of the Peace Prize and his very real desire for international influence only partially explain his choice of the Center.

In the Fall of 1985, I asked Pauling's friend and former student Dr. David Harker what, precisely, Pauling did at the Center. He replied. "I don't know—does anybody?" In fact, Pauling was lost. He had, after so many fruitful years, no clear goals. He said as much himself, in his statement of application for a grant at the Center:

> During the past forty-two years I have carried on both theoretical experimental research in chemistry, physics, mineralogy, biology and medicine. The experimental and theoretical researches have been closely associated. I think that it has been valuable to be able, in association with . . . collaborators, to carry out the experimental studies that have been suggested by my theoretical investigations. At the present time, however, there are so many theoretical problems that I wish to attack that I feel that I cannot afford to devote time to the continued supervision of experimental work. Moreover, I believe that it would be possible for me to get other people to carry out any worthwhile experiments that were suggested by my theoretical work in the future . . . I am not sure about the fields to which I shall devote myself in the future. One of the reasons for my desire for an appointment . . . is that I am looking for new fields to which I might make some interesting contributions by developing a new point of view. . . .[2]

He was not only unsure of what scientific directions he might go in, but undecided even as to which branches of knowledge he would attack next.

Hutchins realized, perhaps better than Pauling himself, that Pauling and theoretical science were not easily parted. He therefore wrote in support of a grant from the National Science Foundation on February 26:

Attention: Molecular Biology. The Center for the Study of Democratic Institutions is a project of the Fund for the Republic . . . Professor Linus Pauling . . . under his appointment . . . is free to carry on research in various fields of . . . science and medicine and also, to the extent that he desires, in other fields, such as war and peace, in relation to democratic institutions and the clarification of basic questions of freedom and justice. . . . For some of his proposed studies in science and medicine, it might be desirable for him to assume residence in a university or medical school especially suited to his research, and for some of his proposed work of writing books and carrying on theoretical research he might desire to live in considerable isolation . . . Application is herewith made for a Grant of $198,924, during the five-year period beginning 1 October 1964, to cover his salary during this period . . .

To convince the NSF that he really did need that much money (which was over and above his $25,000 annual salary from the Center itself), Pauling pulled out all the stops. On his statement for the grant application, he proposed a dazzling and quite unbelievable number of projects, including:

The completion of a book on the molecular basis of biological specificity . . . the completion of a book on science and civilization, . . . theoretical work on the molecular properties of substances with general anesthetic activity, completion of theoretical work on the development of a theory of antiferromagnetism . . . extension of the resonating-valence bond theory of the structure of electron-deficient substances, such as the boranes, . . . preparation of a book on the chemical-bond theory of metals and intermetallic compounds, . . . continuation of the search for information bearing on the question of the molecular basis of mental deficiency and mental illness, continuation of studies of the factors responsible for aging and death, studies of evidence provided by molecular structure about the process of evolution of species, continuation of the development of a somewhat novel theoretical treatment of the structure of atomic nuclei and the nature of the process of nuclear fission.

When someone has that much planned, he has likely planned nothing. Though he accomplished some of his goals, most of this ambitious program would have to wait several years, until the founding of his own Institute in 1973. Professor Swift of the California Institute of Technology commented:

> Linus really wanted to do some serious work, but he was caught between what he wanted to do in biology and all that peace stuff; I think he felt he could probably do it better there than anywhere else, but at the same time, it looked to a lot of us like he was kind of groping, trying to find himself, maybe.

Even if his long-term goals were clouded by doubt and a sense of detachment from his moorings in scientific thought, it was clear that he would participate in some of the political and theoretical discussions at the Center. That was more or less expected of the Fellows—especially in the case of a recent Nobel Prize winner. These discussions were occasional and off-hand; one, however, is of some interest, as it gives insight into Pauling's political views at the time. This discussion, "Table Talk: What Can a Man Do?" was included in the September 1968 issue of *The Center Magazine*, one of the Center's official publications. It is long-winded and rambling, touching on revolution, the CIA, and the abuse of world resources. Pauling, perhaps feeling a little braver now that McCarthyism had subsided, confessed to certain beliefs of which he had long been suspected. After giving a candid endorsement of socialist principles, he gave his views on self-determination and the utility of revolutions, something he had never before spoken about in an open forum:

> I believe that whenever any form of government becomes destructive of these ends, the people have the right to alter it or to abolish it, and to institute a new government . . . our government and the governments of the world are now destructive of the ends of life, liberty and the pursuit of happiness for the great majority of the people. These governments, I believe, must be altered . . .[3]

More disturbingly, Pauling contradicted the principles he had articulated in *No More War!* and for the first and only time in his career hinted at the possibility of the legitimate *violent* overthrow of the government of the United States:

> . . . I don't think that party politics, even if it changes . . . can abolish the evil system of which it is a part . . . I believe in non-violence. The problem is that the Establishment believes in violence, in force, in napalm, in police power, aerial bombing, B-52's, B-58's, nuclear weapons, war. As long as the establishment remains the determining factor, our hope that the coming revolution will be non-violent has little basis in reality.

It is important to put Pauling's comments in perspective, however. Obviously, he was not hedging about where he stood politically. But it was the 1960s and people were disenchanted with the Johnson administration to the extent that many were espousing points of view similar to Pauling's. Pauling had never quite reached that level of exuberance before and never has since. The spirit of the times must be taken into account.

His comments were taken quite seriously by his fellow participants. Norman Tyre, then an attorney for the Center, reacted immediately:

> Dr. Pauling indicates that he would tear up the Constitution because that is what revolution means, so that the Republic that we know will no longer exist in his world . . . The kind of dissent Dr. Pauling refers to, the kind of dissent Bishop Crowther refers to, can go to limits far beyond what we ought to call dissent. Civil disobedience to me is akin to criminal disobedience. Moral codes behind civil disobedience do not make it any less a break of the law.

A strong statement, but moderator Victor Palimeri softened the blow with his response to Tyre: "I think this conversation would get laughed out of a meeting of Students for a Democratic Society."

At any rate, Pauling's stay at the Center does not appear to have been as profitable as other periods of his life, such as the early work at Caltech on crystal structure or his work on sickle-cell anemia. Professor Koepfli of the University of California summed it up: "The Santa Barbara stay was a very short-lived thing [Pauling was actually there for only three years], because there was no science there, and he got mixed up with Hutchins until he got out and went on North."

Pauling did do some scientific work at the Center, despite its lack of laboratory facilities, although far less than his grant proposal indicated. One interesting idea was a new theory of the atomic nucleus. As his close colleague of later years, Dr. Arthur Robinson, described it:

> . . . Pauling came along later and tried to create what was an equivalent of a valence bond theory of the nucleus; it was a different way of looking at nuclei, which was simpler; well it never got anywhere and I think the reason is that physicists felt they already had something superior, but what he did was actually rather pretty and I think had it been done some forty years earlier, before they had the tools they have today, physicists might have found it quite useful. Now it's obsolete before it begins, because they can do better things with their equivalent of molecular orbital theory.[4]

That may be. Certainly an important criterion of any new scientific theory is its usefulness in predicting and explaining raw data. Pauling's theory never really got a hearing—a chance to prove itself. James Bonner relates that:

> . . . Linus started dabbling in nuclear physics, the nucleus of the atom; that was right after 1963 and he got into it for maybe three or four years, then got out of it again, and I'm told by reputable physicists that his ideas were too superficial . . . well, he was into many fields, but it is possible that his insights were not as deep as those people who had been in it all their life . . . furthermore, nuclear physicists are a very, very "in" group, and to have someone like Linus Pauling muscling in on their territory . . .[5]

The charge of superficiality was not new. John Slater had made it a decade earlier in connection with Pauling's work on ferromagnetism. But it is by no means clear that this complaint is justified. Pauling was an intuitive theoretician. As explained in the discussion of the Slater-Pauling imbroglio of the 1930s (Ch. 5), Slater clearly missed the critical point—that there is a real need for intuitive, less rigorously mathematical work in science.

If there was any superficiality in Pauling's ideas, it may have been due to his excessive litigation, and the time and energy it demanded. On July 19, 1964 the *Chicago Tribune* reported that:

> The United States Court of Appeals has upheld the dismissal of a $500,000 libel suit brought [against the *Daily News*] by Dr. Linus C. Pauling . . . The opinion, written by Judge Friendly, had said that Pauling "became an outspoken advocate of causes . . . and individuals sympathetic to communism . . . thereby creating for himself a reputation that could not and did not suffer any damage by reason of the editorial complained of."

On November 9, Pauling initiated a suit against *The Bulletin*, a publication of the New South Wales Australian Consolidated Press Limited, also over printed allegations that he was a communist. And the *National Review* battle was beginning in earnest.

The trouble began on July 17, 1962, when the *National Review* published a provocative editorial by columnist and scholar James Burnham:

> What are we going to do about those of our fellow citizens who persist in a course of collaboration with the enemy who has sworn to bury us? . . . Take . . . Professor Linus Pauling of the California Institute of Technology, once more acting as a megaphone for Soviet policy by touting the World Peace Conference that the communists have called for this summer in Moscow, just as year after year since time immemorial he has given his name, energy, voice and pen to one after another Soviet-serving enterprise . . . Are such persons communists? Some such undoubtedly are, but

there is not publicly at hand the full proof of the kind demanded
by the courts, that they are communists in the total, deliberate,
disciplined organizational sense.

Pauling immediately placed an angry call to his attorney,
Michael Levi Matar, demanding that Matar file litigation papers
immediately. Matar insisted on first writing to *National Review*.
On August 23, he notified the magazine of Pauling's intention
to sue because of the "vicious libel published about him" in the
editorial, which bore the title "The Collaborators." *National Review* was naturally very upset and for good reason. Before the
landmark case of *New York Times vs. Sullivan*, calling a public
figure a communist could be an actionable offense.

However, as *National Review* attorney C. Dickerman Williams said of the magazine's editor William F. Buckley, "Bill was
always ready for a good fight."[5] Refusing to be intimidated, Buckley's only reaction was to pen a second article, *worse* than the
first. Helene Schwarz, part of the *National Review* legal team,
remembered: "When Buckley got the so-called 'lawyer letter,' he
then wrote a column in *National Review* titled 'Are You Being
Sued by Linus Pauling?' That was definitely written by Buckley
and became the subject of the same suit . . ."[6] The Buckley editorial, unlike the Burnham piece, was a direct attack on Pauling.
According to Schwarz, "From a legal point of view, it was much
worse than the first. He came right out and called Pauling one
of the nation's leading fellow-travelers. That was the toughest
thing to defend."

The charges against Pauling were familiar enough by now.
And there is not a shred of evidence that Pauling ever did—or
could—submit to any one else's discipline. He was an iconoclast
with regard to political parties and world opinion. On the other
hand, he did espouse some leftist policies. Certainly his wife did.
Her leftist leanings were becoming more apparent as she became
more and more active politically. On March 13, 1963, she talked
about the role of women in the struggle for peace at the First
Unitarian Church in Pasadena. Ava Helen never disguised her
hopes for world socialism. On many occasions she called for
tolerance of Soviet society: "We must believe the Soviet Union

when they say they want peace, too."⁷ She called the women of the Soviet Union a "great force for peace." Later, in an interview given when she and Pauling were at the Center for the Study of Democratic Institutions in Santa Barbara, she declared that "childbearing is a trap nature has arranged for [Soviet women]." That sort of view is also seen in the Soviet Union. Usually, Ava Helen Pauling was more vocal than her husband on these issues. Professor Cushing Strout of Cornell University recalls a dinner in which he expressed little enthusiasm for Marxist ideas. "Mrs Pauling, something of a Madame La Farge . . . was increasingly scornful and called my position reactionary . . . I soon left."

William F. Buckley had been doing research. On December 12, 1965 Professor Donald Dozer, an authority in international law at the University of California, replied to a query from Buckley:

> Pauling clearly violated the so-called Logan Act when he corresponded with Ho Chi Minh, as reported in the enclosed clipping from the Santa Barbara News Press. The Logan Act . . . provides that "any citizen of the United States, . . . who, without authority of the United States, directly or indirectly commences or carries on any correspondence . . . with any foreign government . . . in relation to any disputes or controversies with the United States . . . shall be fined not more than $5,000 or imprisoned not more than three years or both." You will note . . . that Linus Pauling was named by Louis Budenz in sworn testimony as a person whom he knew to be a Communist.

While Buckley was doing his homework, Pauling approached the suit with characteristic overconfidence. Of course, Buckley's ego is at least as large as Pauling's. But Buckley, in the classic Socratic sense, knows what he does not know. Perhaps this is why he was careful to prepare well for Pauling's suit. Motivation was another factor. While the *National Review* viewed the upcoming battle as crucial for its survival, Pauling, perhaps overly optimistic in the wake of other legal victories, viewed it as just another piece of litigation. His correspondence shows that the *National Review* suit was often at the back of his mind. He wrote to Joe Mayer, for instance, of his intention to absent himself from the trial in order to be present at a dedication ceremony in San Diego. When Pauling did appear in the courtroom, he was lighthearted, even friendly with the enemy team on occasion. Defense attorney Helene Schwartz recalled: "The Matars [Pauling's attorneys], both orthodox Jews, asked for a recess for Passover, and in the intervening days they brought hard-boiled eggs and *matzoh* to court, and Pauling sat there eating with them, and he wished me a happy *seder*."[7] At other times, strict adherence to legal protocol produced some interesting displays. As Helene Schwarz again explained:

> Part of the correct defense in a libel case necessitates showing that the plaintiff has a good reputation; so Pauling had to show he had that, which was rather a joke and he put [Ava Helen] on the stand as a character witness, and they walked into court with a suitcase; they opened the suitcase and there were honorary degrees, awards, medals, and two Nobel Prizes!

In the end, Pauling's tactics and confident demeanor were of no consequence. On April 19, Judge Samuel J. Silverman handed down a significant legal decision. As Buckley explained in his trial summary in *National Review*: "Judge Silverman extended a landmark decision of the Supreme Court handed down in 1964, which held that a public official may not sue a critic for libel unless he can prove what the lawyers call 'actual malice,' which is to say, a 'reckless disregard for the truth.'"[8] The case Buckley refers to, *New York Times vs. Sullivan*, was open to such an extension. If elected officials should find it so difficult to recover for libel, why should it be easier for others in the public eye? If an elected official is by the nature of his position of interest to the public at large, the same holds for anyone widely known, whether elected or not, who, to use the words of the Supreme Court, has "thrown himself into the vortex of the discussion of a question of pressing public concern."

William F. Buckley and *National Review* had won. In its trial summary, the *National Review* concluded:

The strategic importance of the decision is to encourage what the Supreme Court has labeled uninhibited, robust, and wide-open discussion—free of the harassment of the censorious litigators who screech their opinions at the top of their lungs, waving a legal machine gun in their right hand.

In a word, Pauling lost because it was reasonable to conclude that the logic of *New York Times vs. Sullivan* should apply in his case. Though he was not an elected official, he certainly made himself as visible as any elected official, thereby giving the public a right to know as much as possible about the man who was voicing his opinions so widely, loudly, and irreverently. Beyond that, his long-time associations with leftist organizations made the claims of the *National Review* plausible. Pauling was not a communist, but he had aided leftist organizations and had himself often declared that he had considerable sympathy for socialism.

# 17

# On the Way to San Diego and Vitamin C

THE NATIONAL REVIEW SUIT SEEMED TO HAVE TAKEN its toll on Pauling. Although he blasted the Vietnam policy of Lyndon Johnson at a Washington High School reunion in February 1966, the fire was gone from his speech. He seemed to be in an uncharacteristically humble frame of mind. In a slide show recounting the highlights of his work on crystals, he included slides of chemical structures that he had described incorrectly, "to remind myself that I'm not always right." His best scientific work of 1967 was a revision of *The Nature of the Chemical Bond*, which, however, contained little that was new. Titled *The Chemical Bond*, this was an abridged and more manageable version of the original, directed primarily at students. Pauling remained loyal to the views expressed in *The Nature of the Chemical Bond*, including the valence bond approach to molecular structure and bonding. This is surprising, given the amount of work accomplished in the field during the intervening years. The chief rival of valence bond theory, the "molecular orbital" approach which his old friend Joe Mayer of the University of Chicago had taken him to task for ignoring, had acquired even more adherents. In fact Robert Sanderson Mulliken, as dogmatic as Pauling in championing the molecular orbital approach, had won the Nobel Prize in 1966 for this work.

That same year, Pauling also participated in a meeting in Geneva called *Pacem in Terris II*. This was the last important function Pauling participated in while officially associated with the Center for the Study of Democratic Institutions. His message was familiar. In the first *Pacem in Terris* convocation in 1965 he had said: "I accept, as one of the basic ethical principles, the principle of the minimization of the amount of suffering in the world. I do not accept the contention that we cannot measure the suffering of other human beings, that we do not know what is good and what is evil."[1] And in this second meeting he argued that ethical principles can be deduced from scientific laws: "It is sometimes said that science has nothing to do with morality. This is wrong. Science is the search for truth, the effort to understand the world; it involves the rejection of bias, of dogma, of revelation, but not the rejection of morality."

He would return to this highly speculative line of reasoning again in future years. Of course, Hume gave his classic refutation of that notion in the eighteenth century and most philosophers today still accept it. (Interestingly, there have been some thinkers in recent years who have attempted to refute Hume's famous analysis— Professor John Searle of the University of California, for example, as well as Professor Paul Allen of East Stroudsburg University of Pennsylvania. However, such attempts have not yet found universal acceptance. In any event, Pauling's efforts do not have the scope and subtlety of these attempts to deduce moral statements from factual ones.)

Pauling was still upset by his defeat at the hands of the *National Review* and still trying to find the focus he had lost after leaving the California Institute of Technology. The Center for the Study of Democratic Institutions began to seem more and more inadequate to his needs. The solution finally appeared as an appointment to the University of California at San Diego in 1967, where he remained for two years. There were laboratory facilities at his disposal again and he was free of the "unscientific" reasoning he had encountered at the Center. He was already looking deeply into the literature on the relationship between nutrition and mental illness. At this time Pauling was taking about ten grams of vitamin C per day, and already beginning to canvass professional journals for information on the therapeutic role of vitamin C for various human infirmities.

At San Diego he produced one of his most challenging and controversial papers to date: "Orthomolecular Psychiatry," published in the April 1968 issue of *Science*. For the first time in a long while, he had a clearly defined scientific mission. The atmosphere at the University of California at San Diego had Pauling in high gear again.

It was work he had wanted to take up again for some time. He had taken tentative steps towards working out links between mental illness and physiological changes in his last years at the California Institute of Technology, but was stymied by the political atmosphere there, as well as his own growing interest in world peace. So far, there had been no such problems at San Diego. Nor was anyone pressuring him to cut back on his use of space, as had happened at Caltech. Without these hindrances, Pauling made considerable progress, and felt confident enough to publish his findings. This paper, in *Science*, marked the beginnings of a final crusade: to establish the supreme importance of nutrition in human health.

He announced his new theory of nutrition in the very first paragraph:

> The methods principally used now for treating patients with mental disease include psychotherapy . . . chemotherapy . . . I have reached the conclusion, through arguments summarized in the following paragraphs, that another general method of treatment, which may be called orthomolecular therapy, may be found to be of great value, and may turn out to be the best method of treatment for many patients.

In the concluding paragraphs he states his theory:

> The functioning of the brain is affected by the molecular concentrations of many substances that are normally present in the brain. The optimum concentrations of these substances for a person may differ greatly from the concentrations provided by

his normal diet and genetic machinery. . . . Mental symptoms of avitaminosis sometimes are observed long before any physical symptoms appear.

At San Diego Pauling renewed his relationship with Arthur Robinson, once a talented student of his at the California Institute. Robinson had fulfilled the promise of his undergraduate years and now held a tenured post at the University of California at San Diego. He made many valuable suggestions to Pauling, such as an examination of the striking differences between a vitamin analysis of urine from mentally disturbed subjects and that from "normal" subjects. Recent scientific advances also included some improvements in the technique of gas chromatography, allowing Pauling and Robinson to separate and measure the amounts of different substances in body fluids with greater accuracy than was possible previously. Utilizing such techniques, Sonoma State Hospital for the mentally retarded in California had been cooperating with Pauling and Robinson, providing about twenty volunteers. Pauling and Robinson also participated in their own research.

This research had, by 1971, demonstrated that some mentally ill patients had unusually strong requirements for ascorbic acid, niacin, and pyridoxine. At the time, Pauling happily described Art Robinson as "my principal and most valued collaborator."[2]

Unfortunately, problems developed even in this friendly environment. Though Pauling remained comparatively inactive politically at San Diego, some people disapproved of his highly publicized past involvements. As Rae Goodell explains in *The Visible Scientists*, "He and Marxist philosopher Herbert Marcuse were the campus's two controversial celebrities, and the surrounding community voiced continual objections to their presence."[3] James Bonner claims Pauling felt "threatened" there. Goodell describes how Pauling decided to leave: "When Pauling read an item in the newspaper in 1969, saying that Marcuse had been reappointed, implying that reappointments had been made and that he had been omitted, Pauling decided the sensible thing was to accept the job which had been offered at Stanford."

However, political problems were not the sole cause. As Pauling got older, he seemed to do his best and most productive work in isolation, removed from peers, distractions, the telephone, students, everything. As Art Robinson reminisced, "Pauling would go away to the Big Sur ranch, and it was then that he was really a scientist; he'd . . . come back after three or four days with a new paper on the nature of the chemical bond or whatever . . . it'd be about the only time he'd really be happy." The ranch was the renewal point—the touchstone, in later years, for Pauling's creative energies. San Diego was far from the Big Sur and Stanford was not. Pauling was finding it increasingly difficult to do real science away from the Big Sur.

Stanford had another attraction as well: the distinguished physical chemist Harden McConnell was there. Pauling had deepened his relationship with the chemist when he fought to bring McConnell back to Caltech in 1956. Pauling had always been impressed with McConnell's work, particularly his pioneering study of very fast chemical reactions by the use of spin-labeled atom groups, which can be studied by magnetic resonance spectroscopy. (This technique depends on the groups of atoms having an electron with unpaired spin.)

The struggle to bring back McConnell had been a difficult one, because McConnell's personal style was a bit abrasive. As Jack Roberts told me, "About the only time I went to the mat with Linus was when he wanted to bring Harden McConnell back; but it turned out to be a good appointment after all. We were all very pleased."

Jonathan Singer was at Stanford as well. Pauling had also had the greatest respect for Singer's abilities since Singer, along with Itano, had done such brilliant work on sickle-cell anemia twenty years earlier. Yet there was considerable personal friction: Singer to this day remains resentful of Pauling for his spurious addition of Ibert Wells's name to the famous 1949 paper.

However tempting and attractive the Stanford offer may

have been to Pauling, the prospect of the move was not so attractive to his collaborator, Arthur Robinson. Robinson had, after all, a tenured position at San Diego. Working with Pauling would be a considerable strain, requiring him to commute and divide his energy between the two campuses. He would sometimes have to give up vacations to work with Pauling. Nevertheless, in March of 1969 it was announced that Pauling had accepted an appointment as professor of chemistry at Stanford University.

Right from the outset, Pauling did not get the red carpet treatment he had expected. Again, lack of space was a problem. His office in the new chemical engineering building was cramped. There had not even been room for a secretary until a janitor's closet had been converted into an "office." Nor was his lab space sufficient for interesting research. Why such ill-treatment? For one thing, Nobel laureates were nothing out of the ordinary at Stanford. William Shockley was already there, as were Felix Block, Robert Hofstader, Arthur Kornberg, and the great geneticist Joshua Lederberg. There was also professional jealousy. Unlike other professors emeriti, Pauling was being paid. True, most of his salary was supplied through outside grants from the Alza corporation, but they still resented the fact and may well have pressured the administration to be less generous to Pauling.

On the other hand, it was well known in the scientific community that Pauling had never relied very much on exhaustive laboratory research to verify his theories. Slater had scolded him for that back in the 1930s, when Pauling sent him his paper on ferromagnetism. Pauling's son Peter has written that "my father is perfectly willing to stick his neck out." The Goertzels, who have made a thorough study of Pauling's life, wrote in *The Antioch Review*:

> His greatest discoveries have come in periods of intense solitary concentration. Typically, he would retreat to his study for a few days and emerge with a solution to a scientific riddle that had puzzled other investigators for months. This pace of work has

enabled him to rush into print with discoveries ahead of other
scientists who take more time to check and recheck their work.[4]

Doubtless Stanford knew this and they may have felt that it was
perfectly logical not to supply Pauling with much laboratory
space.

Pauling and Robinson made do. Robinson was granted a
year's leave of absence from San Diego and, intent on doing first-
rate research, he set up a laboratory on his own, crowding guinea
pigs, mice, and complicated and unwieldly laboratory apparatus
into some makeshift space, paying most of the expenses himself.
He did laboratory work on nutrition, while Pauling acted out a
"research" scenario he'd developed some years ealier: pick an
issue, exhaustively study most of the literature on it, and then
take a theoretical position. In 1970 he described his attitudes
towards research at this time in his life: "I was . . . too old to
commit large amounts of time to setting up a research organization to perform a research program and carry it out. I'm at
the time of life when I should be devoting my energies to stim-
ulating the thoughts and research interests of younger scientists."[5]

He remained concerned with nuclear power and its consequences, although he was now more worried about peacetime
than wartime uses of nuclear energy. In September of 1970 he
published an article with the title "Genetic and Somatic Effects
of High-Energy Radiation" in the *Bulletin of the Atomic Scientists*. In this piece, he echoed warnings from Berkeley and the
Lawrence-Livermore Laboratories that levels of exposure to radiation had to be drastically reduced immediately, or numbers
of deaths from bone cancer, leukemia, and neonatal problems
would begin to skyrocket.

Soon afterward, in December, Pauling won a small political
victory. The Committee on Internal Security of the House of
Representatives deleted Pauling's name from its list of people
not permitted to speak on college campuses:

> . . . the Committee on Internal Security in reviewing this testimony
> decided to delete Pauling because of the fact that the Budenz

testimony was in the nature of hearsay and thus concluded that this was not a sufficient basis to include Pauling in the report as a Communist Party member.

However, Pauling didn't take much notice; he was busy digging into the literature on vitamin C and the common cold. His approach was quite different from Robinson's; Robinson was more the experimentalist than Pauling and more concerned with calculation, verification, and fact-checking. Robinson says:

> He's a sharp theoretician; he read all the common cold and vitamin C literature . . . We were at Stanford at that point and I told Pauling that one of the undergraduates . . . had an idea on how to do a vitamin C and the common cold experiment on Stanford students; the debate was raging at the time . . . it was a good experiment and wouldn't have cost us too much. So I suggested to Pauling that we do it and Pauling said, "No, everyone knows what I think about vitamin C and the cold. I don't think I need to do any experiment." He doesn't feel the need to do any experiments; people don't understand, they think he's out making discoveries about vitamin C, when he's really taking a theoretical position . . .

Pauling may not have been doing laboratory research, but he was certainly working. Although no really important papers emerged, he did continue his early theoretical work on chemical bonding, molecular structure, and nuclear structure. He attempted to apply some of the concepts of valence bond theory to the nucleus itself, though the idea never really caught on— in part because physicists already had efficient ways of doing this and in part because of academic territorialism.

More important was his research into the literature on the cold and vitamin C. He began reading in this area at San Diego and had accelerated the pace at Stanford, often poring over obscure journal articles until the early morning. As indicated earlier, reading in the field is as much a part of good science as experimental work. (Many of Einstein's views, for example, were not verified experimentally until some time after his initial theoretical papers.) And he made progress. He was beginning to interest a few associates, and had already begun capturing the attention of the general public. He enthralled Stanford undergraduates with his lectures, as he had done with many generations of students in the past. He had even convinced the stubborn, highly respected and tough-minded University of Pennsylvania chemist Jerry Donohue of the great curative powers of vitamin C.

Then he encountered Victor Herbert. Herbert was perhaps a bit like Pauling—brilliant, impatient, and very sure of himself. In 1969 Pauling gave a talk at the Mount Sinai Medical School, before a skeptical audience of medical students and faculty. Thinking he had been well-received, Pauling returned home to Stanford triumphantly with Ava Helen. A few weeks later he received a stinging letter from Herbert. In essence, Herbert told him he was spouting nonsense and challenged Pauling to prop up his speculations with some hard studies. Pauling did come up with some studies, including one by Ritzel which showed that taking a gram of vitamin C per day reduced upper respiratory infections among skiers by over 60 percent.

Herbert responded as scientists sometimes do when presented with studies contradicting their preconceptions: he wrote back saying "I am not impressed by Ritzel's paper." Pauling replied, "I am not impressed by your saying your are not impressed by Ritzel's paper."[6]

But were there any hard facts? There were certainly many papers and studies and opinions which contradicted each other. Pauling was starting to appreciate the colossal ability of the medical establishment to disregard that which contradicts its official positions. While Pauling's studies may not have proved the efficacy of vitamin C, it was not possible to conclusively refute them either. Pauling later stated that his scientific opponents demanded no end of controlled, double-blind studies from him supporting his views, while hardly hesitating to reject what he said on the flimsiest of evidence.

The dogmatism of Herbert and his supporters convinced Pauling that he could hardly hope for an objective hearing from the medical establishment. He had to turn to the general public.

Thus emerged his book *Vitamin C and the Common Cold*. He wrote it in just over a month, immediately stating a revolutionary thesis: "The natural, essential food ascorbic acid (Vitamin C), taken in the right amounts at the right time, would prevent most of these colds from developing and would in most cases greatly decrease the intensity of the symptoms in those that do develop."[7] He criticized what he perceived as the futility of the over-the-counter drug industry, saying that the half a million dollars Americans spend every year on cold medications "do not prevent colds." In the same combative vein, Pauling criticized the drug industry for its "lack of interest" in natural ways of treating illness.

As was to be expected, there were both positive and negative reactions. Hoffman-LaRoche was probably pleased, since they produce tons of vitamin C every year and are of course convinced of its value. More importantly, other respected and trained, albeit popular nutritionists, including Adelle Davis and Dr. Carlton Fredericks as well as *Prevention* magazine, echoed the virtues of vitamin C and good nutrition generally. Numerous individual physicians began to believe there could be some role for vitamin C in preventing or at least alleviating cold symptoms.

Even some of Pauling's strongest medical opponents conceded vitamin C might have value. Dr. Charles Moertel of the Mayo Clinic (one of the authors of two studies of Pauling's claims for the therapeutic link between vitamin C and cancer) writes:

> I am unaware of any clear-cut work defining a definite physiologic effect of large doses of vitamin C. Some comments were made about this in the earlier double-blind studies of vitamin C treatment of the common cold where there was some indication of transient symptomatic benefit.

Other critics were far harsher. In many cases they didn't even focus on the theory itself, relying instead on *ad hominem* assaults. Dr. George Briggs, professor of nutrition at the University of California at Berkeley, claimed that Pauling was meddling in areas outside of his competence. Frederick J. Stare of the Harvard School of Public Health said that Pauling was "lost in the woods."

Pauling has often been, and still is, subjected to these kinds of criticisms. But even from a common-sense viewpoint, it is difficult to understand how someone who developed valid theories about proteins and cracked the secrets of sickle-cell anemia could be "outside his field of competence" in medicine. Furthermore, from a theoretical point of view, medicine is not a specific branch of knowledge; that is, it does not refer to any single theoretical discipline. Rather, the concept of "medicine" takes its ideas from a variety of fields, including chemistry, biology, biochemistry, physics, psychology, and even engineering.[8] Therefore, Pauling, with his training in biochemistry, physics, chemistry, and biology was working in medicine with a far deeper understanding than the average medical-school-trained physician.

Regardless of these considerations, the criticism kept coming. Probably the worst assaults came from Stare's collaborator, Dr. K.C. Hayes, also of Harvard. He noted that:

> Dr. Pauling's nutritional comments of recent times have disappointed us . . . not only because they make no sense in terms of modern medicine or nutrition, but also in the irresponsible way they arouse false hopes in those who have diseases which Pauling feels can be successfully treated by his "vitamin therapy."[9]

Oddly enough, Pauling soon found one of his former adversaries supporting him in his enthusiasm for vitamins. Dr. David Harker, his old *bête noire* from the 1930s, commented, "There is no question that Pauling is right on vitamin C. Pauling certainly isn't made of gold, and has done a lot of wrong things, including misusing my name in support of some of his peace initiatives; but on vitamin C and the cold he is, in my judgment, completely correct."[10] And Dr. John Enloe, then editor of the prestigious *Nutrition Today*, said

Linus Pauling's book should be read by everyone seeking cures for baffling diseases . . . it just might herald the introduction in medical research of a style of thinking which has proved successful in solving the problems of physics and chemistry, and which as yet has hardly been employed in medicine.[11]

Albert Szent-Gyorgi, who first synthesized vitamin C, added his voice: "If the body doesn't get enough ascorbic acid, you don't just get a cold, everything—just everything goes to pieces, and the final stage is scurvy." Of course physicians do not deny that a minimum amount of vitamin C is necessary—but only, in the view of official medicine, to prevent scurvy.

Was Pauling drawing conclusions without presenting hard evidence? To some extent, yes. Pauling, and even Szent-Gyorgi, often spoke about how much "better" they felt after taking megadoses of ascorbate. In scientific terms, this is of course merely "anecdotal" evidence. But there is much in *Vitamin C and the Common Cold* that is more objective and valuable than that. Pauling mentions a study involving 279 skiers in Switzerland: In the study, a 65 percent drop in cold symptoms was reported in the group that received a single gram of vitamin C per day. Since the statistical odds against that sort of result were over 1000 to one, the results were in fact significant.

Just as Pauling seemed well on his way towards providing good prima-facie evidence for his views, some bad news came. In a study conducted at the University of Maryland shortly after the publication of *Vitamin C and the Common Cold*, twenty-one volunteers, taken from a group of prison immates, were isolated for one month. At the start they were free of colds. For the next two weeks, ten of them ingested 3,000 milligrams of vitamin C every day. The rest received placebos. They were then given nasal injections of cold viruses. Pauling was gravely disappointed by the results: all the volunteers developed colds and the University of Maryland group concluded that vitamin C had "no effect."

Pauling soon realized that there were design flaws in the experiment:

All we know from this experiment is that all twenty-one subjects caught colds through this method of virus transmission: we can't tell whether the vitamin C may have had a preventive effect or not—whether it might have protected some of the subjects under normal conditions of exposure to the cold virus.[12]

This is a valid point. A bullet-proof vest may provide fair protection against gunfire under ordinary conditions of combat, but relatively little if a bullet is fired at point-blank range.

To clarify and further support his own findings and views on vitamin C and the common cold, Pauling published a new paper in the *Proceedings of the National Academy of Sciences*. In this paper, Pauling pointed out the possibilities for

> the preservation of good health and the treatment of disease by varying the concentrations in the human body of substances that are normally present in the body and are required for health . . . Ascorbic acid, taken in the proper amounts, decreases the incidence of colds and related infections, and also decreases the severity of individual colds. These arguments were presented in my book *Vitamin C and the Common Cold.* . . . The evidence and arguments presented in this book were not convincing to some physicians and authorities on nutrition. . . . I have decided that, because of the importance of the question, it is desirable to publish a more detailed account of the evidence . . .

He concludes:

> An analysis has been made of all published results of double-blind controlled studies of the effect of ascorbic acid in daily amounts over 100mg on the incidence, severity, and integrated morbidity of the common cold in populations that receive the ascorbic acid (or a placebo) regularly . . . The observations reject with high statistical significance the null hypothesis that under these conditions ascorbic acid has the same effect as a placebo . . .[13]

But does vitamin C really work? This has never been clearly determined. Medicine is just too inexact a science; the same data can be interpreted in many different ways. There is also too much subjectivity in drawing conclusions. The medical community will often dismiss theories, even those supported by research, coming from outsiders. Nor, frankly, was the issue important enough. While the common cold can have serious side-effects, even developing into pneumonia on occasion, it is usually far from life-threatening and, after a while, it appears that everyone, even Pauling himself, wearied of talking about it. Furthermore, the first stirrings of a far more dramatic application of vitamin C were beginning.

At the time of the *National Review* defeat, a little book appeared by a Scottish physician named Ewan Cameron, entitled *Hyaluronidase and Cancer*. In that book, Cameron argued that "the resistance of the normal tissues surrounding a malignant tumor to infiltration by that tumor would be increased if the strength of the intercellular cement . . . that binds the cells of the normal tissues together could be increased."[14] Pauling later became intimately associated with Dr. Cameron and with one of the biggest medical debates of the century. Like Stone, Cameron was a fervent apologist for vitamin C, the "miracle" vitamin. In 1971, in Vale of Leven Hospital, Loch Lomonside, Scotland, Ewan Cameron was starting to give ten grams of vitamin C per day to patients with advanced cancers. Very soon, Cameron noticed a remarkable improvement in patients who'd been taking the vitamin C. Pauling heard of this and in the same month began publicizing these findings. In a dedication of the Ben May Laboratory for Cancer Research at the University of Chicago he said that: ". . . with the proper use of ascorbic acid the mortality from cancer could be reduced by about ten percent."

The press quickly jumped on Pauling. By this time, they had realized that Pauling's controversial activities made for good copy. One newspaper published an article accompanied by a viciously unflattering photo of Pauling—a photo obviously intended to make him look ridiculous. The title of the piece was "Linus Pauling—Orange Juice Freak." In *The Visible Scientists*, Rae Goodell said that:

The media, unable to sort out the evidence, tended to cover the
vitamin C controversy humorously, stressing the faddishness and
the incredible alacrity with which the general public was trying
Pauling's advice . . . As if they sensed a weakness in the godlike
scientists, some journalists made fun of Pauling for probably the
first time.[15]

# 18

# Pauling vs. the Medical Establishment

DESPITE HIS PREOCCUPATION WITH VITAMIN C, PAULING had not forgotten about his research in orthomolecular psychiatry. With prodding from Robinson, who was still very much interested in that field and believed they could make substantial progress in it with a little funding, Pauling applied for a grant from the National Institute of Mental Health. They received $325,255. Robinson was especially enthusiastic because he felt that certain important technological developments that had occurred over the years might now aid them in measuring the amounts of different substances found in various bodily fluids. With more precise measurements, they would be more likely to find correlations between the amounts of these substances (such as vitamins) and abnormal mental states. As Pauling explained:

> We are now performing experiments in which we compare the quantitative molecular composition of humans who are in good mental health and those who are in poor mental health. When individuals are fed a completely defined chemical diet consisting of only the essential nutrients, then the chemical composition of their urine is quantitatively reflective of their biochemical activity. The long-range aim of our research is to develop methods of chemical diagnosis that will determine the chemical environment that a human's biochemical apparatus and diet are providing for his

mind, and that will suggest a chemical therapy to optimize that chemical environment.[1]

Now the vitamin C and the orthomolecular work occupied the same podium when Pauling spoke. The two were closely related, after all. In a way, the study of the link between vitamin C and cancer or the common cold was an "orthomolecular" approach to those diseases, just as focusing on nutrition was an orthomolecular approach to mental disease.

One problem still plagued Pauling and Robinson: the difficulty of making biochemical generalizations when "normal" biochemistry varies so much among individuals. While a certain level of a vitamin might be normal for one person, five times that level might be subnormal for another. In general, it was hard to allow for outside variables that could alter the experimental results. But progress was made in the course of their cooperative work with Sonoma State Hospital for the mentally ill. This period was the calm before the storm however, for the established medical and psychiatric community was already starting to marshall its forces for another assault on Pauling's views.

If 1971 had been a year of many frustrations, 1972 began with a celebration. In April, Pauling was to be awarded the first Dr. Martin Luther King, Jr. Medical Achievment Award for his work on sickle-cell anemia, a disease which mainly affects blacks. Linus and Ava Helen turned out in full dress, surrounded by an appreciative audience that included Muhammad Ali, Ralph Abernathy, Coretta King, and Count Basie at a $100-a-plate dinner in the Philadelphia chapter of the Southern Christian Leadership Conference in Philadelphia's Convention Hall.

If Pauling thought he had found a new audience among American blacks, he soon realized he had only widened the gulf between himself and the mainstream of academic science. On May 1, Pauling received a letter from John Edsall, chairman of the editorial board of the *Proceedings of the National Academy of Sciences*. To Pauling's dismay, the journal would not publish his paper on the link between vitamin C and cancer, "because of its therapeutic implications." Throughout its history, the *Pro-*

*ceedings* had never turned down a paper by one of its own members. In fact, most members of the Academy viewed publication in the *Proceedings* as an almost sacrosanct right.

The blow was all the more surprising given that the editorial board had, in the previous two years, accepted several papers on Vitamin C (though Edsall claimed he had done so with "extreme mental reservations"[2]). Predictably, Pauling was fuming. He reacted immediately, decrying this act of "censorship" and claiming that the editorial boards' powers were purely advisory—that they had no right to reject a paper.[3]

On this point, Pauling was right. Edwin Wilson, managing editor of *PNAS* from 1915 to 1964, admitted that the editorial board members had never acted as "referees" in the usual sense, but had left it up to the member himself to "police" his own article. Nothing significant came of Pauling's protests and lamentations however, as Edsall had made up his mind. Instead, Pauling returned to his newest strategy: ignoring the academicians and taking his case straight to the public. After all, *Vitamin C and the Common Cold* had been well received. He began a campaign of frequent talk-show appearances, interviews in popular magazines, and the like.

In January he spoke to an audience at Stanford that was overflowing with fans, disciples, and curiosity-seekers. The talk, entitled "The Prevention of Disease," was a restatement of his standard views on the therapeutic efficacy of vitamin C for both cancer and the common cold. He was witty and charming, and enthralled the audience with his pyrotechnics, his blasts at the medical community, and his virtuosic display of scientific knowledge.

So disgusted was he with the academic medical community (though not with individual practicing physicians) and its obstinacy about the vitamin C–cancer link, that he began reverting to safer territory—the common cold. Although he had little that was new to say, he felt that these discussions would be more productive than his speculations about cancer. Thus, with less than his usual enthusiasm, he spoke at a meeting sponsored by the Industrial Affiliates of the Chemistry and Chemical Engineering departments at Stanford. This was essentially his last significant speech, and practically his last significant public appeal for acceptance of the vitamin C/common cold theory.

Even Albert Szent-Gyorgi was there, though he admitted to having done little if any research on vitamin C since first synthesizing it some forty years earlier. But the meeting attracted scant attention from the Stanford community and even less from the general public. Apparently, people were bored with the common cold.

During the rest of the year, and well into 1973, Pauling's name was not mentioned in the press very often. He did release a few unexciting comments about the validity of Kissinger's receiving the 1973 Nobel Peace Prize and delivered lectures here and there on nutrition and politics. Stanford had a policy of compulsory retirement and Pauling knew he would soon be losing his position as well as his laboratory facilities. The original grant money which had allowed Pauling and Robinson to come to Stanford in the first place was now nearly gone. In addition, Arthur Robinson was beginning to tire of shuttling back and forth between Stanford and San Diego.

Still, their work might have progressed further had not Pauling, in addition to facing the gloomy prospect of forced retirement, been severely damaged by Task Force Report No. 7, entitled "Megavitamin and Orthomolecular Therapy in Psychiatry," published in 1973 by the American Psychiatric Association. The report harshly attacked his ideas on nutrition and psychology:

> Advocates of megavitamins received substantial support in 1968 when so prestigious a figure as Pauling presented a theoretical paper supporting the possibility that some forms of mental illness might be due to vitamin deficiencies occurring even on ordinarily adequate diets. . . . The rigorous double-blind studies with Vitamin B3 or its enzyme conducted by clinical psychiatrists and psychopharmacologists who were not initial advocates of this treatment rationale have failed to confirm the positive results of megavitamin therapy.[4]

Pauling, of course, was less than pleased. On November 10, 1975, he wrote his old friend and colleague Hardin Jones at the

University of California at Berkeley ". . . I feel that the task force of the American Psychiatric Association did a shockingly poor job in discussing orthomolecular psychiatry in their report." The study did have design defects, which Pauling quickly pounced on. But the sheer credibility of the medical establishment carried the day and interest in Pauling's orthomolecular approach to mental illness dropped sharply.

In recent years it has begun to receive new attention from researchers. There has been a general vindication of Pauling's idea of nutrition-based therapies for mental disorders in the past few years. It is very widely accepted among psychiatrists, for example, that large doses of the amino acid L-Tryptophan, which is a biological precursor of the class of compounds called "neurotransmitters," can be helpful in alleviating depression. The use of niacin, tryptophan, and other nutrients is now taken very seriously indeed in mental health therapy. Whether or not the APA did a "poor job," it does appear that Pauling and Robinson's original insights were at least partly valid.

Pauling continued to believe he could demonstrate a link between megadoses of vitamin C and prevention of cancer. There was reason to hope, since now that Pauling had left Stanford, he and Robinson were able to devote virtually all of 1974 to the planning of a Linus Pauling Institute of Science and Medicine. Robinson began approaching potential donors and hunting for federal research money. Though the planning and groundwork for the Institute proceeded slowly, Robinson was making headway.

Meanwhile, Pauling received some overdue recognition. In 1975, the Watergate affair had all but decimated the highest echelons of the federal government. Richard Nixon, so long a foe of Linus Pauling and, essentially, of most of the scientific community, was no longer in power. Gerald Ford, anxious to heal the nation's wounds, decided to make peace with scientists. On September 18, 1975, thirteen scientists and engineers gathered in the East Room of the White House to receive the National Medal of Science: among them were Ken Pitzer of Berkeley, who would later be president of Stanford University; physicist William Fowler of the California Institute of Technology, and Pauling. Reading the citation for Pauling, President Ford recalled the "extraordinary scope and power of his imagination which has led to basic contributions in such diverse fields as structural chemistry and the nature of genetic diseases."[5]

Despite a sarcastic piece by William F. Buckley, Jr., the response to Pauling's award was positive. The California Institute of Technology held a seventy-fifth birthday party for him in February, 1976. The rift between Pauling and Caltech had healed, and the Institute spared no effort to honor him. Max Delbruck was there, along with Max Perutz of England's Medical Research Council. Pauling's brother-in-law Paul Emmett recalled that "Linus was moved by all the commotion; it seemed to me that it brought him back to the days at Caltech when things were going better, and he was glad everybody was so nice."

Such events were mere footnotes to Pauling's Vitamin C campaign, which occupied him almost constantly. He began to look at reunions, speeches, and other public appearances as distractions. It is no wonder that his relationship with Arthur Robinson deepened—both socially and professionally. Until he married, Robinson spent Christmas with the Paulings at their Big Sur ranch (Robinson's parents had died in the late 1960s). However, even at the most festive times of year, Pauling seldom indulged in idle chatter. As his sister-in-law Lillian explained to me: "Liney didn't go much for . . . small talk; he wasn't unfriendly, but if you couldn't talk to him about the things he was interested in . . . he'd kind of clam up . . ."[6]

By this time, Robinson had retired from his position at San Diego in order to devote all of his energies to Pauling and the vitamin C research. Robinson spent most of his time hunting for support for the Linus Pauling Institute. Eventually, these efforts paid off and the new Institute found its first home in a modest building near the Stanford Linear Accelerator Center in Menlo Park, California. Pauling and Robinson were happy, even though funds were still in short supply. The Institute was supported primarily by donations from a future trustee, Keene Dimick, as well as by Robinson's own private resources.

Around this time, Ewan Cameron's labs in Scotland published a report on the condition of fifty cancer patients treated with vitamin C:

> We should now like to describe what we have come to recognize as the standard response to large dose ascorbic acid supplements in patients with advanced cancer . . . the objective evidence of benefit varies with the individual clinical presentation, but may take the form of relief of particularly distressing pressure symptoms such as pain from skeletal metastases . . . This phase of clinical treatment may be very transient, or it may last for weeks or months, and in a few patients may be so prolonged and accompanied by such convincing evidence of objective benefit as to indicate that permament regression has been induced.[7]

# *19*

# Break from
# Arthur Robinson

EWAN CAMERON'S RESEARCH WAS BEGINNING TO AS-
sume an increasingly important role in Pauling's work. Yet Cameron received very little media exposure—the attention, naturally enough, went to the better-known Pauling. During the mid-
1970s Pauling and Cameron cooperated intensively, both in their
individual work on the vitamin C–cancer link and in the writing
of their book *Cancer and Vitamin C*. However, because of Pauling's love of the limelight, and his tendency to announce theories
and draw preliminary conclusions before doing extensive research, it seemed to some that Pauling had simply "upped the
ante." Dissatisfied with the public reception of his work on vitamin C and the common cold, he was now claiming it would
cure cancer.

Perhaps there is another explanation of Pauling's crusade
for vitamin C in the fight against cancer. In many instances,
scientists, philosophers, and other theorists have, toward the
end of their careers, made one, last, fervent effort to solve a
classic problem in their fields. Einstein, for example, devoted
his later years to a fruitless effort to construct a unified field
theory.

Professor Norman Malcolm of Cornell, nearing the end of
a long and distinguished career in epistemology and analytic
philosophy, published a daring and tricky defense of St. Anselm's

classic proofs for the existence of God. Pauling, too, may have wanted to make one final contribution.

Pauling's fruitful work with Cameron and the founding of the Institute were little consolation for a developing personal tragedy. In 1975, Ava Helen was diagnosed with stomach cancer. The saddest irony of Pauling's life was that despite all their research, he and Robinson would be able to do little for Ava Helen. The Paulings continued with as normal a life as possible, maintaining the usual regimen of lectures and research. At the time, Ava Helen still appeared radiant and healthy. It would be some years before the signs of illness became clearly visible.

Pauling and Cameron still felt secure enough in their faith in vitamin C to begin a second study of patients in the Vale of Leven Hospital, where Cameron had done his original work on the efficacy of vitamin C as a cancer treatment. This time, 100 ascorbate-treated cancer victims were compared with 1000 who had not received any vitamin C. These experiments were better planned than Cameron's early studies. Although he had done his best under difficult clinical conditions, Cameron had been criticized because of the use of "historical" controls—comparison of current treatment with records of patients who had lived and died years earlier. Historical controls always leave open the possibility that other factors might influence the results of the study. Professor Thomas Jukes, in the fall of 1984, suggested to me that the Scottish patients in the original Vale of Leven studies may have already had grossly deficient diets. If that was true, the early Cameron experiments would only have demonstrated that Vitamin C was useful for patients *already* grossly deficient in the vitamin—deficient even by low FDA standards. It would not necessarily follow that megadoses of vitamin C would help patients who already had adequate amounts of vitamin C in their diets.

In the new studies, the patients treated with vitamin C all had similar types of tumors, and were of the same sex and roughly the same age. Pauling and Cameron, in fact, were rigorous in their application of the scientific method through all future experiments. As Pauling said of his 1978 studies in *Vi-*

*tamin C and Cancer*, "Of the 1000 control patients, 370 were completely concurrent with the ascorbate-treated patients."[1]

In 1977, Arthur Robinson made plans to marry—a development which curtailed the amount of leisure time he spent with Pauling at the Big Sur ranch. And although Robinson continued searching for money for the fledgling Institute, the hiring of some experienced fundraisers had lifted that burden from his shoulders. Consequently, he had time to begin his own cancer research.

In following his own developing interest in vitamin C, Robinson found a new source of inspiration: a book called *How I Conquered Cancer Naturally*, by Edie Mae Hunsburger, published in 1975. Hunsburger, the wife of a California elevator manufacturer, faced a diagnosis of breast cancer in 1973. The couple tried the usual routes, but the cancer continued to worsen. Hunsburger then drifted into the cancer therapy counterculture. She headed for Boston and placed herself on the raw fruits and vegetables diet of the Hippocrates Health Institute.

Edie Mae Hunsburger's health improved, and she resumed a normal life. After reading her story, Robinson invited the Hunsburgers to spend some time at the Institute. Since he had been testing the effects of vitamin C on cancer, the Hunsburgers raw fruits and vegetables diet seemed a natural corollary to Pauling's "orthomolecular" approach to cancer treatment. (After all, Pauling himself had always suggested that one of the great virtues of vitamin C was that it was a food, rather than a drug.)

Robinson designed a complex experiment, intended to test both vitamin C therapy and Hunsburger's "natural food" approach to cancer. The first step was to induce a form of skin cancer called "squamous cell carcinoma" in a special breed of hairless mouse. One group of mice was then fed a normal diet; the second group received only raw fruits and vegetables. A third group got the same diet as the second, but supplemented with heavy doses of vitamin C. He did the same for twelve more groups of mice, varying the percentage of natural foods and vitamin C.

The results were remarkable. First, the raw foods diet alone significantly reduced the number of cancerous lesions. Roughly the same result occurred when mice were fed an ordinary diet combined with enormous doses of vitamin C (roughly the same as a human ingesting 50,000 milligrams).

These were impressive results, but the combination of raw foods and vitamin C produced *phenomenal* results. After just a few months of therapy, the mice being fed the raw foods and vitamin C diet suffered 3500 percent fewer cancerous lesions than the control group.

At first glance, it would seem vitamin C really did have the remarkable curative powers Pauling had claimed for it—at least in combination with natural foods. However, in the group fed an ordinary diet plus the human equivalent of 10 grams of vitamin C per day, the number and severity of cancerous lesions actually *increased* slightly.

These experiments raised more questions than they answered. Robinson wanted to answer them—to continue the research and publish the results. He never got the chance. For in 1978, Pauling did an abrupt about-face. In January, he was still on Robinson's side, praising him in an article in the *New Scientist* for obtaining federal grants in excess of two million dollars for the Linus Pauling Institute. But by June, the relationship between Pauling and Robinson had disintegrated. Robinson was growing more independent, even deciding to venture onto the political lecture platform himself. Early in 1978 he delivered a speech before a San Francisco audience. The speech was saturated with free-enterprise and laissez-faire philosophy. It openly avowed and embraced everything Linus and Ava Helen Pauling had always detested. Furthermore, at the Cato Institute on May 13, 1978, Robinson declared that "Capitalism, laissez-faire, free enterprise, is the usual economic relationship that naturally comes into existence between free men and women. Freedom, the God-given right to life, liberty and property, is fundamental to human existence."[2]

Consequently, in June of that year, Pauling stormed into Robinson's office, demanding that he resign, immediately leave the building, and turn over all his research data and equipment, as well as all monies alloted to him for research. According to Robinson,

> . . . he was also to complain that this work would draw attention away from vitamin C and create controversy and that I was inappropriately out of my field in that I was a protein chemist. He claimed that his famous name gave him the right to absolute control over all ideas and research work at the Institute. Linus informed me that he would have me fired disgracefully from all of my positions, including that of Tenured Research Professor, and that he would take several other actions ruinous to my professional career if I did not agree to his demands.

Pauling refuses to discuss the matter, except to say that Robinson's studies of mice were "amateurish" and that "it would be quite improper of me, as it would be for Dr. Robinson, to discuss any of the preliminary results." Eventually, he did speak just a little more freely:

> Someone here pointed out that Art had got into the habit of thinking of the Institute as his. . . . Perhaps he thought I had got to an age where I should be sitting under a tree—smoking a pipe—I don't smoke of course—so that for him no longer to be president might have been too much to bear . . . He had a brusque way of dealing with people . . . a good number of people quit at least partly in protest of Art.[3]

The question of whether or not Robinson was still, in fact, "employed" by the Institute was unclear from a legal point of view. For a while, he was able to act as if he were still at the Institute mainly because, for assorted technical and legal reasons, he was still on salary. Thus, he decided to bring in a group of pathologists to inspect the cancerous mice. The visiting pathologists (plus a well-known dermatologist) were stunned when they were met at the door by Emile Zuckerkandl, an Austrian geneticist who had recently been appointed vice-president of the

Institute. Zuckerkandl threatened legal reprisals if Robinson and his pathologists so much as went near the mice.

Zuckerkandl claims there was merely a bit of confusion over protocol: "We wanted our own pathologists to examine them first, and Dr. Robinson to wait his turn. In only a few days, his own pathologists would have had free access."[4] In fact, Robinson's group did have a chance to examine at least some of the mice, before Pauling carried out his threat to have them destroyed. But if this situation resolved itself relatively easily, the matter of charges against Art Robinson and the confused issue of his employment at the Institute did not. Robinson was, by this point, feeling insulted and ready for a fight with Pauling. Not only had his office been moved to an obscure corner on the second floor, but even the trustees were accusing him of incompetence and failure to fulfill his duties.

All this led to an unpleasant confrontation with both the trustees and Pauling over a so-called "bill of particulars." In a March meeting, one of the trustees angrily waved a thick document in Robinson's face, and, as Robinson told me, he responded: "This is supposed to be a list of reasons why [Pauling] has taken the action he's taken and you're about to have him read it, is that correct? Fine. In view of the fact that Pauling has been alleging possible criminal activities, I want an attorney present."

Pauling and the trustees were apparently shocked by Robinson's resistance; the meeting stopped abruptly. They asked him to leave the room. After a tense hour, he was called back into the meeting. To Robinson's amazement, Pauling was no longer chairman of the meeting and the "bill of particulars"—which Pauling had threatened him with for many weeks—had vanished. When Robinson asked about the bill, he was told there existed no bill of particulars. Robinson responded, "There must be some charges; the guy wants to fire me from all of my jobs and throw me out of here and take my research from me; there must be some charges."

There were no charges and the group continued to insist that Robinson leave anyway. Evidently they had no specific

charges of wrongdoing or incompetence against him. Still, firing
Robinson was a complicated matter, partly because he had ten-
ure claims, and because he held a variety of posts at the Institute.
Robinson has said:

> The problem is they didn't have anything to justify the action.
> So the upshot was that they first made him president, took that
> job away from me, and then their lawyer said, "Now you have
> a tenured job, but what we're going to do is to keep paying
> you but make it impossible for you to work, so you'll have to
> leave"; and the result was that they locked up my data . . . and
> wouldn't allow me to use my own laboratories, and they sent
> things around to the post-docs, saying they weren't to work with
> me and finally Pauling sent me a note in which he said I was to
> refrain from all direct contact, that is, all oral discussion . . . in
> the building.

So there was nothing left for Robinson but legal redress.
For a while, he acted as his own attorney, but he eventually had
to hire counsel. Of course the financial strain was considerable
on both Robinson and the Pauling Institute. The Institute records show that up to $200,000 per year was spent on attorneys'
fees over the five-year course of the litigation. Robinson's problems were of a slightly different kind: his initial legal motions
were, to his surprise, stymied. Judge Thomas Jenkins of the
State Superior Court ruled that Robinson's case simply wasn't
strong enough to constitute a cause of action. Robinson had
been basing his case on an oral contract, claiming, among other
things, that he had a tenured position at the Institute. According
to the bylaws, which he had helped Pauling write, he was to
have university-style tenure until age sixty-five. However, the
Statute of Frauds holds that any oral contract, in order to have
force for more than one year, has to be confirmed in writing.
There had been no confirmation in writing from either Pauling
or the Institute, and so the whole case had to be redrafted by
Robinson's attorneys, to his great frustration and, of course,
added expense.

Despite this modest victory, Pauling was being attacked on

all sides by disgruntled employees. Fred Westall, another biochemist with interests similar to Pauling's, was also filing suit. Westall did not have nearly as long and close an association with Pauling as Robinson, but he had been warmly welcomed by Pauling in February of 1978.[5] Now Westall too was claiming he had been unfairly dismissed from a tenured research position. His firing, in May of 1979, was abrupt and without warning. In his suit, he too accused Pauling of fraud, breach of contract, and slander.

Not surprisingly, Pauling connected Westall with Robinson. On February 15, 1978, he wrote Westall again—but the tone of the letter was far different from the welcoming missive of one year earlier. Referring to Westall as a "salaried employee," Pauling wanted to know the precise relationship of his work to Robinson's. Not long after that, he wrote Westall again, this time claiming he was not a salaried employee, but was in fact dependent on Robinson's research funds.

The implications were ominous: since Robinson was being forced out, Westall would no longer be on salary either. After the ensuing litigation was over, Westall commented: "I had understood the position at the Pauling Institute was tenured, or I wouldn't have accepted it . . . I stopped pursuing a position at Oregon State because I'd accepted this one."[6] The Westall case was eventually settled out of court in 1983, with all the parties unable to discuss it further.

The Robinson case was also settled out of court in 1983. Robinson commented: "It's a question of just how much justice you can afford. We won, but I don't know that we won, because we lost our research; we lost what we went after and tried to save, won a bunch of money but no great compensation." Robinson offers numerous possible explanations for the break with Pauling and the final truth will probably never be known. Undoubtedly, the experiments showing that megadoses of vitamin C could, at least in laboratory mice, actually hasten the growth of cancerous tumors, were an important factor. Robinson was worried about that possibility. He didn't allow the issue to be buried, either. As late as March, 1984, Robinson wrote Pauling with even more evidence that vitamin C in the doses Pauling was recommending might well cause cancer in human beings. He ended the letter by saying, "I currently believe that a public warning should be issued concerning this. However, I feel obligated to consider any arguments that you have formulated regarding it."[7] Pauling never answered.

There may well have been an even more troublesome and personal dimension to the Pauling–Robinson feud. It was bad enough that Robinson had evidence that massive doses of vitamin C might hasten the growth of cancer. Surely, this worried Pauling, who had been promoting vitamin C's curative powers. But to make everything worse, Ava Helen, at the time of Pauling's battle with Robinson, was nearing death from stomach cancer. In a 1984 interview with Dr. John Grauerholz, Robinson urged that:

> . . . it appears increasingly that vitamin C is mutagenic in large amounts in aerobic solutions, and it's not at all clear that you don't increase the chances or the risk of cancer if you pour 10 to 20 grams a day into people's stomachs and intestines for years . . . at that time [1970] he put himself and his wife on at least 10 grams a day of vitamin C, and they were on it for the next decade. His wife contracted stomach cancer and died. I pointed out that she was bathing her stomach with an enormous amount of mutagenic material for ten years. I don't know if that's why she got it; there are no statistics there either but that's the sort of thing I would worry about in the long-term effect.[8]

It is true that the results of the studies on mice may not apply to people. It was later suggested that there is in fact a critical difference, in that mice make their own vitamin C while humans do not. Consequently, large additional amounts of vitamin C in the mice might have "confused" their vitamin C regulatory mechanisms, in turn producing far greater amounts of vitamin C in their systems than those which would be present due to the externally ingested vitamin C. As Robinson himself summarized, "It didn't necessarily follow that people would get cancer from taking vitamin C because the mice did." However, the possibility had arisen, and Pauling refused to consider it. In an interview at Oregon State University in May of 1980, Ilona J. Fry asked Pauling: "Does vitamin C have any side effects on long term use of, let's say, gram quantities?" Pauling's answer was brief: "No."

Ava Helen died of stomach cancer seven months after that interview.

As early as 1978, Pauling could not have failed to notice an ominous possibility: the "miracle" vitamin he had been touting for so long might in fact be carcinogenic; it might even have caused Ava Helen's illness. Pauling may have felt some guilt, given Robinson's observations. Robinson, who had uncovered the disturbing results and directly pointed out the possible connection between Ava Helen's illness and her intake of vitamin C, would thus be a logical target for Pauling's anger.

It is likely that guilt merely exacerbated tensions between Pauling and Robinson which were already present. Differences in political philosophy were probably at the root of these tensions. While Pauling knew of Robinson's conservatism, Robinson had, until his 1978 lectures, always confined his views to private conversation. On the other hand, Robinson may also have taken too many liberties with his position as president of the Institute. For one, he summarily dismissed Richard Hicks without consulting Pauling (though he was technically within his rights in doing so). Robinson has asserted that the firing of Hicks was justified. Hicks, a retired stockbroker, had taken over the job of fundraising from Robinson. He was supposedly a great admirer of Pauling. However, according to Robinson, Hicks had become involved in some infighting at the Institute, and was spreading misinformation, including a report that Pauling was senile. Whatever the truth of the matter, Pauling was not convinced that Hicks had done anything untoward, and was not happy when he found that Robinson had dismissed Hicks.

In an effort to further probe the Pauling–Robinson fiasco, the *Antioch Review* published a general discussion of the incident in their Summer 1980 edition. In response, Pauling wrote:

> It was indicated in the article that it was a dispute about my investigation of the effect of nutrients on the development of skin cancer in mice, with which Dr. Robinson was helping me, that caused the board of trustees of the Linus Pauling Institute to remove him as president and director and, some time later, as a member of the staff. . . . It was not because of any dispute about the mice but rather for other reasons that the board took these actions.[9]

Here Pauling's credibility is debatable. Although he describes Robinson as merely "helping" him with the cancer research, Robinson both designed and conducted the entire experiment and tabulated the results. This is one of the reasons Pauling had been drawn to Robinson in the first place: unlike himself, Robinson was an experimental scientist. Pauling, on the other hand, was the "idea" man, often ready to formulate a theory without much experimental back-up.

In his reply to the *Antioch Review* article, Pauling also refuses to give any specific reasons for dismissing Robinson. The vitamin C controversy is obviously a personal crusade for Pauling (like Einstein and his quest for a Unified Field Theory), and performing a long series of objective experiments to measure the vitamin's effects did not interest him, deeply committed as he was. One of Robinson's supporters, Professor Thomas Jukes, comments:

> People spend their nickels and dimes for the great Dr. Pauling who's going to find a cure for cancer, you see. He only cooperates with people willing to praise him lavishly. Robinson himself is a brilliant young scientist, who just happened to have been dazzled by Pauling's showmanship early in his career. As far as I can tell, everything Robinson has claimed about that nasty business at the Institute is correct.[10]

Amazingly, Robinson remained productive throughout the ordeal, even publishing papers on the problem of human aging while embroiled in his dispute with Pauling. He has put the past behind him, working at the Oregon Institute of Science and Medicine on problems similar to those he worked on at Pauling's Institute.

# 20

# In Defense of Vitamin C

AS IF THE CONTROVERSY WITH ROBINSON WASN'T TROU-
ble enough for Pauling, he received another setback with the
first really systematic study of his views by the medical establishment, performed by the Mayo Clinic in 1978. It proved to be
an irony of the first order. For years he had been trying to convince the medical community and the National Cancer Institute
to conduct such studies, having been refused by the N.C.I. for
over seven years. Finally, the renowned cancer specialist Dr.
Charles Moertel and his group at the Mayo Clinic decided the
controversy over vitamin C was great enough that an experiment,
under the toughest controlled conditions, was justified.

They did the experiment and published their results in the
September 1979 issue of the prestigious *New England Journal
of Medicine*. Their conclusions dovetailed with Robinson's findings: "In this selected group of patients, we were unable to show
a therapeutic benefit of high-dose vitamin C treatment." In a
paper delivered by the Mayo group before the American Society
of Clinical Oncology in New Orleans, they repeated the same
conclusions.

Pauling could not easily dismiss their findings, for not only
did the Mayo Clinic have prestige and credibility, but their experiments were also far better designed than the early Vale of

Leven trials conducted by Ewan Cameron. Instead of the less-than-ideal "historical" controls used by Cameron, the Mayo group took 150 patients, all with advanced cancer, and divided them into two groups. One group received vitamin C in the doses recommended by Pauling; the other received a placebo. The Mayo trials were also "double-blind"—neither the patients nor the researchers knew which group was receiving vitamin C and which group the placebo. They also used patients of similar age and sex and with tumors in roughly the same parts of the body.

However, Pauling found one critical point in which the Mayo Clinic had erred. Many of the patients used in the Mayo clinic experiments had received extensive previous chemotherapy, while the Vale of Leven patients had not. The clinic failed to attach any significance to this fact in its published report. The difference was crucial, and went right to the core of Pauling's entire conception of how vitamin C was supposed to work—by strengthening the body's immune system.

In the Mayo experiments, according to Pauling, the patients' immune systems had been rendered worthless because of extensive chemotherapy. And if, as Pauling believed, vitamin C works by energizing the immune system, then, the vitamin C failed to work simply because the patients' immune systems had already been decimated.

Pauling was right, and the Mayo Clinic later had to redo the study. One has to wonder why the Mayo clinic erred, since Pauling had actually written to Moertel in August of 1978 to warn him of the necessity of using only patients who had no prior chemotherapy if he wanted to do a valid test of Cameron's earlier work:

> In my last letter to you I pointed out . . . that the patients studied by Dr. Cameron had not received chemotherapy. The cytotoxic drugs damage the body's protective mechanism, and vitamin C probably functions largely by potentiating these mechanisms. Accordingly, if you hope, as you stated in your letter, to repeat the work of Cameron as closely as possible, you should be careful to use only patients who have not received chemotherapy.

Moertel had to concede. In his reply to Pauling's letter he said:

Certainly in any presentation of this data I can assure you we will call attention to the fact that the majority of our patients had had prior chemotherapy, whereas in the study conducted by you and Dr. Cameron, it was clearly stated that none of the patients had had prior chemotherapy.[1]

But despite this promise and all their communication, Pauling and Moertel reached no agreement. Not satisfied with the final form in which the Mayo results were presented, Pauling himself sent, in May of 1980, a letter in to *New England Journal of Medicine* claiming that the Mayo Clinic group "published a misleading report. The title of their paper should have been 'Failure of High-Dose Vitamin C (Ascorbic Acid) Therapy to Benefit Patients with Advanced Cancer Who Have Received Prior Chemotherapy: A Controlled Trial.' " He ended the letter by arguing that: "We are quite convinced that in the not-too-distant future supplemental ascorbate will have an established place in all cancer-treatment regimes."

Moertel and Creagan of the Mayo Clinic themselves replied, to Pauling in the *Journal*, claiming that they had never promised him that they would study only patients previously unexposed to chemotherapy. Worse still, they expressed skepticism as to whether the original Vale of Leven patients had or had not received chemotherapy, despite Pauling's assurances that they had not. It was a battle of scientific findings: but it was also a clash of personality and a test of faith and mutual trust.

A deadlock had been reached. Since Pauling had so long maintained that the health of the immune system was critical to the success of vitamin C therapy for cancer and since the Mayo group had completely ignored that element in Pauling's theory, they had no choice. A second study was necessary. But even the second study failed to completely clarify matters. The research was planned and conducted in the years following Pauling's complaints about the first one. It was more like the original Vale of Leven studies, in that colorectal cancer patients were used. Nevertheless, these patients too had received extensive previous chemotherapy and Pauling's central hypothesis still remained unexamined by the medical establishment.

Moreover, some of the claims made by the Mayo Group in defense of its methodology appear more than a little problematic. In a 1985 letter to me, for example, Moertel reports that "[Pauling] felt that prior chemotherapy exposure would somehow depress the patients' means of responding favorably to vitamin C. The rationale for this claim is a bit obscure from a scientific standpoint."[2] Moertel did not elaborate further, but it is hard to see why Pauling's claim is "obscure." The devastating effects of chemotherapy are certainly well established and there is hardly a bodily function that isn't affected by the tissue-poisoning properties of these immensely powerful drugs. Even sperm counts are drastically lowered in men receiving chemotherapy. It would not be surprising to find that the immune system is also affected.

On the other hand, it is hard to blame Moertel and his group for testing only those patients who had already received the best that modern medicine could offer—including chemotherapy. There is an ethical problem, because as a general rule, clinicians are reluctant to conduct any study that involves deliberately withholding a tested therapy in order to check into a speculative and unproven one. There are human lives at stake. And time is of the essence with rapidly spreading malignancies.[3]

However, all the patients who figured in these studies were terminally ill. Though chemotherapy, surgery, and radiation might have prolonged their lives and eased their suffering, death was inevitable. The issue is then one of free choice. A cancer patient has an absolute right to try any sort of alternative therapy he or she wants, including vitamin C. Once informed of the choices, a certain percentage of terminal patients will always opt for vitamin C over conventional treatments. That percentage will yield a group of patients who could test Pauling's claim— terminal patients who have not received chemotherapy.

Still, these are technical matters. There is a more general question that has cast an ugly cloud over what should be normal scientific controversy. Throughout his career, Linus Pauling has, at times, become his own worst enemy, venturing into fields like solid-state physics where his methods simply would not work. At other times, he has publicly attacked politicians, seemingly without iron-clad reasons for doing so. That is his style. Yet at so many points in his career, both the general public and the scientific community have confused style with lack of substance, and viewed his intuitive genius as mere showmanship. Professor Jack Roberts discussed this theme with me:

> I was interested in physics, and Linus told me once when he'd been down to give a talk in San Diego, he was really pleased when Maria Goeppert Mayer had really listened to him and asked good questions about his molecular theory; I asked a physicist once about this [Pauling's working on nuclear theory] and he said, "Well, what would you do if a physicist started telling you about the Lewis-Langmuir theory at this stage?" I'm not sure that's fair. If physicists had taken the time to see what he was doing, they would have seen he didn't do trivial things.

Moertel has echoed John Slater's earlier charges that Pauling is not rigorous and does not do enough experimentation. Professor Sten Samson of Caltech expresses another point of view: "As soon as he [Slater] gets an idea he works it out to the end before he gets a new one. *But that is also dangerous* [emphasis mine] of course, because you look at the trees and you don't see the forest; Pauling is a man that looks at the forest but does not explore the individual trees. . . ." Pauling had not "abandoned scientific discipline" in his vitamin C crusade. On the contrary, a different *kind* of discipline characterizes Pauling's scientific mind. It is the discipline that keeps a man generating idea after idea, day in and day out, year after year, despite inevitable failures in the midst of many successes.

Eventually, the public controversy over the Mayo Clinic trials abated, and Pauling returned to what he knew best: strictly scientific work in physics and chemistry and the general promotion and advocacy of vitamin C. Talk-show appearances, endorsements of others promoting the vitamin, and the usual gamut of public lectures filled much of his time. Meanwhile, Ava

Helen's health continued to fail. She was losing weight and fighting fatigue and the other debilitating effects of her metastasizing stomach cancer.

On December 5, 1981, she died quietly. Yet she had remained active right until the last possible moment, giving lectures on sexual equality, disarmament, and exploitation of the American workers by the military—all favorite themes of hers in the last part of her life.

The effect on Pauling was devastating. According to his old friend Verner Schomaker, at the University of Washington: "We were all very worried about him; he just didn't seem like he'd be able to go on; they were close all their lives. Finally, it was his interest in science that helped him pull through."

Despite all of the contradictory findings and the doubts raised by Robinson, her death seems not to have caused Pauling to renounce his long term faith in vitamin C. When questioned about the fact that vitamin C did not seem to help Ava Helen, he has usually responded simply by saying: "We didn't know as much about vitamin C then as we do now."

In any event, the work of the Institute went on as before. Both he and Ewan Cameron continued their research. Pauling was buoyed, too, by the immense outpouring of money for vitamin C research, due to Arthur Robinson's skillful fund-raising. His spirits were also raised by tributes and sympathy for him in the aftermath of his wife's death. All of this culminated in the establishment of the Ava Helen Pauling Lectureship for World Peace at Oregon State University in 1982. Each year, the university brings a speaker to the campus to provide a forum for exploring the issues that Ava Helen was concerned with throughout her life.

Inspired by the establishment of the lectureship, Pauling escalated his own trips to the podium. In late June of 1982, he spoke to a crowd of over 1000 people at the United Methodist Church in Portland, Oregon, urging that "For many years I advocated treaties, and a few have been made . . . But we have seen that this process is extremely slow, and I am afraid the world will be destroyed before the treaties can be made."

Some brilliant new work was going on at the Institute while

Pauling was on the road. In 1982, for example, John Leavitt, a senior research scientist who had been doing ground-breaking work at the National Institutes of Health isolating genes responsible for cancer, came to Pauling's Institute to continue his work.

Then history repeated itself with the publication of a second Mayo Clinic report on vitamin C, entitled "High-Dose Vitamin C Versus Placebo in the Treatment of Patients With Advanced Cancer Who Have Had No Prior Chemotherapy."[4] In the report, Moertel repeats his skepticism about Pauling's objections to the previous Mayo studies, but acknowledges that "because the issue of the possible effectiveness of vitamin C for advanced cancer remains one of public concern, we thought an additional study was warranted."

He goes on to explain his resolution of the ethical dilemmas involved in giving a speculative treatment when established ones are available:

> We felt ethically justified in studying this group of patients without first offering cytotoxic drugs because in our opinion there is no known form of chemotherapy for colorectal cancer that has been demonstrated to produce substantive palliative benefit or extension of survival.

Moertel concludes by very confidently asserting that:

> It is very clear that this study fails to show a benefit for high-dose vitamin C therapy of advanced cancer. Certainly, these were patients who presumbably would have had their protective mechanisms as intact as possible in the presence of incurable cancer.... none had received prior chemotherapy, and only 4 percent had received prior radiation therapy (a proportion substantially smaller than in the study of Cameron and Pauling). We chose for study the tumor type that was most commonly treated by Cameron and Pauling and that in their study showed a striking survival advantage for vitamin C therapy. In spite of this seemingly ideal setting, vitamin C performed no better than a dummy medication. No patient had measurable tumor shrinkage, the malignant disease in patients taking vitamin C progressed just as rapidly

as in those taking placebo, and patients lived just as long on sugar pills as on high-dose vitamin C.

The final blow is delivered in the following passage:

> In the face of this evidence it would seem appropriate to ask why the 100 patients with cancer who were selected by Cameron and Pauling for high-dose vitamin C lived many times longer than their selected historical control patients, whereas our patients who were randomly assigned to vitamin C treatment had no survival advantage whatsoever over those assigned to the control group. Certainly, prior chemotherapy can no longer be considered an important factor, and we are left with the inevitable conclusion that the apparent positive results of Cameron and Pauling were the product of case-selection bias rather than treatment effectiveness.

In a similar vein, in his letter to me, dated May 7, 1984, he writes of Mayo:

> Here we have employed patients who have had no prior chemotherapy exposure and we have used the particular tumor type . . . most commonly represented in Dr. Pauling's study—colorectal cancer. . . . Certainly we feel that claims of this kind can only be confirmed by randomized concurrently controlled studies. Historically controlled studies are notorious for producing false positive results. In view of the rather heated debate surrounding the use of high dose vitamin C we felt it was also essential that we conduct a double-blind placebo controlled study to avoid any conceivable bias on either our part or the patient's part that might influence the results of treatment.

Of course, Pauling and the staff at the Institute were extremely upset, and with some justification. For one thing, it is not completely clear that the second Mayo Clinic study really did duplicate Cameron's original Vale of Levin experiments, even if it came closer to doing so than the first study. Dr. Cameron and his associates began the study of the value of high doses of vitamin C, 10 grams per day, for patients with advanced cancer in 1971. Since 1973 they have published many papers about their observations and the well-known book, *Cancer and Vitamin C*, which appeared in 1979. The results of that book at least, do show that virtually all of the patients responded favorably to vitamin C, compared to *control* patients who received no vitamin C. The vitamin C patients lived substantially longer.

Cameron's patients took the Pauling-recommended doses of vitamin C from the time when they began it until they either died or until 1985. Some have lived as long as twelve years.

Consider, however, the Mayo Clinic's methodology: their patients, in the second study, received the Pauling-recommended doses of vitamin C for only about 2.5 months. Also, a point Moertel et al. do not emphasize is that *none* of the Mayo Clinic patients died while receiving vitamin C. They died once vitamin C was discontinued.

Thus, Pauling immediately began to answer the most recent Mayo Clinic study. On Saturday, January 26, at 11 A.M.—just nine days after the release of the second May study, Pauling released his counter-salvo; he pointed to a possible flaw in the Mayo Clinic report. At one point, the group says:

> The remaining patients reported regular drug intake according to instructions, usually stopping treatment only when symptoms of disease progression developed. The median duration of drug intake was 2.5 months with vitamin C (range one day to 15.6 months) and 3.6 months with placebo. . .

But that is a much shorter treatment period than that of Cameron's patients. As Pauling indicated:

> Dr. Cameron's patients received high-dose vitamin C from the time when they began to take it until they died or until the present time, some of them for as much as 12 years. On the other hand, the Mayo Clinic patients received high-dose vitamin C for only a short time, median 2.5 months. Moreover, none of the Mayo clinic patients died while receiving vitamin C. Their deaths occurred only after the vitamin C had been taken away from them.[5]

Pauling makes the further point that there is a "rebound" effect with vitamin C. Anyone who takes high doses of it for a while and then suddenly stops, risks having blood vitamin C levels fall precipitously. Following Pauling's theory, it would be reasonable to surmise that ". . . the control of cancer might be less at this time."

This effect may have a theorectical basis: for one thing, "rebound" is a well-known, potent biological phenomenon. It is exploited therapeutically, for example, in such therapies as "testosterone rebound" therapy, given to treat male infertility. In this procedure, physicians administer very large doses of the male hormone testosterone for several weeks, and then abruptly discontinue it. It is known that the body tends to "fight" against the sperm-depressing effects of testosterone during the period of administration of that hormone. But once discontinued, the testosterone "barrier" to sperm production is lifted and sperm levels often soar to enormously high levels—often 100,000,000 sperm per cc or more. In other words, the body's sperm-producing "factory" has "rebounded" to levels far in excess of normal. For brief periods, at least, this, when it works, amounts to a cure for infertility.

Much the same physiological principles are involved in the vitamin C "rebound" phenomenon. Anyone who takes very large doses of vitamin C for a long time and then suddenly discontinues it will show a significant drop in the vitamin C concentration in the blood. In same cases, there are even chances the persons involved will start showing symptoms of scurvy. It is at least possible that the body's ability to fight off cancer might be depressed during this time. That this could have happened to some of the Mayo Clinic patients, is not beyond the realm of possibility. (The rebound phenomenon, incidentally, is not mentioned in the Mayo Clinic paper.)

Still another vexing question is, *did* they give vitamin C for too short a time? That is difficult to answer clearly. It is interesting to note, however, that there is enormous pressure on the scientists in such studies to make the studies as short as possible. In an article in *The Journal of Medicine and Philosophy*, November, 1986, Dr. Kenneth Schafner of the University of Pittsburgh writes: ". . . There is in addition, the desire not to prolong a trial unnecessarily long—thus depriving others of the better therapy of subjecting patients in the trial to a less advantageous treatment."

And in another article in the same issue Dr. Loretta Kopelman writes: "If studies are stopped too quickly, then errors are more likely to result, setting false standards of care; if they are continued too long, then some subject-patients may be harmed or denied optimal care."

Surely the Mayo group was aware of this problem: their attitude toward vitamin C had to be slanted against it from the start, since their previous study had had a null result. Doubtless, therefore, they would not have wanted the patients receiving vitamin C to be receiving it any longer than necessary. And given the well-deserved ethical reputation of the Mayo Clinic, the trial could easily have been too short to get a fair *scientific reading*, just as Pauling points out.

And there is a deeper problem with the Mayo study, one which Pauling, so far as I know, does not discuss. The insidious aspect of it is the insinuation that historical controls (as used by Cameron in the original Vale of Leven Trials) are just this side of quackery, by comparison with the much-touted "randomized" clinical trials. Consider Moertel's choice of words in his letter to me:

> Certainly we feel that claims of this kind can only be confirmed by randomized concurrently controlled studies. Historically controlled studies are *notorious* [emphasis mine] for producing false positive results. In view of the rather heated debate surrounding the use of high dose vitamin C we felt it was also essential that we conduct a double-blind placebo controlled study to avoid any conceivable bias on either our part or the patient's part that might influence the results of treatment.

But Moertel's description is in part misleading and in another part simply wrong. Despite Moertel's insinuation that "historical" controls are practically worthless, there is a large body of opinion urging that randomized studies are very much overrated and that historical controls are, in fact, excellent methodologies.[6]

Schaffner, in the above-mentioned essay, expresses sympathy for such a view in his article, "Ethical Problems in Clinical Trials," which appeared in the November, 1986 issue of the *Journal of Philosophy and Medicine* saying ". . . there are theorists such as Freireich and Gehan (1979) who contend that RCT's [randomized controlled trials] are highly overrated and that more extensive use of historical controls is desirable."

But there is still another reason for doubting the value of RCT's (randomized controlled trials). From a more theoretical point of view, there has been a great deal of recent research which is beginning to show that the very *foundation* of the experimental design of such trials as the Mayo clinics "randomized" trials may be theoretically inferior. In effect, many have argued that the basic *concept* of RCT's is flawed.

There is another, entirely different statistical approach which is taken very seriously by many statisticians, physicians and other scientists. This is the so-called "Bayesian" concept: it refers to a theory of probability and experimental testing that is radically different from the classical approach usually adopted by scientific researchers (including the Mayo group). Classical statistical ideas undergo radical change in a Bayesian world. In effect, its proponents suggest a clinical approach that would completely *abandon* controlled trials. As Schaffner puts it in his article:

> Notions that are standard from the classical statistical perspective become reinterpreted in a Bayesian world, and some writers such as Clayton view this approach as perhaps suggesting a formal model in which we would in effect abandon controlled trials and return to a reliance on clinical judgment. . . .

Such approaches are still new of course, and controversial. But they are taken very seriously. Indeed, the greatest testimony to the attractiveness of the Bayesian approach may be seen by the fact that Johns Hopkins Medical School has approved some forms of the Bayesian approach for clinical studies.

But what is the "Bayesian" approach? *It is merely an application of the old "stochastic" method that Pauling developed so many years ago*, which advocates the relevance of intuitive judgment over mere data-collection. In a way, the battle of classical statistics vs. the Bayesian approach is the Pauling-Slater controversy all over again in new dress. It is also the approach to scientific research generally that is endorsed by no less a figure than Nobel-Prize winner Professor P.W. Anderson of the department of physics at Princeton, as outlined in his letter to me of October 14, 1988. In that letter, Anderson wrote: ". . . in fact, I admire his [Pauling's] semi-empirical approach much above the modern crank-turning "all-electrons, a priori" [Slater, e.g.] methods in chemistry, which are of very limited usefulness."

Note too, that even *opponents* of historical controls neither endorse ramdomization necessarily, nor dismiss historical controls as seriously deficient as the Mayo group does. In the article "Consent and Randomized Clinical Trials," by Loretta Kopelman in the same issue of *The Journal of Medicine and Philosophy*, she says:

> The use of historical controls then, generally offers less adequate assurances than concurrent controls, that the control and test groups are comparable . . . Some non-randomized prospective trials, however, do not use historical controls. These include matching similar subjects into the test and controls groups, or blocking comparable groups of subjects into the test and control groups. In addition, non-random assignment in prospective trials may use sequential assignment to maximize the efficiency of the study and achieve statistical significance as soon as possible. . . . *It is a matter of ongoing debate* [emphasis mine] when or if non-randomized prospective trials are ever, from a scientific view, as good or better than randomized trials.

And there is still more trouble with the much-vaunted randomized control trial. Physicians' attitudes can affect patients negatively. Consider the following comment by Kopelman:

A *second* reason for refusing to enroll patients in RCT's is that *discussions of the uncertainty about treatment options and random assignments is bad for patients....* Some [physicians] hold open discussion of uncertainty are bad because they may compromise physicians' effectiveness by diminishing their authority . . . or by weakening the patient's trust, hope and morale.

Perhaps worst of all, however, is the fact that Dr. Moertel, in his letter to me, is simply *wrong* in saying that the Mayo Clinic's methodology eliminated "any conceivable bias." That is, while it is possible that Cameron's results were due, at least in part, to "case-selection bias." One has to note that *exactly the same charge might be made against those, like the Mayo group, who rely on so-called "objective" randomized studies.* As Dr. Kopelman points out in the same article, such researchers may inject bias in other ways. Dr. Kopelman delivers this assault against experiments like the Mayo's random trials when she urges that:

RCT methods, however good, are not ideal tools of inference or perfectly objective methods because, first, personal choice must be used in selecting both what variables to randomize and what is to count as a random method of assignment. Second, chances assignments can result in imbalances. Reviews conducted at the end of studies show that not infrequently, groups differ in important variables despite random assignment, making it difficult to interpret apparent differences in outcome.

And slightly further on she says:

The disturbing problem for those seeking an entirely objective method, however, is that there is no guarantee that randomized assignments eliminate nuisance variables. That investigators do not happen to know of differences, offers no guarantee that differences do not exist, and, of course, there are an indefinite number of possible sources of error. The personal judgments neccessary to assess what variables are relevant (such as age, [as in the Mayo trials]) and which are not (such as the color of one's drivers license) shows *randomization cannot guarantee elimination*

*of all nuisance variables, and that this methodology provides no*
*purely objective basis for scientific inference.*

The only conclusion possible is that the Mayo Clinic's charge
of "case selection bias" on Cameron's part has no force what-
soever, since randomized controls are just as open to the same
kind of charge.

I have dwelt on the question of the alleged "objectivity" of
randomized controls for several reasons. For one, that methodology is the reigning orthodoxy in establishment medicine.
Usually, conclusions based on such trials are offered to the public as if they were the very essence of neutrality and objectivity,
and that historically controlled trials are the very essence of
quackery. The May group does not openly make such a charge,
as noted earlier, but the tone of their writings and their choice
of words when discussing historically controlled studies ("no-
torious" for producing false positives, e.g.") makes it appear as
if randomized vs historically controlled trials is a special instances of good vs evil.

What I have tried to argue, by contrast, is that while the
Mayo group was both following an accepted methodology and
proceeding in the most ethical manner possible, and while they
may be correct in saying that the Cameron-type of study does
allow bias to creep in, the randomized studies of the Mayo Clinic
do so as well. Put more positively, both types of studies are
reasonable methodologies, but neither is perfectly objective either. That is why some physicians even prefer historical controls.
While neither historical nor randomized studies eliminate bias
completely, at least historical controls do not generate ethical
problems. (One reason for this, as noted earlier, is the fact that
in RCT's you must withold an *accepted* therapy from some patients in order to test the *experimental* one: Moertel himself discusses this problem in his article in the *New England Journal of
Medicine.*)

Beyond that we should note that there is a new method, the
"Bayesian" approach, which has many advocates and which may
be better than both historical *and* randomized studies.

Ultimately, further studies of vitamin C are clearly needed.

Researchers, for the sake of truth and comprehensiveness, must design tests based on all three methodologies—historical, randomized and Bayesian, if we are ever to know the truth about vitamin C. These studies must also be of longer duration than the tests of the second Mayo Clinic study.

There is another problem with the Mayo Clinic studies, part of which is due, ironically, to Pauling himself. Over the years, Pauling's claims about the efficacy of vitamin C against cancer have bordered on the unbelievable. In the November 1977 issue of *Prevention* magazine, for example, he states that: ". . . my present estimate is that a decrease of 75 percent [in cancer mortality] can be achieved by use of vitamin C alone, and a further decrease by use of other nutritional measures."

Seventy-five percent is an astonishing claim. Suppose one grants, for the sake of argument, that the second Mayo study is correct and it constitutes a refutation of Pauling's claims. The critical question is: *What* has been refuted? The claim that vitamin C cures 75 percent of all cancers, or the claim that vitamin C might have a smaller positive effect on cancer patients? Clearly the former rather than the latter. In order to show that vitamin C has *no* positive effect on cancer at all, a much subtler experiment would have to be done (one which would, for example, distinguish between, for example, a slightly greater longevity in vitamin C-treated cancer patients compared with non-vitamin C-treated cancer patients.) This kind of experiment has not yet been done, and must be done if we are ever to learn the truth about vitamin C. For, as indicated earlier, even Dr. Moertel himself said that there have been some reports of at least symptomatic benefits from vitamin C in cancer patients.

Not only is the vitamin C controversy still very much alive, but there seem to be a few salient observations worth making about the medical community as a whole. A comment I heard all too often in my research was that the vitamin C theory "must" be wrong since, if there were any evidence to support it, the medical community would be the first to embrace it. Unfortunately, the medical establishment is not always so open to new developments, however promising. For example, many psychiatrists still resist the "chemical revolution" in psychiatry. In a letter to Lawrence Kubie of Columbia University, psychiatric researcher Ronald Frieve observes,

> Even today, many psychiatrists, and most psychoanalysts . . . cling to the psychoanalytic explanation of the major mood disorders despite compelling scientific evidence to the contrary. The medical model with an emphasis on heredity and brain chemistry is obviously replacing it . . .

So much for the much-vaunted openmindedness and flexibility of the medical community.

I choose psychiatry as an example for still another reason, however. Earlier in his career, Pauling devoted considerable energy to establishing the view that megavitamin therapy, niacin in particular, was useful in treating mental illness. The Task Force Report of the American Psychiatric Association in 1973, however, virtually killed Pauling's theory. Today, most practitioners are either unaware of Pauling's views or simply disregard them. Interestingly, however, even that "discredited" view may have some life in it, as some of the younger medical practitioners are taking a new look at megavitamin therapy. In their book *Mind, Mood and Medicine*, for example, Drs. Paul Wender and Donald Klein of the University of Utah and Columbia University Medical Schools respectively, ponder Pauling's ideas on megavitamin therapy and mental disorders:

> In the area of dietary factors, Linus Pauling's vitamin-deficiency theory has not yet been confirmed, but there is a suggestive correlation between schizophrenia and a digestive disorder (celiac disease), and between schizophrenia and high wheat and rye consumption. Schizophrenia patients on gluten-free diets in two clinical trials have shown greater improvement than the control patients . . .

Although they do not specifically argue for Pauling's proposed link between diet and mental health, they do defend the connection between mental health and diet in general, which is a first step toward reconsidering Pauling's views. And in any event, their wording makes it evident that they believe Pauling might be right, and that he should at least be taken seriously.

In short, all of the Mayo Clinic's criticisms of Pauling might equally well apply to them. This is not to say that Pauling is right; it is only to say that he may be suffering from the bias of the medical establishment. The objective truth about vitamin C has yet to be revealed. It may have no effect on cancer. But considering the fact that there is solid scientific evidence showing that it does have an effect on cancer (this is not to deny, of course, that there is also evidence against it), it would be foolish and unfair to the public to simply dismiss Pauling's claims. More work is needed.

# Postscript

NO ONE KNOWS WHEN OR IF THE MEDICAL COMMUNITY will conduct a study that really duplicates Cameron's work or if this is even possible. Since there are so many conceivable factors that can affect the outcome of experimentation, differing results from one experiment to another can, in theory, always be traced to some factor not yet considered or allowed for in an experiment. Work, however, continues at the Linus Pauling Institute. Ewan Cameron has completed studies indicating that vitamin C may be of some benefit for patients with cancer that has spread to other locations. Researchers at the Institute are also comparing cancerous cells and nonmalignant ones; the difference may be due to certain proteins found in cancer cells but not found in normal cells. There is other work going on as well, such as an investigation of the link between viruses and AIDS.

But the Pauling Institute is suffering from financial difficulties. Donations have dropped off in recent years. Regardless of the controversy surrounding Pauling's theories, the loss of the Institute would be tragic. Institutions like the Pauling Institute provide a counterforce to reigning orthodoxy in medicine. History has repeatedly shown the dangers of allowing too much power and influence to accumulate in the hands of any one person or group of persons.

Today, Pauling remains as busy and active as ever. Cancer

research continues at his Institute, along with AIDS research and study of many other problems in molecular medicine.

Pauling does not devote all of his time to vitamin C. In fact, he has recently published scientific papers on high-temperature superconductivity. One such paper appeared in *Physical Review Letters*. Again, he attacked this problem from the chemical bonding point of view, much as he had attacked the problem of ferromagnetism years earlier. Perhaps most importantly, one of the foremost physicists of our time, Professor P.W. Anderson of Princeton, has taken Pauling's resonating valence bond approach and himself applied it to the problems of superconductivity. True, he has refined it and worked out the details, but the original concept was Pauling's and Anderson credits Pauling in his published writings.

Pauling's approach to superconductivity remains a minority view at the present time, but the minority does include some of the world's most distinguished physicists. It remains to be seen whether Linus Pauling's most recent theory will be proven correct.

# Notes

## Chapter 1: THE EARLY DAYS

1. Linus Pauling, interview by John Heilbron, Pasadena, 27 March 1964.
2. Ibid.
3. Ibid.
4. Ibid.
5. "In Their Own Words," interview with Pauling's two sisters, Frances Lucille Jenkins and Pauline Darling Ney, conducted by the Oswego Public Library, Lake Oswego, Oregon, 1976.
6. Pauling, interview by John Heilbron, Pasadena, 27 March 1964.
7. "Teacher Remembers Linus Pauling," *The Oregonian*, 17 December 1963.
8. Pauling, interview by John Heilbron, Pasadena, 27 March 1964.
9. Ibid.
10. Florence Meiman White, *Linus Pauling: Scientist and Crusader* (Walker & Co., Inc. 1980), 15.
11. Pauling, interview by John Heilbron, Pasadena, 27 March 1964.
12. Philip Mervyn Stephenson, interview by Linda Brody of the Oregon Historical Society, 7 July 1982 (transcript provided courtesy of the Oregon Historical Society).
13. Pauling, interview by John Heilbron, Pasadena, 27 March 1964.
14. Ibid.

15. From transcript of "Nova," program aired originally in June 1977 by KOAP–TV (transcript provided courtesy of WGBH–TV in Boston).
16. Pauling, interview by John Heilbron, Pasadena, 27 March 1964.
17. Quoted in Florence Meiman White, *Linus Pauling: Scientist and Crusader* (Walker & Co., Inc., 1980), 24.
18. Derek Davenport, "Vintage Pauling," *Chemtech*, Dec. 1982, p. 15.
19. Pauling, interview by John Heilbron, Pasadena, 27 March 1964.

Chapter 2: PROBING THE STRUCTURE OF CRYSTALS

1. Linus Pauling, "Fifty Years of Progress in Structural Chemistry and Molecular Biology," *Daedalus*, May 1970, p. 988.
2. Pauling, interview by John Heilbron, Pasadena, 27 March 1964.
3. Ernest Swift, interview with author, Pasadena, 1984.
4. Pauling, interview by John Heilbron, Pasadena, 27 March 1964.

Chapter 3: FROM CALTECH TO EUROPE

1. Pauling, interview by John Heilbron, Pasadena, 27 March 1964.
2. Ibid.
3. Linus Pauling, "Fifty Years of Progress in Structural Chemistry and Molecular Biology," *Daedalus*, May 1970.
4. Pauling, interview by John Heilbron, Pasadena, 27 March 1964.
5. Ibid.

Chapter 4: MAKING STRIDES IN QUANTUM MECHANICS

1. Pauling, interview by John Heilbron, Pasadena, 27 March 1964.
2. Ibid.
3. Ibid.
4. Linus Pauling, "Fifty Years of Progress in Structural Chemistry and Molecular Biology," *Daedalus*, May 1970.
5. Horace Freeland Judson, *The Eighth Day of Creation* (Simon & Schuster, 1979), 76.

## Chapter 5: AT HOME AT CALTECH

1. Horace Freeland Judson, *The Eighth Day of Creation* (Simon & Schuster, 1979), 73.
2. Pauling, interview by John Heilbron, Pasadena, 27 March 1964.
3. Pauling to Slater, 6 June 1930.
4. Slater to Pauling, 21 January 1931.
5. Pauling to Slater, 7 February 1931.
6. Linus Pauling, "Fifty Years of Progress in Structural Chemistry and Molecular Biology," *Daedalus*, May 1970.
7. E.F. Freundlich, "Star Photographs Leave Einstein Effect in Doubt," *Science Service*, 16 Aug. 1933.
8. Linus Pauling, "Chemical Achievement and Hope for the Future," *American Scientist*, Winter 1947.

## Chapter 6: PAULING VS. DOROTHY WRINCH

1. Horace Freeland Judson, *The Eighth Day of Creation* (Simon & Schuster, 1979), 77.
2. Linus Pauling, "Fifty Years of Progress in Structural Chemistry and Molecular Biology," *Daedalus*, May 1970.
3. Quoted in Horace Freeland Judson, *The Eighth Day of Creation* (Simon & Schuster, 1979), 72.
4. Quoted in Florence Meiman White, *Linus Pauling: Scientist and Crusader* (Walker & Co., Inc., 1980), p. 39.
5. Pauling to Noyes, 3 November 1935.
6. "The Scientific Work of Linus Pauling", *Folia Humanistica*, 2 (1964), 197–208.
7. Jack Roberts, interview with author, Pasadena, Aug. 1984.
8. Marjorie Senechal, "A Prophet Without Honor: Dorothy Wrinch, Scientist, 1894–1976," *Smith Alumnae Quarterly*, April 1977.
9. Michael Polanyi to Dorothy Wrinch, 23 May 1935.
10. Quoted in Sibilla E. Kennedy, "Dorothy Wrinch and the Rockefeller Foundation Grants" (Paper presented at the National History of Science Meeting, Norwalk, Conn., 28 October 1983).
11. Ibid.
12. Ibid.
13. Quoted in Marjorie Senechal, ed., *Structures of Matter and Patterns in Science* (Cambridge, Mass.: Schenkman Publishing Company, Inc. 1980), 155.

14. Ted, Mildred, and Victor Goertzel, "Linus Pauling: The Scientist as Crusader," *The Antioch Review*, Summer 1980, p. 38.
15. Irving Langmuir to Linus Pauling, 17 May 1987.
16. Pauling to Professor William Scott, 14 February 1956.
17. Marjorie Senechal, conversation with author, Smith College, October 1984.
18. David Harker, telephone conversation with author, 12 Oct. 1984.
19. Marjorie Senechal, "A Prophet Without Honor: Dorothy Wrinch, Scientist, 1894–1976," *Smith Alumnae Quarterly*, April 1977.
20. Pauling to David Harker, 8 July 1940.
21. Quoted in Marjorie Senechal, "A Prophet Without Honor: Dorothy Wrinch, Scientist, 1894–1976," *Smith Alumnae Quarterly*, April 1977.
22. Roy Benedek, telephone conversation with author, 14 July 1987.
23. Ruth Hubbard, telephone conversation with author, March 1984.
24. Jack Roberts, conversation with author, California Institute of Technology, July 1984.

Chapter 7: MOLECULAR MEDICINE

1. Quoted in Horace Freeland Judson, *The Eighth Day of Creation* (Simon & Schuster, 1979), 140.
2. Linus Pauling, "Fifty Years of Progress in Structural Chemistry and Molecular Biology," *Daedalus*, Fall 1970, 1007.
3. James Bonner, interview with author, Caltech, August 1987.
4. Linus Pauling, *The Nature of the Chemical Bond* (Ithaca: Cornell University Press, 1939), ix.
5. Joe Mayer, review of *The Nature of the Chemical Bond* (manuscript version), American Institute of Physics Publications, Summer 1939.
6. Ibid.
7. Jack Roberts, conversation with author, Pasadena, 1984.
8. Joe Mayer, review of *The Nature of the Chemical Bond*.

Chapter 8: THE WAR YEARS

1. Edward Hughes, conversation with author, California Institute of Technology, 1984.

2. "Linus Pauling," *Fairfield Chronicle*, 28 March 1981.
3. Professor Koepfli, telephone interview with author, 1985.
4. "Dr. Pauling Wins Medal," *Oregon State Barometer*, 25 October 1940.
5. Ibid.
6. "The Unretiring Paulings," *San Francisco Examiner & Chronicle*, 21 Aug. 1977.
7. Edward Hughes, interview with author, Pasadena, 1984.
8. Documents on World War II scientific activity at Caltech, from the Robert Andrews Millikan Library at the California Institute of Technology.
9. Verner Schomacher, interview with author, University of Washington, June 1984.
10. From transcript of "Nova," program produced by WGBH–TV, Boston: first transmission, PBS, 1 June 1977 (transcript provided courtesy of WGBH–TV in Boston).
11. "Reed Speaker Decries Oppenheimer Ruling," *The Oregonian*, 2 Oct. 1954.
12. Robert Millikan to Robert Oppenheimer, 31 August 1941.
13. Ibid.
14. William R. Nelson, *The Politics of Science* (New York: E.P. Dutton, Inc. 1968), 25.

## Chapter 9: POLITICS AND THE POSTWAR YEARS

1. Mildred and Victor Goertzel, unpublished biography of Pauling.
2. Seagers to author, 11 April 1984.
3. Excerpt from the mimeographed pamphlet, "Additional Remarks on Fritz Ephraim's *Inorganic Chemistry*" fourth English edition, 1943, written in February 1947 (see book reviews in American Mineralogist, 32, 97–104, 1947, by Kasimir Fajans)
4. Quoted in Horace Freeland Judson, *The Eighth Day of Creation* (Simon & Schuster, 1979), 82.
5. From transcript of "Nova," program produced by WGBH–TV, Boston: first transmission, PBS, 1 June 1977 (transcript provided courtesy of WGBH–TV in Boston).
6. Quoted in Judson, *Eighth Day of Creation*, 72.
7. Jonathan Singer to author, 20 May 1985.

Chapter 10: THE MCCARTHY ERA AND THE "RACE" FOR DNA

1. Robert Andrews Millikan to Robert Moore, 21 December 1949.
2. Quoted in Horace Freeland Judson, *The Eighth Day of Creation* (Simon & Schuster, 1979), 86.
3. Quoted in Judson, *Eighth Day of Creation*, 86.
4. "Chemist Rips H-Bomb Move," *Daily Worker*, 7 February 1950.
5. Robert Olby, author of *The Path to the Double Helix*, wrote to the author on 23 November, 1988: The alpha helix has an amino acid repeat (or residue repeat) or 1.49 Å along the axis. This short repeat should produce a "wide-angle" reflexion on the meridion (since it is a repeat along the axis of the fibre and since the X-ray diagram is in reciprocal space, short distances in the crystal are represented by long distances on the diagram—hence "wide angle"). This reflection had not been observed in any protein or polypeptide when Pauling advanced the alpha helix. Furthermore, there existed the well known meriodional repeat for alpha keratin at 5.1 Å, a very strong reflexion. The 1.49 Å reflexion had not been observed for two reasons: in proteins like haemoglobin it was not obvious; you needed to look for it, hoping to find it. Pauling detected it in the Fournier maps that Perutz showed him when he [Pauling] was Eastman Visiting Professor in Oxford, but he did not divulge this information to Perutz at that time. Second, nearly all diffraction patterns from fibres did not go out far enough to pick up the wide-angle reflexion of 1.49 Å. As I explained over the telephone, MacArthur in Leeds did record such a reflexion for porcupine quill in the 1940s; I think it was 1943. But he, like Astbury, was looking for narrow-angle reflexions which they believed were evidence of long-chain repeats in accordance with the hypothesis of repeating (chemical) sequences, the rare amino acids in a protein occurring only at regular widely separated positions.

   Hence it was not until Perutz received the number of the PNAS which contained the alpha helix paper that he realized it should be possible, by going out far enough on the meridion to record a strong reflexion at 1.49 Å. He did this that very weekend—see my book, p. 293.

   I should also remind you of the account I give of the Cambridge group building as one possible model for a polypeptide chain, a 4/13 helix which is very close to Pauling's alpha helix (Fig. 17.11) and has planar peptide bonds. The reason they rejected it concerned evidence they had to the effect that the peptide bond is not planar (the fact that it was known to be planar in diketopiperazine did not mean that it was so in a polypeptide chain), see p.289 ff [in my book].

Finally, on the subject of non-integral helices, it is surely only fair to note that Huggins expressly noted that he had drawn integral helices, but that they did not have to be integral. Also, as I remark (p62 and Fig. 5.2.c, p.61) Sauter has advanced a non-integral helix for polyoxymethylene in 1933.

6. Pauling to Albert Einstein, 19 May 1952.
7. Albert Einstein to Dean Acheson, 21 May 1952.
8. Einstein to Pauling, 21 May 1952.
9. Linus Pauling, "Molecular Architecture and the Processes of Life" (Twenty-first *Sir Jesse Boot Foundation Lecture*, quoted in Robert Olby, *The Path to the Double Helix*, 120)
10. Robert Olby, *The Path to the Double Helix* (Seattle: University of Washington Press, 1974), 204.
11. Quoted in Olby, *Double Helix*, 366.
12. James Watson, *The Double Helix*, New York: Atheneum, 1968, 156.
13. Verner Schomacher, interview with author, Seattle, 1984.
14. Horace Freeland Judson, author of *The Eighth Day of Creation* wrote to the author on 15 October 1988: Pauling always liked to be first, but he was in no race with [Watson & Crick] so far as he knew. I think I made clear in *The Eighth Day of Creation* that the race was a creation of Watson's manipulative imagination. At the time, early 1953, Watson knew that *Bragg* harbored a competitive resentment against Pauling of two decades' standing; so Watson used the idea of Pauling's getting DNA first to secure Bragg's permission for W & C to go back to building models. The real race was against Kings College, London. Then when Watson wrote the book eventually published as *The Double Helix*, he could hardly admit manipulating Bragg fifteen years earlier. He used the idea of the race with Pauling for dramatic interest. And he needed once more to recruit Bragg to his side: Bragg in fact strove mightily, against the vociferous objections of Crick, Pauling, Wilkins, and others, to get that book published. Some other factors were at work, too, but that's enough to show you why Watson made up the competition the way he did in *The Double Helix*.
15. Anne Sayre, *Rosalind Franklin and DNA* (New York: W.W. Norton, 1975) 143.

## Chapter 11: ON THE WAY TO HIS FIRST NOBEL PRIZE

1. Pauling to John Slater, 30 November 1953.
2. Roy Benedek, telephone interview with author, Chicago, 23 Feb. 1986.
3. Sten Samson, interview with author, 1984.
4. Pauling to Astbury, 2 November 1954.
5. Pauling to Albert Einstein, 1 June 1954.
6. Einstein to Pauling, 8 June 1954.

## Chapter 12: ON THE TRAIL OF A CURE FOR MENTAL ILLNESS

1. Peggy Kiskadden, telephone interview with author, 11 Feb. 1984.
2. James Bonner, interview with author, Pasadena, June 1984.
3. Jack Roberts, interview with author at the California Institute of Technology, June 1984.
4. Herman J. Muller, speech in acceptance of Kimber Genetics Award, 1 April 1955 (as reported in *Saga*, May 1962).
5. *U. S. News and World Report*, 30 March 1953.
6. John C. Burger, memorandum to W.F. Libby, 18 April 1955.
7. Willard Libby to Pauling, 6 May 1955.
8. "Legion Hits Nobel Lecturer at UI," n.p., 29 February 1956.
9. Joel Hildebrand to Pauling, 20 May 1957.

## Chapter 13: PEACE CRUSADING IN HIGH GEAR

1. Fulton Lewis, Jr., in the *Washington Report* (King Features Syndicate), 19 June 1957.
2. "Science Near Discovery of Life's Secret, Say 2," *Daily News*, 30 Aug. 1957.
3. Quoted during "Fallout and Disarmament: The Pauling-Teller Debate," KQED–TV, San Francisco, 20 February 1958 (transcript provided courtesy of KQED–TV).
4. Edward Hughes, interview with author, Pasadena, June 1984.
5. Jack Roberts, interview with author, Pasadena, June 1984.
6. William Friedlander, telephone interview with author Oct. 1984.
7. FBI data sent to author in 1984.
8. "Meet the Press" (NBC Television), 11 May 1958.
9. Linus Pauling, *No More War* (Dodd Mead, 1958), 87.

10. Linus Pauling, commencement address given at Reed College, 7 June 1959.
11. From transcript of "Nova," program produced by WGBH–TV, Boston: first transmission, PBS, 1 June 1977 (transcript provided courtesy of WGBH–TV in Boston).
12. Linus Pauling, address to the American Humanist Association, Cleveland, 17 March 1961.

## Chapter 14: A BRUSH WITH DEATH

1. "Dr. Pauling Rescued From Fog-Cloaked Cliff," *Los Angeles Times*, 1 February 1960.
2. "Linus Pauling Hopes Hearings Will Be Open," *The Washington Post*, 27 June 1960.
3. Report of the Subcommittee to Investigate the Administration of the Internal Security Act and Other Internal Security Laws to the Committee on the Judiciary: United States Senate, 87th Cong., 1st sess., "Testimony of Dr. Linus Pauling," 21 June and 11 October 1960.
4. Ibid., 5.
5. UPI release 212, Washington Capital News Service, 26 August 1960.
6. Subcommittee report, 5.
7. "Linus Pauling Talks Up at Tea," *The Washington Post*, 17 October 1960.
8. From text of "Conference Against the Spread of Nuclear Weapons" (manuscript of proceedings provided to the author courtesy of Dr. Frances Herring).
9. Linus Pauling, "Colossal Deception: Analysis of the Shelter Program," *Liberation*, November 1961.

## Chapter 15: AT WAR WITH HERMAN J. MULLER

1. "Spieth Decides Pauling Not Competent on Disarmament," *The Highlander*, 7 February 1962.
2. Quoted by William F. Buckley, Jr. in "Ford Award Did Not Ennoble Pauling Politics," *Washington Star*, 1 October 1975.
3. Barry Goldwater, "Good Chemist, No Realist," *New York Times*, May 1962.

4. Quoted by Pauling to Herman J. Muller, 9 July 1962.
5. C. Dickerman Williams, interview with author, Yale University, August 1984.
6. Helene Schwarz, telephone interview with author, April 1984.
7. "Mrs. Pauling Recognizes Role of Women in Fight For Peace," *The Oregonian*, 15 March 1963.
8. From transcript of "Nova," program produced by WGBH–TV, Boston: first transmission, PBS, 1 June 1977 (transcript provided courtesy of WGBH–TV in Boston).
9. "The Controversial Chemist," *Christian Science Monitor*, 14 October 1953.
10. "A Weird Insult From Norway," *Life*, 25 October 1963.
11. Rae Goodell, *The Visible Scientists* (Boston: Little Brown, 1975), 74.

## Chapter 16: SQUARING OFF WITH WILLIAM F. BUCKLEY, JR.

1. *The Center Magazine*, April 1968 (back cover).
2. Linus Pauling, application to the Center for the Study of Democratic Institutions, 14 February 1964.
3. *The Center Magazine*, September 1968, 68.
4. Arthur Robinson, telephone interview with author, May 1984.
5. James Bonner, interview with author at California Intitute of Technology, June 1984.
6. Linus Pauling, "The Social Responsibilities of Scientists and Science" (article based on 1966 talk at the National Science Teacher's Convention), *The Science Teacher*, May 1966.
7. Helene Schwarz, telephone interview with author, March 1984.
8. William F. Buckley, Jr., "Linus Pauling: TKO," *National Review*, 3 May 1966.

## Chapter 17: ON THE WAY TO SAN DIEGO AND VITAMIN C

1. Linus Pauling, from talk given at *Pacem in Terris* Convocation, 18 February 1965. *As quoted* in "The Social Responsibilities of Scientists," L. Pauling, *The Science Teacher*, May, 1966, p. 17
2. Arthur Robinson, "To the Editor," *Antioch Review*, Summer 1981.

3. Rae Goodell, *The Visible Scientists* (Harper & Row), 76.

4. Ted, Mildred, and Victor Goertzel, "Linus Pauling: The Scientist as Crusader," *Antioch Review*, Summer 1980, 32.

5. Quoted in Rae Goodell, *The Visible Scientists* (Harper & Row), 82.

6. Ibid.

7. Quoted in Stanford University News Release, 18 November 1970.

8. This idea is not my own: I am indebted to conversations with Prof. Israel Scheffler of the Philosophy Department at Harvard, my advisor when I was a special student at Harvard in the spring of 1972.

9. Stanford University News Release, 16 March 1973.

10. David Harker, telephone interview with author, Feb. 1985.

11. Stanford University News Release, 16 March 1983.

12. Stanford University News Release, 1 December 1971.

13. "The Significance of the Evidence About Ascorbic Acid and the Common Cold," *Proceedings of the National Academy of Sciences*, vol. 68, no. 11, 2678–2681.

14. Ewan Cameron, *Cancer and Vitamin C* (New York: Warner Books, 1979), p. x.

15. Rae Goodell, *The Visible Scientists* (Harper & Row), 83.

Chapter 18: PAULING VS. THE MEDICAL ESTABLISHMENT

1. Stanford University News Service Release, 30 March 1971.

2. "Academy Turns Down a Pauling Paper," *Science*, November 1972.

3. Ibid.

4. "Megavitamin and Orthomolecular Therapy in Psychiatry," Task Force Report 7 of the American Psychiatric Association (July 1973), vi.

5. William F. Buckley, Jr., "Ford Award Did Not Ennoble Pauling Politics," *Washington Star*, 1 October 1975.

6. Author's interview with Pauling's sisters-in-law, Seattle, 14 May 1984.

7. Linus Pauling and Ewan Cameron, *Cancer and Vitamin C* (Warner Books, 1979), xi.

## Chapter 19: BREAK FROM ARTHUR ROBINSON

1. Linus Pauling and Ewan Cameron, *Cancer and Vitamin C* (Warner Books, 1979), 139.
2. Arthur Robinson, "Tax Financed Research: Is it Ethical? Is It Effective?" (talk presented at the Cato Institute), San Francisco, 13 May 1978.
3. Linus Pauling, "Of Mice and Men," *Barron's*, 11 June 1979.
4. Quoted by Jerry Carroll in "The Perils of Pauling," *New West*, 8 October 1979.
5. Pauling to Frederick Westall, 17 February 1978.
6. "Of Mice and Men," *Barron's*, 11 June 1979.
7. Robinson to Pauling, 26 March 1984 (not answered by Pauling).
8. Arthur Robinson, interview by Dr. John Grauerholz, *Economics*, 28 August 1984.
9. Linus Pauling, letter to the Editor, *Antioch Review*, Spring 1981.
10. Thomas Jukes, telephone interview with author, 18 September 1984.

## Chapter 20: IN DEFENSE OF VITAMIN C

1. Charles Moertel, as quoted by Pauling in a letter to the editor of the *The New England Journal of Medicine*, 20 March 1980.
2. Charles Moertel to author, 7 May 1984.
3. Certainly the best and most comprehensive examination of ethical issues in clinical trials appeared recently in *The Journal of Medicine and Philosophy* for November, 1986. Of particular importance for such typical trials as the Mayo Clinic used is the article "An Argument that All Prerandomized Clinical Trials are Unethical," by Don Marquis.
4. Charles Moertel, et al., "High-Dose Vitamin C Versus Placebo in the Treatment of Patients with Advanced Cancer Who Have Had No Prior Chemotherapy: A Randomized Double-Blind Comparison," *New England Journal of Medicine*, 17 January 1985.
5. Press release, Linus Pauling Institute of Science and Medicine, 26 January 1985.
6. One such opinion appeared in "The Limitations of the Randomized Clinical Trial," in V. DeVita and H. Busch, eds., *Methods in Cancer Research: Cancer Drug Development.* xvii, Part B. New York: Academic Press, 1986, pp. 277–310.

# Selected Bibliography

"Academy Turns Down a Pauling Paper." *Science*, August 4, 1972

Allison, Helen C. "Outspoken Scientist." *Bulletin of the Atomic Scientists*, December 1960.

Baum, Rudy. "Linus Pauling Wins ACS's Highest Award in Chemistry." *Chemical and Engineering News*, July 11, 1983.

Bragg, Sir W.L., J.C. Kendrew and Max Perutz. "Polypeptide Chain Configuration in Crystalline Proteins." *Proceedings of the Royal Society* 203A, 1950.

Brink, Susan. "Linus Pauling Raises Standard." *Statesman-Journal*, Portland, Oregon, June 4, 1982.

Buckley, William F. Jr. "Are You Being Sued by Linus Pauling?" *National Review*, September 25, 1962.

Cameron, Ewan, and Linus Pauling. "Ascorbic Acid and Glycosaminoglycans." *Oncology* 27, 1973.

Cameron, Ewan, and Linus Pauling. "On Cancer and Vitamin C." *Executive Health*, January 1980.

Cameron, Ewan, Linus Pauling, and Brian Leibovitz. "Ascorbic Acid and Cancer: A Review." *Cancer Research*, March 1979.

Carroll, Terry. "The Perils of Pauling." *New West*, October 8, 1979.

*The Center Magazine* 6, September 1968.

Chargaff, Erwin. "On the Nucleoproteins and Nucleic Acids of Microorganisms." Cold Spring Harbor Symposium on Quantitative Biology 12, 1947.

"Chemical Crystal's Secrets Revealed by Dr. L. Pauling." *The Oregonian*, October 25, 1931.

Chowka, Peter. "Linus Pauling: Conversation with a Nutritional Revolutionary." *Whole Life Times*, June 1984.

"Communist Exploitation of Radiation 'Fall-Out' Controversy." *F.B.I. Documents*, June 12, 1957.

Cochran, W. and Francis Crick. "Evidence for the Pauling-Corey Alphahelix in Synthetic Polypeptides" *Nature* 169, 1952.

Corner, G.W. *A History of the Rockefeller Institute, 1901–1953: Origins and Growth*, New York, n.d.

Cousins, Norman. "Linus Pauling and the Vitamin Controversy." *Saturday Review*, May 15, 1971.

Crick, Francis. *Of Molecules and Men*. The John Danz Lectures at the University of Washington. Seattle and London, 1966.

Crick, Francis, et al. *General Nature of the Genetic Code For Proteins*. *Nature* 192, 1961.

"The Development of X-ray Diffraction in the U.S.A." in Ewald, P. (editor), n.l., 1962.

Dunn, L.C. *Genetics in the Twentieth Century; Essays on the Progress of Genetics During its First Fifty Years*. New York, 1951.

"Dyssymmetry in Nucleotide Sequence of Desoxypentose Nucleic Acids." *Journal of Biological Chemistry*, vol. 187, 1950.

Einstein, Albert. "On the Moral Obligation of the Scientist." *The Bulletin of the Atomic Scientists*, March 1979. Einstein speech delivered in October 1952.

Fruton, J.S. *Molecules And Life: Historical Essays on the Interplay of Chemistry and Biology*. New York, 1972.

Fry, William F. Jr. "What's New With You Linus Pauling?" *The Humanist*, November/December 1974.

Goodell, Rae. *The Visible Scientists*. New York, 1975.

Grant, James. "Of Mice and Men." *Barron's*, June 11, 1979.

Grosser, Morton. "Linus Pauling: Molecular Artist." *The Saturday Evening Post*, Fall 1971.

Herman, Frank. "Elephants and Mahouts: Early Days In Semiconductor Physics." *Physics Today*, June 1984.

Hoagland, M.B. *Discovery: The Search for DNA's Secret*. Boston, 1981.

Ingram, Ralph. *Hemoglobin and Its Abnormalities*. n.l. 1961.

Jukes, Thomas H. and Jack Lester King. "Evolutionary Loss of Ascorbic Acid Synthesizing Ability." *Journal of Human Evolution* 4, 1975.

Kalven, Harry, Jr. "Congressional Testing of Linus Pauling." *The Bulletin of the Atomic Scientists*, December 1960.

Kasha, M. and R. Pullman, eds. *Molecular Disease Evolution and Gene Hetergeneity, Horizons in Biochemistry.* New York, Academic Press.

Kennedy, Sibilla E. "Dorothy Wrinch and the Rockefeller Foundation Grants." Paper presented at the National History of Science Meeting, Norwalk, Conn., October 28, 1983.

Lake Oswego Public Library. "In Their Own Words: Linus Pauling, a Famous Member of an Early Family." Reminiscences of Early Oswego, Oregon.

"Linus Pauling TKO." *National Review,* May 3, 1966.

*The Linus Pauling Institute of Science and Medicine Newsletter*

"Mayo Clinic Studies of Vitamin C and Cancer." Newsletter of *The Linus Pauling Institute of Science and Medicine,* Spring/Summer 1985.

*Megavitamin and Orthomolecular Therapy in Psychiatry.* American Psychiatric Association, Task Force Report 7, July 1973.

McCormmach, Russell. *Historical Studies in the Physical Sciences.* Princeton, Princeton University Press.

Charles Moertel et al. "High-Dose Vitamin C Versus Placebo in the Treatment of Patients with Advanced Cancer Who Have Had No Prior Chemotherapy." *New England Journal of Medicine,* January 17, 1985.

"National Review Vindicated." *National Review,* May 3, 1964.

Navy Department Bureau of Ordinance. Navord Report 43–45, *German Powder Development from 1918 to 1942.* A translation of the German book *"Die Geschutzladung"* done under the direction of Linus Pauling. Washington, D.C., September 15, 1945.

"New Kind of Synthetic Medicine Made." *Oregon Journal,* August 21, 1942.

Olby, Robert. *The Path to the Double Helix.* University of Washington Press, 1974.

O'Neil, Paul. "The Vitamin C Mania." *Life,* July 9, 1971.

"Oregon's Nobel Winner." *The Oregonian,* November 8, 1954.

"Pauling Honored." *The Oregonian.* September 18, 1979.

Pauling, Linus. "Orthomolecular Psychiatry." *Science,* April 19, 1968.

———. "The Significance of the Evidence About Ascorbic Acid." *Proceedings of the National Academy of Sciences,* November 1971.

———. *No More War!* New York, 1962.

———. "Chemistry." *Scientific American,* September 1950.

———. "Five Ways to Live Longer." *Saturday Evening Post,* October 1974.

————. "Chemical Achievement and Hope for the Future." *American Scientist*, Winter 1947.

————. "The Social Responsibilities of Scientists and Science." *The Science Teacher*, May 1966.

————. "The Need to Understand." *New Scientist and Science Journal*, June 24, 1971.

————. "Fifty Years of Progress on Structural Chemistry and Molecular Biology." *Daedalus*, Fall 1970.

Pogash, Carol. "The Great Gadfly." *Science Digest*, June 1981.

"Progress Report on Development of the Pauling Oxygen Meter." In National Archives, March 18, 1947.

Release: *Linus Pauling Institute of Science and Medicine*. January 26, 1985 (A Response to the Mayo Clinic Report).

Rich & Davidson, eds. *Structural Chemistry and Molecular Biology*, 1968. (Memorial volume dedicated to Linus Pauling.)

Roberts, John D. "Studies of Conformational Equilibria and Equilibration by Nuclear Magnetic Resonance Spectroscopy." Division of Chemistry and Chemical Engineering, California Institute of Technology, 1966. Centenary Lectureship of the Chemical Society of London.

Robinson, Arthur. "Research on Nutrition and Preventitive Medicine." Excerpt from address to Canadian Schizophrenic Foundation Conference on "Troubled Children," June 2, 1979.

Sayre, Anne. *Rosalind Franklin & DNA*. New York, 1975.

Smith, Alice Kimball. *A Peri and a Hope: The Scientists Movement in America, 1945–47*. Cambridge, Mass., 1965.

Strout, Richard. "Win a Prize: Get a Passport." *Life*, November 28, 1955.

Sullivan, William Cuyler, Jr., "Nuclear Democracy: A History of the Greater St. Louis Citizen's Committee for Nuclear Information, 1957–1967." Washington University.

Tamplin and Goffman. "The Radiation Effects Controversy." *The Bulletin of the Atomic Scientists*, September 1970.

# Index